Journey
THROUGH
THE Psalms

JOURNEY
THROUGH
THE Psalms

revised and expanded

Denise Dombkowski Hopkins

CHALICE™
PRESS
ST. LOUIS, MISSOURI

Scripture quotations are the author's translation unless otherwise noted.

Those quotations marked NRSV are from the *New Revised Standard Version Bible*, copyright 1989, Division of Christian Education of the National Council of the Churches of Christ in the United States of America. Used by permission. All rights reserved.

Those quotations marked RSV are from the *Revised Standard Version of the Bible*, copyright 1952 [2nd edition, 1971], by the Division of Christian Education of the National Council of the Churches of Christ in the United States of America. Used by permission. All rights reserved.

Excerpts marked NJB are from *The New Jerusalem Bible*, copyright 1985 by Darton, Longman & Todd, Ltd., and Doubleday, a division of Bantam Doubleday Dell Publishing Group, Inc. Used by permission.

Biblical quotations marked (JPS) are taken from *The TANAKH, the new JPS translation according to the traditional Hebrew text*, copyright © 1985 by the Jewish Publication Society. All rights reserved. Used by permission.

Cover art: © Digital Stock Corp.
Cover design: Lynne Condellone
Interior design: Elizabeth Wright
Art direction: Elizabeth Wright

This book is printed on acid-free, recycled paper.

Visit Chalice Press on the World Wide Web at
www.chalicepress.com

10 9 8 7 6 5 4 3 2 1   02 03 04 05 06 07

Library of Congress Cataloging–in–Publication Data

Hopkins, Denise Dombkowski.
    Journey through the Psalms / by Denise Dombkowski Hopkins.—Rev. and expanded ed.
        p.   cm.
    Includes bibliographical references and index.
    ISBN 0-8272-1714-5 (alk. paper)
    1. Bible. O.T. Psalms—Criticism, interpretation, etc.   I. Title.
BS1430.52 .H66   2002
223'.206—dc21
                                                        2002002587

Printed in the United States of America

Contents

Preface

During the twenty years I have spent teaching and preaching the Bible in seminary and in local churches, one thing has remained constant: the passion and openness that laity and clergy alike have shown for the book of Psalms, more than for almost any other part of the Bible. This book is filled with testimonies to that passion from former students at Lancaster and Wesley Theological Seminaries in the form of "communication events" that showcase creative understandings of the psalms, in quilts, music, liturgies, poetry, prayer, and paraments. These "events" remind us that the psalms draw us in not simply intellectually, but as whole persons. I am grateful for the contributions of these men and women and for their company over the years on our continuing journey through the psalms.

My special thanks go to Bill Wright, office of faculty support, for helping me in so many ways while I was working on this book; to Mary Bates-Washington, executive assistant to the President, for her patient help with my computer problems; to Carol Wilson for preparing the indices; to Mark Schaefer for his work with the musical scores; and to DL, for showing me how to walk in the Spirit.

This book is dedicated to my brother, Brian S. Dombkowski, June 7, 1955 to September 3, 1978. I miss you.

Ash Wednesday, 2001

CHAPTER ONE

Praying the Psalms,
Praying into Wholeness

One of the main reasons for the powerful hold that the psalms have on us is that they offer us what Roland Murphy calls "a school of prayer," not simply in the sense of a collection of prayers, but rather as lessons in how to pray.[1] The psalms teach us that there are many different kinds of prayer and many different ways of praying to God that articulate the entire range of human emotions: fear, praise, anger, thanksgiving, joy, despair. All the feelings that mark our struggle for faith from day to day appear in the Psalter. Psalm language grasps for us the many facets of God and our relationship to God, whom we experience as both present and absent. Psalms allow us to be honest and whole before God as we express our faith in good times and bad and every time in between. A journey through the psalms is the journey of the life of faith.

Several years ago, I attended a United Church of Christ Conference workshop on "How to Talk about Your Faith" led by the Reverend Dr. Bill McGregor. Ours was a large group of about forty laity and clergy who were a bit apprehensive about the topic, but who wanted to be more confident about sharing their faith. As part of the workshop process we paired up, with 'A' asking 'B,' "Why are you a Christian?" At the end of five minutes, 'A' asked 'B' the question again. Then the procedure was reversed, with 'B' asking and 'A' answering, twice. In the plenary session, we all shared what we had learned. To a person, we had not responded to the question "Why are you a Christian?" with doctrine or creedal statements, but with our personal stories. Since most of us had not even been asked the question before, we were surprised by the form our answers took and by the feeling of empowerment rather than embarrassment that accompanied our storytelling. Furthermore, none of us produced one smooth narrative, but rather, a series of mini-stories punctuated by memories of joy and cries of pain, often accompanied by tears. We learned firsthand the truth of the Kiowah saying: "Laughter and tears are first cousins."[2] Realizing that we never would have guessed the burdens others were carrying, we acknowledged the importance of the listener in our sharing, especially in accepting the "negative" parts of our story. We saw that asking the question twice offered a way to stay with each other and leave room for the voicing of the pain, the questions, and the joy of each story. We trusted one another to hear, and gave one another permission to voice whatever was in our minds and hearts.

Looking back on that workshop experience, I can see that what we did that day by telling our stories was to produce our own collections of psalms, mini-Psalters that expressed the whole range of our emotions and life experiences before God. No wonder, then, that so many of us are drawn to the book of Psalms in the Bible—the psalms offer us ready vehicles for the telling of our whole story. Just as we gave each other permission in our workshop pairings to tell and hear our stories, so too does the canon of our faith, which includes the book of Psalms with its laments, thanksgivings, and praises, give us permission to take our whole range of human experience to God in prayer. A journey through the psalms from the beginning of the collection to the end mirrors the storytelling we did that day.

A psalms journey takes us on a roller-coaster ride from praise to doubt and back again with a swiftness that takes one's breath away. No matter how fast or how low the roller coaster dips, however, it never leaves the track. Even the angry psalm prayers filled with doubt and questions lead us to God. As Kathleen Billman and Daniel Migliore note, prayer has both a summer and a winter voice: the hallelujah of psalm 150 and the anguished cry out of the depths of Psalm 130; the voice of Christmas and Easter and Handel's "Hallelujah Chorus," as well as the voice of the wilderness, the exile, the cross, and the Negro spirituals; the voice of Rachel weeping, refusing to be comforted (Jer. 31:15) and the voice of Mary, accepting and rejoicing (Lk. 1:46–55).[3] Rachel and Mary are bound together in Christian tradition, reminding us that "the danger of praise without lament is triumphalism, and the danger of lament without praise is hopelessness."[4]

To sit down and skim the book of Psalms rapidly is to embark on the roller-coaster ride of prayer, from summer to winter prayer and back again. Yet we end the ride in praise. Some people cannot see this movement from the beginning to the end of the collection, because they focus only on their favorite psalms, ignoring those psalms that are different or unfamiliar. But a closer look shows a preponderance of praises toward the end of the Psalter. More laments are found in the first half of the Psalter, more hymns in the second half. One cannot trace this movement along a straight line, but "the shift of emphasis is noticeable. To go through the book of psalms is to be led increasingly toward the praise of God as the final word."[5] Psalm 1 is intentionally placed at the beginning of the Psalter to call Israel to obedience to Torah[6] and to assure Israel about the good consequences of obedience. The Psalter concludes with Psalm 150, placed intentionally at the end of the collection to engage Israel in unconditional praise.

How do we move from obedience to praise, from Psalm 1 to Psalm 150? Not directly, for that is too simple and not at all characteristic of the life of faith. Walter Brueggemann suggests that we move from Psalm 1 to 150 "by way of the suffering voiced in the complaints and the hope sounded in the hymns."[7] Lived experience intervenes between obedience and praise, and it is in this between place "where Israel mostly lives...the obedience of Psalm 1 and the praise of Psalm 150 are not simply literary boundaries but the boundaries for Israel's life and faith."[8] As Renita Weems puts it, "this is the spiritual journey, learning how to live in the meantime, between the last time you heard from God and the next time you hear from God."[9] The movement toward praise is punctuated by lurches into despair, but these are not faith relapses or aberrations. "Doubt and despair are not mere side-steps in an otherwise optimistic faith. They are in fact integral to the faith experience."[10] "Israel's lament is never simply an emotional outburst or an exercise in self-pity. It is a cry for relief from suffering so that God may once again be praised."[11]

Over the years, my students in seminary and local churches have been surprised to find so many angry laments in the book of Psalms. They had never encountered them in church before or paid attention to them in their reading of the psalms. Their surprise is understandable. Unfortunately, the church has been quite selective in designing the curriculum for the "school of prayer" that is the psalms. Despite the fact that more than one third of the Psalter contains lament psalms, Christian tradition has drawn heavily only from the seven penitential laments (Pss. 6, 32, 51, 102, 130, 143), especially during the Lenten season.[12] Perhaps the church's theological tradition has viewed laments as a violation of "an assumed prayer etiquette."[13] Though not denying the need for penitential lament, Roland Murphy wonders "if we have lost the art of complaining *in faith* to God in favor of a stoic concept of what obedience or resignation to the divine will really means."[14] Theologian Martin Marty recognized this when he decided not to read lament Psalm 88 to his dying wife during one of their nightly readings of the psalms, because he thought that neither he nor she could take it. She insisted that it be read: "I need that kind most."[15]

The church has inherited the lament from Judaism, which rooted its understanding of lament in the biblical covenant tradition. Darrell Fasching argues that "the covenantal understanding of faith as a dialogue in which the Jew was not only expected to trust and obey God but was also allowed to question (and even call into question) the behavior of God seems to have disappeared in Christianity. The complex dialectic of faith as *trust and questioning* came to be reduced in Christianity to a very different understanding of faith as *unquestioning trust and obedience.*"[16] Questioning and persistence mark Israel's relationship with God as expressed in Jacob's wrestling with God at the Jabbok River (Gen. 32:22–30),[17] in Job's angry poetry (Job 3—42:6), and in Abraham's arguing with God (Gen. 18:16–33). This *hutzpah,* as it is known in Jewish tradition, appears in a few places in the New Testament: "Ask, search, knock" (Mt. 7:7; Lk. 11:9–13); the Canaanite woman (Mt. 15:21–28; Mk. 7:24–30); the woman with the issue of blood (Mk. 5:24–34); the persistent widow (Lk. 18:1–8).[18] Belden Lane explains the virtual absence of the *hutzpah k'lapei shamaya* ("boldness with regard to heaven") tradition in Christianity both theologically and sociologically.[19] Theologically, it is rooted in Paul's emphasis on the patient bearing of suffering in light of the cross and the imminent resurrected world to come. God shares in the suffering through Jesus. Eschatology (doctrine of the end time) makes suffering temporary and honorable. Sociologically, the loss of daring prayer in Christianity can be traced to the church's socioeconomic prosperity and security, which blunted the eschatological impatience for God's reign; prayer reflects this situation.[20]

One of the most appreciated Lenten Bible studies I have ever led focuses upon the angry lament psalms as a way of accompanying Jesus to Good Friday and the cross. As one initially skeptical parishioner told me after a Lenten lament study: "I thought God would shut me out when I told God I was just so sick of God not making things better. Instead, I feel closer to God than I ever have. Do you think that maybe by being so honest there was somehow more room in me for God? I guess being an Easter people and lamenting are not mutually exclusive. Honest praise can't happen if you're filled with pain."[21] On our way to Easter, Lent invites the use of laments. Recognizing this, Victoria Bailey has created "A Service of Silence and Lamentation for Good Friday or Holy Saturday," whose purpose is "to allow us to enter into the experience of apparent abandonment by God as Jesus expressed it in His cry from the cross and as some of His followers must surely have felt during the interim between His crucifixion and resurrection." She sees this service as a way to enter into "our own sense of abandonment and despair, which many of us experience from time to time but are not always encouraged, allowed or enabled to voice."[22] See the appendix for this service. We need more liturgies like this one that name our experience and take it before God within the liturgical rhythms of the church year.

Without the angry laments, we are cut off from the opportunity to be honest and whole in our prayer before God. This recognition, however, bumps up against liturgical renewal begun in the 1960s, which "attempted to recover earlier forms of eucharistic celebration, with the result that an emphasis on thanksgiving, celebration, and victory over sin and death replaced the earlier severe emphasis on contrition and penitence."[23] This move "has, in effect, driven the hurtful side of experience either into obscure corners of faith practice or completely out of Christian worship," warns Brueggemann; the church's "failure of nerve" regarding the lament is clear.[24] The emphasis on celebration coincided with what sociologist Robert Wuthnow calls the move from a "spirituality of dwelling" anchored in houses of worship, denominations, and neighborhoods in the 1950s to a "spirituality of seeking" in the 1960s, when people moved beyond established religious institutions, and new spiritual centers emerged throughout U.S. society in the form of support and small groups: Twelve Step, Bible study, survivor classes. The result was a kind of "spiritual consumerism."[25] The emphasis was on feeling good and satisfying our interests. The problem with that emphasis is, when we do not or cannot feel good, what do we do?

The psalm lament certainly extends what the church has for too long seen to be the traditional range of prayer. That the church has restricted our praying of the psalms in worship is clear from a glance at the responsive psalm readings in the back of most hymnals. I call this the scissors-and-paste method of liturgical psalm use. When angry laments *are* used, the guts of the lament are cut out, with the psalm jumping immediately from petition to praise, skipping over the angry questions.[26] Check your own church's hymnal to see whether or not the psalms have been cut and pasted in the responsive readings and which psalms have been left out altogether. What do you find? Lester Meyer[27] surveyed the *Lutheran Book of Worship*, the Episcopalian *Book of Common Prayer*, and the *Lectionary for Mass: The Roman Missal* and found that the majority of psalms omitted from liturgical use are the laments. I have found that the same is true for *The Hymnal of the United Church of Christ* and *The United Methodist Hymnal.*

One of my favorite exercises for helping people to discover the range of prayer available in the book of Psalms has produced the same results year after year.[28] I put verses from six different psalms on newsprint: Psalm 1:6, a wisdom psalm focusing on obedience; 13:1, an angry lament; 23:1, a confession of trust; 30:2, an individual thanksgiving; 51:1, a penitential lament confessing sin; and 107:1, a communal thanksgiving. I ask each participant to choose one verse that best expresses what he or she would pray if praying right now. Each person reads that verse several times prayerfully, then turns to the psalm within which that verse is found and reads the whole psalm. The person then turns to a partner and reads the whole psalm out loud. The reader shares with his or her partner why that particular psalm was chosen and what words or images in the psalm are particularly powerful. The partner then reads his or her psalm to the other. Everyone will be talking at once, but no one will notice. Hearing the psalm, read or sung, is an important part of appropriating it, though it is not the only way. Psalms may also be appropriated visually; art images can evoke the divine presence and reveal the human condition in the psalms.[29] Liturgical artist Patrick Ellis insists that the psalms are "the closest thing to visual art I've encountered in the Bible."[30] For the deaf and deaf/blind communities, feeling, not hearing or seeing, is the key to psalm appropriation.[31] Indeed, many psalm images are not visual or auditory, but felt, such as "all my bones are out of joint" (Ps. 22:14, NRSV).

In whatever way a psalm is appropriated during this psalm-praying exercise, few people, it seems, are drawn to the lament psalm on the list. Every year, without fail, the psalms most often chosen in this prayer exercise are 23, 30, and 107, which express confession of trust and thanksgiving respectively. Psalm 23 is a perennial favorite. Even Garrison Keillor notes that in Lake Woebegon on Memorial Day, schoolchildren recite Psalm 23 along with Lincoln's *Gettysburg Address;* William Holladay calls Psalm 23 "an American secular icon."[32] Every funeral I have attended has included a recitation of Psalm 23; some people even know it by heart. By contrast, I can name only a handful of people who can identify their favorite lament psalm. This is in part because, as Renita Weems observes, "not enough has been written about the long dry seasons" of our spiritual journey, when we "feel as if we have hit a brick wall and our prayers have been met with silence."[33] For Weems, lament psalms such Psalm 42 afford a meeting with "a kindred spirit" who has felt her own abandonment by God. She testifies that "if these psalms and similar writings were absent from the Bible, my spirit might have withered away long ago."[34]

It is clear that many of us embrace a narrow understanding of prayer that excludes the angry laments. The definition of prayer that one brings to the book of Psalms will shape the way in which one enters into the wide-ranging prayer of the Psalter (or not). Take a minute and complete the sentence, "prayer is ____," after reflecting on when, where, how, and what you pray. Many of my students over the years have defined prayer as listening to God in a virtual one-way conversation that makes no room for lament questions. A submissive prayer posture of head bowed and eyes closed makes it difficult to clench a fist in angry lament. This understanding of prayer as listening owes much to theologian Karl Barth,[35] who argued in response to the crises of the twentieth century that prayer is a matter of obedience to God, listening to God, turning toward God and away from self, and of ministering to the world though petition and intercession. Weems speaks of listening *for* God, but this listening is undergirded by honesty that allows for protests, doubts, and glimpses of God in both the noisiness and silence of ordinary life.[36] Others have described prayer as dialogue, honest conversation, or connecting with the Divine, with eyes open. My colleague at Wesley Bobby McClain reminds his preaching students that one couldn't bow one's head to pray on the steps of the Selma, Alabama, courthouse during the 1960s civil rights marches with snarling dogs and angry mobs everywhere.[37] One student offered this definition: "When I pray, I take off the clothes of my heart before God; I make myself vulnerable, take risks." Prayer in this sense is a way to articulate and cope with the experiences of life before God, "a means of maintaining dialogue"[38] in the midst of chaos. Another student defined prayer as "spiritual breathing" that covers all aspects of our life. Patrick Miller defines prayer as "often a spontaneous outcome of life at its heights and depths."[39] Does your definition of prayer embrace the whole emotional range of the psalms and of your life of faith? If not, why not?

Not only is our range of prayer challenged and broadened by the psalms, but our hymn singing is as well. Not many hymns draw their inspiration from angry lament psalms. A quick check will bear this out. Look in the back of your church's hymnal, in the index that deals with scripture passages related to the hymns. Count the number of psalms represented in the hymnal. Are certain psalms represented more than once? Which ones? In *The United Methodist Hymnal*, for example, Psalm 23 has given rise to four hymns, and Psalms 46, 51, 104, and 150 each have given rise to two hymns. In *The Presbyterian Hymnal*, Psalm 23 is presented in seven hymns, and Psalms 46, 98, and 150 in five hymns each. Just as with responsive readings of the psalms, the laments are noticeably absent as hymns.[40] Furthermore, some hymns not based on the psalms discourage any expression of doubt and questions, for example, hymn no. 326 in *The Presbyterian Hymnal*, "Spirit of God, Descend Upon My Heart," stanza three, lines two and three: "Teach me the struggles of the soul to bear, To check the rising doubt, the rebel sigh." Another example is "Leave It There," hymn no. 522 in *The United Methodist Hymnal;* though the hymn recognizes that the life of faith is difficult "when your enemies assail, and your heart begins to fail," the refrain insists "if you trust and never doubt, he will surely bring you out, take your burden to the Lord and leave it there."

If "we are what we sing," then we are in trouble in terms of expressing the reality of the life of faith. The result of the absence of lament hymns and the restraint of existing hymns contributes to worship that Elaine Ramshaw describes as "unrelentingly positive in tone,"[41] worship that cannot embrace the realities of a life of faith. This optimism is reflected in the music of many contemporary artists whose lament music is indistinguishable from music for hymns and thanksgivings; I call it la-la music, even and sweet, music that does not match the raw, emotional intensity of the angry laments. One exception is the Reverend Robin White,[42] who has written and sung music for Psalm 13. Her music captures the anguish and movement within the lament, even for those who do not know Hebrew. How often do we hear music like this in church? Also powerful is the cantata "I Will Lift Up Mine Eyes" by Adolphus Hailstork, III, for tenor solo, chorus, and small orchestra, reflecting the black church experience. Hailstork expresses the Christian spiritual journey from initial conversion (Ps. 121, "I Will Lift Up Mine Eyes"), trials and tribulations (Ps. 13, "How Long?"), and renewal (Ps. 23, "The Lord is My Shepherd. Alleluia").[43]

Furthermore, though many of the songs in our hymnals claim to be based on particular psalms, a comparison between hymn and psalm often shows that the two have little in common except for a few words or phrases. What is at issue here is not the christological interpretation of the psalms (reading the psalms in the light of the Christ event), but rather, a basic reinterpretation of the theology (talk about God) and the anthropology (talk about human beings) of the psalms. Look up one or two of the psalms represented to see what kinds of emotions and thoughts about God and human beings are expressed. Do these emotions and thoughts match what the psalm has to say? Often, they do not.

Many Christians would argue that such comparisons do not matter anyway; we don't need the psalms, because our hymnals provide prayer and song for worship! Unfortunately, we forget that the Psalter was the hymnbook of the Second Temple and of the early church, which read the psalms as scripture, recited them as prayers, and sang them as hymns. Psalms were taken up by the later church for use in liturgies and the Daily Offices.

Saints, mystics, and monks through the centuries have turned to the psalms as their devotional book. The hymnody of the reformers drew heavily from the psalms. The psalms are a part of our Christian heritage from the very beginning. Although the hymnbook is a relatively modern development, it seems to have displaced rather than supplemented the psalms in today's worship. We may encounter some psalms cut and pasted in the back of our hymnals as responsive readings; religious houses may pray psalms faithfully daily; and liturgical reforms among some denominations may have recovered the use of psalms in eucharistic liturgies. But by and large, for too many Christians the psalms are not preached from, prayed from, or sung in worship services nor studied as much as they could be. Psalms are often treated as little more than poetic appendages to our liturgies or as catchy introductions to church committee meetings. For most of us, psalms—and only certain favorites at that!—function at best as the vehicle of our private devotions and meditations; psalms we do not like or understand are ignored.

Yet at the same time, a spiritual hunger gnaws at Christians across the ecumenical spectrum.[44] As a trip to any bookstore will substantiate, new translations and paraphrases of, meditations on, and musical settings for the psalms appear with regularity. This interest testifies to the yearning for renewal of worship and prayer in our time, especially among Gen Xers (people born between 1964 and 1978). Gen Xers, unlike their Baby Boomer parents, are connected to institutions, to denominations, and to spiritual direction and other spiritual disciplines, despite media claims to the contrary. "New York publishers are tripping over each other to turn out snappy prayer books. Christians increasingly speak of going to their spiritual director, as though it were as ordinary as going to the hair dresser."[45] That many of the new prayer books being produced have little or nothing in common with the Hebrew text of the psalms, however, ought to warn us against too readily digesting such spiritual junk food. The psalms cannot say whatever we want them to say, but a careful study of the psalms can contribute to a faithful renewal of the worship life of contemporary Christians. As one Xer argues, "churches that want to lure Xers should give up their glitzy, poppy entertainment strategies and stick with the elements of tradition. Some Xers...may like synthesizers and hymns that were written last week, but many Xers like... 'the comfort of something older.'"[46] I would suggest the comfort and challenge of the "older" psalms.

The flood of prayer pamphlets and "a religious form of do-it-yourself techniques for helping people cope" cannot fill the "spiritual vacuum"[47] at the center of our lives. In 1994 *The Washington Post* ran a feature article on the "trend" of random kindness as part of the self-help movement in America.[48] Remember the bumper stickers proclaiming, "Practice Random

pop
spirituality

Acts of Kindness and Senseless Acts of Beauty"? The experts interviewed in the newspaper article felt that the "feel good" reaction to doing random acts of kindness appealed to American individualism but could not sustain the movement; what was needed was a sense of communal responsibility. It is not surprising that I never see that bumper sticker anymore.

That a spiritual vacuum still exists is caused in part, I think, by the split within much of contemporary theology between the doctrine of God (theology) and prayer.[49] A reappropriation of the psalms can contribute to the reunification of theology and prayer. Kathleen Norris recognized this possibility during her immersion in Benedictine liturgy, reciting or singing the psalms at morning, noon, and evening prayer, praying the whole Psalter every three or four weeks. "During my year among the Benedictines I found that as their prayer rolls along, daily as marriage or doing dishes, it tends to sweep away the formalities of systematic theology and church doctrine."[50] She quotes British Benedictine Sebastian Moore: "God behaves in the Psalms in ways he is not allowed to behave in systematic theology."[51]

Psalm prayer can serve as a criterion for the "prayability" of our doctrine of God: "Is this a God to whom we can pray in the full range of biblical prayer?"[52] The criterion of "prayability" is absent for many in Harold Kushner's best-seller *When Bad Things Happen to Good People*.[53] Kushner argues that bad things that happen to us are "not really God's fault"; we should *"be angry at the situation"* rather than at ourselves, others, or God. "Being angry at God erects a barrier between us and all the sustaining, comforting resources of religion that are there to help us at such times."[54] In his picture of a God who is still creating and facing pockets of chaos to be overcome (based on God's speeches from the whirlwind to Job in Job 38—41), there is no room for the psalm lament and thus for the full range of biblical prayer.

Yet many find comfort in Kushner's theology, as I learned firsthand at a conference at Hershey Medical Center in Pennsylvania in 1983. Kushner was there to discuss his book with a panel of physicians, pastors, and seminary faculty, including me, relatively new to seminary teaching. As it happened, I was the only panelist to disagree with Kushner's theology and to ask where the psalm laments fit in it. After the conference ended, I was accosted by a group of fifteen or so angry people who backed me up against a wall and demanded to know how I could dare to disagree with Rabbi Kushner. Didn't I know that he was redeeming his son's death with this book? (Kushner's son, Aaron, died at age 14 of progeria, "rapid aging"). The irony of the situation was that I had made a conscious decision that morning when introducing myself to the five hundred or so people assembled, not to mention that this very day would have been the twenty-eighth birthday of my only brother, Brian, who had drowned at age twenty-three. I shared with this angry group afterward that my work with the psalms, particularly with the laments, was my way of redeeming Brian's death. What Kushner had called "the comforting resources of religion" had tormented me by pushing me too soon to acceptance. The laments were my only lifeline to God and the church in my anger and confusion, and without them, I would not be speaking to them today. Their hostility melted—now they understood what I had been saying as a panelist.

That encounter has remained vivid in my memory after all these years. First, it illustrates how deep our pain can be and how much we want to be able to make sense of it, to redeem it. Second, it shows us how emotional and risky our prayers can be if we allow ourselves to let them match our experiences. Third, the confrontation reminds us that one person's experience is not normative for all of us; my pain "credentials" resonated with this group alongside Kushner's. As a counter to Kushner twenty years later, I raise Samuel Balentine's question: "If one cannot question God, then to whom does one direct the questions? If God is a God whom we cannot question, then what kind of God is this to whom we are committing ourselves?"[55] Thankfully, poets such as Ann Weems have declared that "our only hope is to march ourselves to the throne of God and in loud lament cry out the pain that lives in our souls."[56] Her laments are for "those who weep and for those who weep with those who weep."[57] Her God is prayable in the style of the biblical laments. Weems' poignant psalms written in response to her son's early death have struck a chord with many across the nation.

My experience with Rabbi Kushner convinces me that rather than move exclusively from a systematic and theoretical construct of God to prayer and experience, the community of faith needs to move also in the opposite direction. Does the experience of different people, as it is articulated in prayer, square with the picture of God that theology has sketched? If not, then what becomes of that experience? Must it be denied or negated? Can a person be whole before God in the face of such denial? Can one group of people control another group of people with the picture of God (a theology) that denies the experience of the other group? Prayer and theology go together; loss of their dialectical relationship can lead to the atrophy of both and an erosion of the community of faith. As Patrick Miller argues, theology "is not simply a matter of believing and then praying to God in the light of what one believes. That very belief is shaped by the practice of prayer. So prayer and theology exist in relation to each other in a correcting circle."[58] Psalm prayer can offer much correction for theology.

Preaching in our churches has also suffered from the clergy's unwillingness to embrace the entire psalms range as the stuff of proclamation.[59] In a collection of twenty-five sermons preached by Christians, Jews, and Muslims the Sunday after the Oklahoma City bombings in 1995, only five psalms were referenced, and among the five, only one lament, Psalm 22 (in a sermon by a rabbi). Psalms 23 and 46 were cited by three different preachers. Not only did preaching in this tragedy suffer from a reticence to embrace the range of psalm prayer, but it suffered as well from our reluctance in America to think theologically about public issues and public problems in the midst of our privatistic inclinations.[60] The same pattern repeated itself more recently in the wake of the 9/11 attacks on the World Trade Center and the Pentagon. In my random sampling of area pastors, no one had preached from a lament the Sunday after 9/11; many chose the comfort of Psalm 23. A local rabbi preached from Lamentations, and several African American pastors preached from the prophets.

Erhard Gerstenberger boldy challenges Christian preachers to take up the theme of enemies and evildoers in the laments as "one of the most crucial issues of our times." The "enemy" problem has not disappeared today but has simply been reformulated in our mechanistic, impersonal world. We must ask today who is responsible for suffering and dehumanization. Christians have kept few church services to help the individual and the community in suffering or in naming and dealing with "enemies." Only to the extent in which worship "includes or embraces present- day reality" can our Sunday services claim to "represent the heart of a Christian congregation."[61]

Along with preaching, churches need to reconsider other aspects of the worship service in light of the psalms, especially the use of banners and paraments. How often do we see paraments like those crafted by artist Susan Stevens with its anguished figure in purple on a burlap background crying out, "My God, Why?"[62] The visual arts can powerfully communicate the range of psalm prayer.

To what kind of God do the psalmists pray? This is a question about the theology of the psalms. Make up a list of adjectives and nouns describing God as you skim the psalms: deliverer, warrior, judge, rock, protector, creator, refuge, asleep, hidden, enemy, king, gracious, compassionate, giver of Torah, relentless, absent. Unfortunately, many of us bring to our reading of the psalms an image of God shaped by our hymnals, an image that Brian Wren calls the KINGAFAP metaphor, an acronym for "King-God-Almighty-Father-Protector" who mirrors the domination of males over females in society.[63] By analyzing English hymnody, Wren seeks to document how "God-language in Christian worship is heavily preoccupied with power-as-control."[64] This metaphor of an omnipotent God who protects us makes the hiddenness and absence of God in the psalms that much more uncomfortable for us and distances us from the angry laments. God is called to account and much more vulnerable in the lament psalms, as we shall see.

The image of an all-powerful God can be especially damaging for women. As Rebecca Chopp argues, modernity is divided into public/private or primary/secondary domains that are gendered.[65] The public is the domain of the man and the private the domain of the woman. Tasks and values are assigned to each domain: the public/male realm is objective, scientific, competitive, powerful; the private/female domain is the locus of all the public rejects—relationships, caring, mutuality, physicality, embodiment. Chopp argues that knowledge is lodged in the public realm and religion in the private realm, where it is devalued as full of feeling. How ironic that the church struggles within the private realm about what constitutes "acceptable feeling" in its avoidance of the laments. The language of our hymns mimics the language of the public realm, as does some psalm language (the enthronement psalms—"the LORD reigns," for example), yet psalm language is also saturated with feeling, emotion, and physicality. As one of my students put it, the psalmists are "body-conscious people": lips, tongue, teeth, eyes, bones, hands, face, feet, and heart are graphically functional in their responses to life; body parts are personified and express the feelings of the psalmists.[66]

Our assessment of the picture of God in the psalms stands in inverse proportion to our assessment of the picture that the psalmists draw of themselves. Our penchant for seeing a loving, powerful God in the psalms dictates a contrast with sinful, weak humanity. Skim the psalms to generate a list of nouns and adjectives for the psalmists. My students have described the psalmists as either sinners and self-righteous protesters, or as afflicted, poor, and oppressed. The more transcendent the view of God, the lower the view of humanity. The audacity of *hutzpah* in the psalm laments does not sit well with those who see a loving, powerful God. One of my students who had fled the devastating civil war in Liberia describes how worship services in Liberia usually opened with the following exchange: Pastor: "God is good"; Congregational response: "all the time"; Pastor: "all the time"; Congregation: "God is good." The student shared how angry that made him feel as neighbors killed neighbors and people were marched out of their villages and slaughtered in death treks every day. What we needed, he said, were the angry laments, but our opening declaration silenced them. Those who sentimentalize Jürgen Moltmann's suffering God into a passive God will not be comfortable with laments, either. Liberation, feminist, and womanist theologians speak not of a passive God, but of "a compassion that resists tragic suffering."[67]

In order to understand who we are as worshiping Christians, we must reclaim our psalms heritage. To do that is to stand today in continuity with our tradition, in touch with our roots. In this sense then, "the Psalms are something like a family album; they remind us of who we are and of things that happened to us."[68] They tell our own stories. Because the psalms are the common heritage of all churches, they also provide a ready base for ecumenical worship. Furthermore, "communal recitation of the Psalms works against our narcissism, our tendency in America to turn everything into self-discovery."[69] When we can't pray, the psalms pray for us, pulling us along, "out of private prayer, into community and then into the world, into what might be termed praying the news," not as voyeurs but as ones who take responsibility for the violence of that news.[70]

In our noisy world of cell phones, videos, TV, and the Internet, in which we can be instantly in touch with anybody at any time, and in which we fool ourselves into thinking that we are in control, we stumble upon God's absence and God's silence, and we panic. This was Renita Weems's experience: "I had grown so accustomed to believing in a God who spoke thunderously and in spectacular ways that I didn't think I could survive when it came time to stumble in divine silence."[71] Barbara Brown Taylor warns that our reaction to the silence shows us that "our language is broken."[72] When God is silent, we cannot talk more. Preachers must show homiletical restraint and be matchmakers; they must "choose the fewest, best words that will allow them [God and people] to find one another and then to get out of the way."[73] I would suggest that the psalms can help facilitate this matchmaking; they are "the fewest and best words" of our tradition.

A journey through the psalms can be a path to wholeness, healing, and rootedness. The psalms engage our whole person. They demand our aesthetic response to the beauty and power of the poetry, our theological response to the picture of God that is drawn, and our emotional response to the humanness of the psalmists. Psalms speak "both *for* us as they express our thoughts and feelings, fears and hopes, and *to* us as we hear in them direction for the life of faith and something of God's way with us."[74] To sing the psalms, pray them, study them, and hear them preached calls us into continuity with our tradition and joins us with other Christians past and present in the struggle for faith in God.

CHAPTER TWO

The Synagogue, the Church, and the Psalms

When I ask people to guess what book of the Bible is quoted most often by Jesus, the usual response is Isaiah. They are surprised to learn that Isaiah comes in third behind Deuteronomy and the Psalms. In the New Testament there are at least fifty-five quotations (by one count) from more than sixty of the psalms.[1] Among the sayings of Jesus in the gospels, there are more quotations from Psalms than from any other book of the Hebrew Bible.[2] Jesus uses Psalms 22 (Mk. 15:34), 31 (Lk. 23:46), and 69 at Calvary, quotes 110, 118, and 41 in his teaching, and sings the Hallel Psalms (113—118) in the upper room (Mk. 14:26). The evangelists used many psalm texts in reference to Jesus' baptism (Mt. 3:17 and parallels quoting Ps. 2:7) and temptation, his ministry and teaching, and especially his passion (Pss. 22, 31, and 69). In his sermon at the church's first Pentecost, Peter cites texts from Joel and Psalms 16, 110, and 132 (Acts 2:25–35) as pointing to Christ's resurrection and ascension. Paul references the Psalter thirty-one times, orienting it to the event of Jesus Christ and faith in him as Messiah.[3]

This frequent use of the Hebrew Bible psalms in the New Testament does not mean that the early Christian church composed no psalms or hymns of its own. Many sayings of Jesus in the gospels are poetic in form,

16

notably the Beatitudes and many of the discourses in John. Many hymn fragments are scattered throughout the New Testament, for example, the Magnificat in Luke 1:46–55, the Benedictus (Canticle of Zechariah) in Luke 1:68–79, and the Philippian hymn in Philippians 2:6–11. These have found a permanent place in the liturgies of the church. It is not likely, however, that these Christian hymns displaced the psalms, which were reinterpreted by the church in the light of the Christ event. As Clinton McCann observes, "the church used the psalms both as liturgical materials in the early Christian worship and as a theological resource."[4]

Where did these early Christians get their knowledge of the psalms? From the Hebrew Bible, which was their Bible, and from the public worship in the temple and the synagogue, where Jews met for worship and instruction on the sabbath and during the week. The books of First and Second Chronicles seemingly record the organization of choirs in the time of David and Solomon (1 Chr. 6:31–48), but more probably they give us information about the Second Temple (built after the return from Babylonian exile, 520–515 B.C.E., and destroyed by the Romans in 70 C.E.) and its worship. The names of some choir guilds are found in several psalm superscriptions (that is, titles written above the psalms): Asaph (50, 73—83); the children of Korah (42—49, 84—85, 87—88); Heman (88; 1 Chr. 25:6, NRSV, suggests that the sons *and daughters* of Heman were "all under the direction of their father for the music in the house of the LORD"); Ethan (89); and Jeduthun (39, 62, 77). In the Second Temple, psalms were sung by choirs of priest singers from the tribe of Levi (Levites), whose job was to supervise temple worship; they were to "play loudly on musical instruments, on harps and lyres and cymbals, to raise sounds of joy" (1 Chr. 15:16); (compare 2 Chr. 5:13; 7:6). At various places in the singing and playing of instruments, people responded with praise shouts of hallelujah or with refrains, for example, "For God's *hesed* endures forever" (2 Chr. 5:13).[5]

The superscription indicates the psalm's liturgical use in the temple. The superscription of Psalm 100, for example, reads *mizmor letodah,* a song accompanied by a stringed instrument for the *todah,* or thanksgiving sacrifice; see also the superscriptions for Psalms 30, 38, 70, and 92. Other superscriptions may give titles of psalm melodies to be used, for example, "according to the *sheminith*" in Psalm 6 (compare with Pss. 5, 8, 12, 22, 57, 69, and 77). Superscriptions in the Septuagint (Greek translation of the Hebrew Bible begun in 250 B.C.E. by the Greek-speaking Jews of Alexandria, Egypt) text of the Psalms indicate that Psalm 24 is recited on Sunday, Psalm 48 on Monday, Psalm 82 on Tuesday, Psalm 93 on Friday, and Psalm 92 on Saturday.[6] The technical term *selah,* which appears in many of the psalms, is understood by some to indicate an orchestral interlude, a silent pause, a congregational response, or a recitation[7] of a story from Israelite tradition. Fifty-five psalms are entitled "for the leader" (or director or choirmaster). Musical instruments are mentioned in eight psalm superscriptions.

In the synagogues (prayer or meeting houses), prayer, accompanied by scripture reading and exposition, replaced the sacrificial offerings of the temple. The rise of the synagogue during the Second Temple period symbolized "the democratization of religion"; the entire community, rather than a priestly elite, was to place every act and moment of life in God's service.[8] Nearly half the psalms were incorporated eventually into the fixed prayers of the synagogue service, including the daily psalms, which the Levites used to sing in the Temple. The rabbis preached extensively from the psalms, so much so that "there is not a single chapter of Psalms—indeed, hardly a single verse—which is not expounded somewhere in the Talmud and Midrash."[9] In the synagogues, psalms were sung by cantors rather than by Levitical choirs, with the people joining in with chanted refrains. No musical instruments were used.

The New Testament makes it clear that psalms "have been the staple diet of the Church's singing."[10] In 1 Corinthians 14:26, Paul lists the spiritual gifts individual members share with one another in worship: a hymn (*psalmon* in Greek, or psalm), a lesson, a revelation, a tongue, an interpretation. Colossians 3:16–17 urges Christians to teach and admonish one another "and sing psalms and hymns and spiritual songs with thankfulness in your hearts to God" (RSV); compare with Ephesians 5:19–20 and Acts 2:42. The church father Tertullian (c. 200 C.E.) affirms the place of the psalms in the Sunday liturgy of the church: "The Scriptures are read and the psalms sung, sermons are delivered and petitions offered."[11] In the same period, Clement of Alexandria and Origen mention the use of psalms and hymns and the melodies used for them. Some scholars suggest that the word *psalmon* was not restricted to the psalms of David in the Bible, but included many nonbiblical compositions, especially in the third and fourth centuries.[12] Singing songs after banquets was a universal practice in the ancient world, and many Christian writings criticize the erotic nature of these songs accompanied often by drinking and fighting, in contrast to the Christian singing of psalms and hymns (Greek: *hymnon)* at meals and vigils; some of these songs were from scripture, and some were new compositions.[13]

Biblical psalms were frequently quoted and preached from in the first to the fourth centuries, and Jerome even advised women and children to learn Hebrew so that they might be able to read and sing the psalms in their original tongue. Such knowledge was often required for ordination, a fact of which I remind my seminary students, much to their distress! Early Christian exegesis was different for the psalms than for other biblical books.

Exegetes were concerned with clergy and monks rather than ordinary believers; they aimed to promote the internalization of psalms so that thoughts and feelings could be purified and transformed. In this sense, the psalms were medicinal and therapeutic, teaching what to say and do to heal. Church fathers did not comment on the content of psalms, but on their sweetness and beguiling qualities; one could find delight in praising God with psalms, which were read and sung as poetry for spiritual growth.[14]

The oldest liturgies of the church, both East and West, require at least three lessons: from the Hebrew Bible, from the epistles or Acts, and from the gospels. After the Hebrew Bible lesson, a psalm was sung as a response to the previous reading. In the Latin church, this psalm came to be known as the Gradual because it was sung from the step (*gradus* in Latin) of the pulpit from which the lesson was read. As early as the second century, each psalm was followed by the Gloria Patri (glory be to the Father) to show that the psalms were accepted as Christian expressions with specific references to Jesus. The early church used the psalms to help it interpret Christ, and Christ became the interpretative key for unlocking the psalms.

No evidence exists for a fixed schedule of daily lessons and psalms in the liturgies of the early church. The Gradual was chanted by a cantor (a practice taken over from the synagogue), with the congregation and later a choir responding with a refrain. This responsorial model can be seen in the psalms themselves (Pss. 42, 43, 107, and 136). Since liturgical development was slow during the first to the fourth centuries, the music of the Gradual was originally very simple. However, the melodies of the Gradual were eventually taken over by professional soloists, so that Pope Gregory the Great in 595 assigned the Gradual to lesser ministries, arguing "while search is made for a good voice, no care is taken to provide that the life shall be such as harmonizes with the holy ministry."[15]

After Constantine's conversion to Christianity in 312, when the church enjoyed peace from persecution and support from wealthy benefactors, the churches and the liturgy both became more elaborate. Choirs supplemented congregational responses to cantor melodies, and antiphonal singing (the singing of psalm verses alternately by two groups of singers) developed out of Antioch in the mid-fourth century. This style spread quickly to monastic communities. The use of the antiphon also arose; one or two verses from the psalms would be sung at the beginning and end of the psalm. The seasons of the year determined the choice of antiphon. Changing antiphons could underscore different themes within the same psalm. In addition to the Gradual, three antiphonal psalms in the ancient Roman liturgy (Introit, Offertory, and Communion) functioned as devotional accompaniments to processions within the service.

In the Middle Ages, the use of psalms in worship declined radically. Processions were shortened, and communion was limited to a few times per year because of a lack of resident clergy, the fact that few cantors or choirs could read the Latin of the service and chant the psalms, and the fact that books and music were too expensive for most parishes. All the parts of the liturgy were copied in a one-volume Missal, and psalmody was reduced to a few verses read by the priest.

Despite their decline in medieval worship, the psalms had continued to serve as the central focus for the daily devotions of monks in monastic communities since the development of monasticism in the fourth century. The church had taken over this practice of daily prayer from the Jews, who were required to pray twice a day (morning and afternoon), these times corresponding to the *Tamid* sacrifice in the temple.[16] By the end of the second century, the church had increased the number of daily prayer times from two (morning and evening) to six. Rather than being tied to times of corporate worship, these Daily Offices (times of prayer) were meant to promote reflection on Christ's death and resurrection.[17] Whereas cathedral psalmody had been designed for the liturgical instruction of illiterate lay participants to counter the private psalmody used by heretics to propagate false doctrine, monastic psalmody promoted meditation on the psalms rather than liturgical experience.[18] In the monastic communities, East and West, seven Daily Offices were prayed to accord with Psalm 119:164: "Seven times a day I praise you for your righteous judgments." The psalms were distributed so that all 150 were sung once a week, with double offices on major saints' days.

Elaborate illustrated Psalters were produced for members of the nobility who prayed the Offices. The illustrations were frequently of New Testament scenes to which the psalms were thought to refer, or made reference to the times of day and occasions for reading the psalms. Also, the monastic practice developed of saying a certain number of psalms for particular sins as penance.[19] The psalms also found their way into folk customs. The opening verse of Psalm 91, for example, "He who dwells in the shelter of the Most High, in the care of the God of Heaven will abide," was a favorite inscription for protective amulets.[20] By the fifteenth century, hand-copied manuscripts of the Prymer (first prayers) were used by people who could read for private devotions and for teaching the young how to read. The Prymer originated as additional prayers to the daily prayers of the monasteries. Sixty-three psalms are common to all the Prymers in different countries.[21]

By the sixteenth century, the seven Daily Offices became too much for priests living outside the monasteries. Many reformers followed Martin Luther, who valued the daily reading of the psalms but cut them back to twice a day, midnight and 6 p.m., each with three psalms. Luther also adapted psalms for congregational singing. Psalms within worship enjoyed renewed status, especially when John Calvin argued that "only God's Word was worthy to be sung in God's praise"; he allowed no music in worship except that of the metrical psalms.[22] His Genevan Psalter (1562), with its regular rhythms, was singable by most congregations with a songleader; trained choirs were not required. In many American hymnals, "All People That on Earth Do Dwell," based on Psalm 100 and sung to the tune of "Old Hundredth," remains as an example of this metrical psalmody.[23] In the psalms, Calvin found a world similar to his own, in which people were traumatized by fear and violence; he also found hope in the midst of that trauma.[24]

English-speaking congregations of Calvin's time also sang metrical psalms; no hymns were introduced until the eighteenth century. Given this situation, it is no surprise that the first book printed in the American colonies was the *Bay Psalm Book* (1640). In Dutch Reformed churches, the organ came to replace the songleader, and psalm singing with the organ continues unbroken to this day. I recently experienced a congregational psalm sing in the Dutch Reformed style for the first time;[25] the pace was slow and ponderous, but it allowed us to concentrate on what we were singing, so that the effect was one of meditation and awe-inspiring worship.

In the early eighteenth century, Isaac Watts, "the father of English hymnody," who complained of wretched psalm singing in his church, began to paraphrase, modernize, and christianize the psalms. His hymns, such as "Joy to the World" (based on Ps. 98), were published in 1707. After Watts's death, it took almost one hundred years for hymn singing to become firmly established in England and America. At any rate, by the end of the eighteenth century, psalms were on their way out as the centerpiece of song in worship.

Ironically, it is the singing of the metrical psalms in worship that stimulated this development. Watts's adaptation of psalms, however, became an important part of the devotional life and liturgy of slave Christians and their free descendants. In mainline Protestant African American churches today, psalms are part of the repertoire of the spiritual leaders of the church, the deacons; the sermon following the psalm-centered deacon's prayer offers answers to the supplications of that prayer, moving the congregation from tragedy to transformation.[26]

Today, Roman Catholics in the wake of Vatican II, Lutherans, Episcopalians, and United Methodists have all returned to the use of psalms at points in the liturgy in which psalms were once customary. The Presbyterian Church (U.S.A.) published a new hymnal and liturgical Psalter in 1990. The charismatic movement has been using psalms in worship since the 1960s. The Christian Reformed Church in America still uses psalms for half of its congregational singing. The Revised Common Lectionary uses 110 of the psalms for the Sundays of the three-year cycle, along with special readings for special days. Yet the old pattern of the use of psalms in the call to worship and as responsive readings still permeates most Protestant worship services. The recovery of the psalms for our prayer and song in worship is under way but incomplete. Pay attention to the use of psalms in your Sunday liturgy the next time you worship. At what points in the liturgy are the psalms used?

The Development of the Psalter

It is important to keep in mind that the Psalter in its present form is not the result of one single act of collecting by a single person or group of persons. There was no editor in ancient Israel working feverishly to meet a publisher's deadline, no catchy press releases. We can see this just by looking at the Psalter itself, which shows traces of growth over a long period of time, probably many centuries.

The Psalter as we now have it is divided into five books, each of which is marked off by a closing doxology (a speaking of praise to God). Editors of modern translations of the Bible (NIV, NRSV) have added the words "Book 1," "Book 2," and so forth at the beginning of each division to make this clear, but these notations are not found in the Hebrew text of the psalms. The fivefold psalm division mirrors the fivefold division of the Torah, or Pentateuch, the first five books of the Hebrew Bible. Book 1, for example, includes Psalms 1 through 41. Verse 13 of Psalm 41, which is not a part of the literary whole that is Psalm 41, functions as the closing doxology for Book 1: "Blessed be the LORD, the God of Israel, from everlasting to everlasting. Amen and Amen" (NRSV). See also Psalms 72:18–19; 89:52; and 106:48 for the closing doxologies of books 2, 3, and 4, respectively. The whole of Psalm 150 concludes not only book 5 (Pss. 107—149) with doxology but the entire Psalter as well.

This fivefold division is an artificial construct superimposed on various independently circulating collections of psalms. One can think of the Psalter as composed of different little psalters and psalm collections that were in circulation before the book assumed its final form.[27] This view is supported by several clues within the book of Psalms. For example, in the editorial postscript of Psalm 72:20, which ends book 2, we read: "The prayers of David, the son of Jesse, are ended." Most of the psalms within Books 1 and 2 bear the superscription "*leDavid*," "a psalm of/to/for David." But other "psalms of David" are found, for example, in Book 5 (Pss. 108—110 and 138—145). This means that only at one stage in the history of the formation of the Psalter, or for one group of worshipers in a particular region, did the psalms of David end there. How these various collections were created we simply do not know. Books 1 to 3 probably came together before Books 4 and 5, in which the name of David and individual psalms are less frequent.

That there were separate psalm collections can be supported by the superscriptions[28] (117 of the 150 psalms have superscriptions). In addition to providing liturgical instructions, as discussed above, psalm superscriptions indicate types of psalms. The Hebrew word *mizmor* occurs most frequently, fifty-seven times. The Septuagint translates this Hebrew word as *psalmos* (a song accompanied by a stringed instrument), from which we get the English word *psalm*. Our word *Psalter* comes from one Greek manuscript that uses the word *psalterion* ("harp") for the whole collection. A cluster of psalms with the term *psalmos* in their superscriptions occurs in Psalms 47—51, which may indicate an earlier collection. Another frequent designation of psalm type in the superscriptions is *shir,* which means "song." Thirteen psalms contain both *mizmor* and *shir* in their superscriptions, for example, Psalm 87; the difference between the two designations is not clear.

Clusters of psalms with *maskil ("didactic poem")* in the superscription occur in Psalms 42—45 and 52—55. The term *miktam* ("writing," "inscription"?) is clustered in Psalms 56—60. Personal names in the superscriptions may also point to smaller psalm collections. Most psalms in Book 1 show *leDavid* in their superscriptions; so, too, do Psalms 51—72 in Book 2. Psalms 42—49 mention Korah in their superscriptions; Psalms 73—83 cite Asaph (see above for a discussion of temple guilds). "Song of Ascents" is found in the superscriptions of Psalms 120—134, perhaps indicating that these short, easy to memorize psalms were used by pilgrims traveling to Jerusalem to celebrate a festival. Several references to Jerusalem and Zion are made in these psalms, and there are many liturgical elements in them. Psalm 120 seems to mark the beginning of the journey to Jerusalem, while Psalm 134 suggests a blessing as pilgrims are leaving it.

Doublets (the same psalm or part of a psalm appearing twice) also suggest separate psalm collections. Psalm 14 is repeated in Psalm 53; 40:13–17 is the equivalent of 70; 57:7–11 plus 60:5–12 are repeated in 108. These were probably popular songs that found a place in more than one collection. Also, Psalms 1—41 and 42—83 use different Hebrew terms for deity. Psalms 42—83 are called the Elohistic Psalter, since they use the divine name *Elohim,* translated "God," more frequently (244 times) than in Psalms 1—41 (49 times) or in Psalms 84—150 (70 times).[29] This so-called Elohistic Psalter may have existed independently before being incorporated into the final collection, as a look at the doublets suggests. Psalm 14 uses the divine name *Adonai* (the vocalization of pious Jews of the Hebrew Tetragrammaton, four consonants revealed to Moses at the burning bush), translated in most Bibles as LORD or *Yahweh* (the latter term is not used by pious Jews).

The psalms in each of the five books of the Psalter are not all related to one another in the way that songs are grouped according to theme or liturgical season in our modern hymnals. The collection as we have it probably took final shape after the fall of Jerusalem in 587 B.C.E., either in exile in Babylonia or after the return to Judah from exile in the Persian period, or at least before 200 B.C.E., since we find the collection pretty much as we have it now in the Septuagint. Many of the psalms in the Psalter are quite old and probably were used much earlier in Israel's worship life. In this sense, calling the Psalter "the hymnbook of the Second Temple" is misleading. The Psalter reflects a long history of worship before the Second Temple came into being. Skim the psalms again and look for these superscriptions, doxologies, and book divisions. Be careful to note lines above the psalm superscriptions that come from the editors of the English translation you are using; these lines are meant to sum up and characterize the psalm for you. I think they are intrusive.

Psalm Interpretation

Unlike our modern hymnals, the book of Psalms does not identify for us the author or date of each psalm. The ancient world was little interested in the question of authorship; no one worried about copyright infringement. We can say nothing concrete about psalm authors; they remain anonymous. Nor do we find any absolutely clear indications of the date of particular psalms, except perhaps Psalm 137: "By the waters of Babylon, there we sat down and wept"; here the Babylonian exile in the sixth century B.C.E. seems to be in view.

Psalms were not always treated this way, however. At the turn of the last century, scholars tried to match situations depicted in the psalms with particular events in King David's life or in the history of Israel. In this historicizing interpretation, David was considered to be the author of most of the psalms. The fact that seventy-three of the psalms in the Psalter were connected with David through their superscriptions was claimed as support for this view. The superscription of Psalm 41, for example, reads: "to the choirmaster, a psalm *leDavid*," which most Bibles translate as "a psalm of David." The Hebrew phrase is made up of the preposition *lamed* and the proper name David. This phrase need not suggest authorship. Instead, the range of the Hebrew preposition allows for translations such as "to David," "in the style of David," "in honor of David," or "according to the direction of David."

It was natural for Israel to tie the psalms to David, who enjoyed a great reputation as singer, musician, and poet. David, as the story goes, was introduced into Saul's court for that very reason. "So Saul said to his servants, 'Provide for me someone who can play well, and bring him to me'" (1 Sam. 16:17, NRSV). "And whenever the evil spirit from God came upon Saul, David took the lyre and played it with his hand, and Saul would be relieved and feel better" (1 Sam.16:23, NRSV; see also Am. 6:5). It was also David who made Jerusalem the political and religious capital of his kingdom by bringing the ark of the covenant into it (2 Sam. 6) and by proposing to build there a permanent house for the Lord (2 Sam. 7). As we have seen above, 1 Chronicles credits David with organizing the choir guilds and worship of the temple.

To strengthen this association with David, later editors of the psalm collection developed biographical notes and attached them to the superscriptions to indicate the historical situation in which David composed or recited the psalm (see, for example, Pss. 3, 7, 18, 34, 51, 52, 54, 56, 57, 59, 60, 63, and 142). Thus the superscription of Psalm 51, a penitential lament in which the psalmist begs for God's forgiveness, reads: "A psalm of David, when the prophet Nathan came to him, after he had gone in to Bathsheba" (NRSV). This tendency to associate psalms with David continued in the Septuagint. Fifteen more psalms were tagged with *leDavid*, even Psalm 137! In the New Testament, David was seen as the author of psalms (see Mk. 12:35–37; Acts 4:25–26; and Rom. 4:6–8).

Patrick Miller points out that superscriptions such as the one in Psalm 51 can give us some clues about how the psalm was understood in ancient Israel. Superscriptions "are a way of saying that the psalms over which the superscription is written make sense in just such a context."[30] A variety of human experiences that come forth from a biblical story can also provide a context for a psalm's meaning; we need not be tied to a search for only one explanation. Thus, David's sin with Bathsheba is one way, not *the* way, of understanding Psalm 51.

By contrast, Gerald Wilson argues that psalm superscriptions give us *the* way of uncovering psalm meaning. He focuses on the purposeful editing of the Psalter and suggests that psalm superscriptions about David were added to psalms that already had cultic, technical superscriptions firmly fixed in the tradition. These additions were meant to obscure the original worship setting of these psalms and to ensure individual access to what had been mainly public, communal psalms. By linking them to biblical narratives, editors created a new context for interpreting the psalms, a context that emphasized the private life of devotion and individual access to God. David's inner, spiritual life was opened up to the reader as a model for individual response. This "movement toward personalization"[31] argument unfairly denies the possibility that there can be pious and personal moments in Israelite worship. An older, very negative view of Israelite worship also insisted that personal piety and individual relationship with God could only emerge when worship was freed from formality and the temple. This kind of thinking has helped to drive a wedge of discontinuity between Second Temple Judaism and early Christianity, and has sometimes inadvertently fueled the fires of anti-Judaism throughout the church's history.

Wilson has identified intentional editorial activity most clearly at the "seams" of the psalms collection, that is, at beginnings and ends of collections or books.[32] Royal psalms dealing with the king are found near the beginning of Book 1 (Ps. 2) and at the end of Books 2 (Ps. 72) and 3 (Ps. 89), forming an envelope or bracket for those books. Psalms 2, 72, and 89 progress from an intimate relationship between God and the king to God's rejection of the Davidic covenant in Psalm 89:38–45 and the anguished king's pleas in 89:46–51: "Lord, where is your steadfast love of old?"(89:49, NRSV). Wilson concludes that books 1—3 show the failure of the Davidic covenant underscored by the destruction of Jerusalem in 587 B.C.E. and Babylonian exile, and these books call out for response. Books 4 and 5 respond to the theological crisis caused by the loss of land, temple, and king by proclaiming God's reign and reminding Israel that its only true king is God, not the Davidic king. Wilson suggests that the enthronement psalms (93, 95—99), which declare that "the LORD is king!" are "the theological heart" of the Psalter.[33]

In Wilson's view, one cannot call the Psalter "the hymnbook of the Second Temple" because it "is a book to be *read* rather than to be *performed*, to be *meditated* over rather than to be *recited from*."[34] The continued relevance of the psalms depends on this shift. Clinton McCann has adopted this approach in his commentary on psalms in *The New Interpreter's Bible*,[35] yet at the same time he allows that the early church used the psalms as liturgical resources (see above). McCann and others make much of the intentional placement of Psalms 1—2 at the beginning of the Psalter. These psalms "set the interpretive agenda and provided an orientation for reading the whole book of Psalms,"[36] rather than praying or singing them. Psalm 1 says that "happy" (1:1; 2:12) means being open to "instruction" *(torah),* and Psalm 2 gives the content of that instruction—God rules. The rest of the psalms show that God's rule is constantly opposed and shows how one lives a faithful life amidst that opposition.

Walter Brueggemann rightly criticizes those who embrace a too simple one-dimensional move from the cultic to the didactic, from worship to study. The psalms are polyvalent, feeding Israel's imagination in many ways. The emphasis on the final, canonical form of the Psalter "may be less interesting and less productive for our understanding."[37] The whole Psalter provides a "paradigmatic act of imagination" that struggles with the "too simple" settlement of issues in Psalm 1 and the reality of lived experience. In the same way, David Pleins argues that we should experience the psalms "with both canon and context in mind," immersing ourselves at many different stages of the tradition that mark the changing usage of the psalms in communities of faith over the centuries; no matter at which point we plug in, "the issues of suffering, social justice, and worship continually confront us."[38]

Still helpful today in interpreting the psalms is the form-critical approach pioneered by Hermann Gunkel in the 1920s, which focused on psalm types rather than on authors and their personal experiences, or on the final form of texts.[39] Gunkel identified several distinctive literary types, among them the hymn, the lament, the thanksgiving, and the royal psalm; each type had its own special form and content growing out of a distinctive setting in life in which that psalm type functioned. A lament, for example, may have been prayed in the temple when enemies defeated Israel in battle, or prayed at home when illness struck a family; a thanksgiving may have been offered up after a good harvest or recovery from sickness. In this sense a psalm cannot be pinned down to one particular time in Israel's history or associated with one particular person and can be more readily appropriated by worshipers of any time and place.

We exercise form-critical judgments whenever we write letters or read the newspaper. We do not normally send a business letter to a best friend telling about the birth of our first baby, nor do we send a friendly, chatty letter to the bank requesting a loan. We do not usually read an editorial in the same way that we read a news article. E-mail today is producing a whole new range of abbreviations and spellings that would be unintelligible in most other forms of written communication. The expectations connected with each situation govern the form and content of our communication in that situation. This is the central concern of form criticism.

Claus Westermann argues that there are two basic psalm categories— praise and lament. The setting in life of the psalms is unimportant, because praise and lament are the two "basic modes of thought when [humans] turn to God with words."[40] These two categories reflect our human movement between lament and praise on the continuum of prayer. The movement within the lament psalms from alienation to praise and thanksgiving also expresses this dynamic of the God/human encounter.

Walter Brueggemann builds on Westermann and focuses on the function or "social usefulness" of the psalms. It is not enough, he argues, to say that the function of a lament is to lament. Instead, we must ask how the psalms function as voices of faith in the life of a community of believers. To answer this question, he rearranges the form-critical categories of psalm type according to the themes or "seasons of life" they express, the seasons of *orientation, disorientation,* and *new orientation.*[41] These seasons are beautifully represented in a sketch by the Reverend Chris Suerdieck entitled "Three Figures in Prayer."[42]

Orientation is a season of well-being, order, security, and trust in the reliability of God's good creation. Psalm hymns to God as creator, hymns to the God of Zion, wisdom psalms, and Torah psalms articulate the orientation of this no-surprise world. Which of the figures in the sketch do you think represents the season of orientation? Many people are torn between choosing the figure on the right and the one on the left. One could argue that the figure on the right generates all the energy that a well-ordered world supports. But the figure on the left radiates the serenity of security. It is a calm figure, with arms folded across the chest, almost as if to shut out the pain of the real world. The hands can either be seen in  a posture of prayer or in a defensive position as if to say: "Everything is fine with me, thank you—don't come any closer and mess it up!" This one has life and God all figured out. This is the security of the status quo, which can be oppressive for those peripheralized on the edges of order.

Disorientation is a season of disorder, suffering, and alienation. Psalm laments bring this pain of shattered order to expression. Most everyone agrees that the figure in the sketch that represents disorientation is the one at the bottom, which seems to have sunk into the dust, head bowed. Is the head bowed from consciousness of sin and unworthiness, or from the weight of pain and unanswered prayer, the taunt of enemies, or the feeling of being abandoned by God? The sketch, is, I think, deliberately ambiguous here. One of my students who had accompanied me on an immersion trip to the

Holocaust sites in Poland saw this figure as a naked, contorted prisoner in one of the concentration camps. Others see a figure crouched while being beaten, with hands up as a last effort to get help, perhaps a victim of spousal abuse. Some see a clenched fist in anger; others see hands hiding the face in shame. The arms, contorted in pain and supplication, communicate the urgency of the lament petition: "Forgive me, or answer me, God, *now;* my life has fallen apart."

New orientation is a season in which a surprising new gift from the sovereign God is received just when one was not expected; disorientation is reversed. Thanksgiving psalms and hymns to God the sovereign (the so-called enthronement psalms) articulate this season of life. The figure on the right in the sketch opens its arms wide in thanksgiving and amazement as it emerges out of the pit of disorientation. Perhaps because the pain of disorientation is still fresh, this one can be open and sympathetic to the pain of the world. The figure is bigger than the other two, not because suffering is good for you and makes you grow, but because of the joy from the unexpected gift, and because after the experience of the pit, we can never be the same again; we are different, changed. This figure represents, I think, what James Cone describes as happening in black worship services; people are no longer named by the world that humiliated and oppressed them six days a week, but by the Spirit of Jesus. "Liberation is no longer a future event, but a present happening in the worship itself. That is why it is hard to sit still in a black worship service."[43] The figure on the right cannot sit still either. Arms are flung wide open as if to say: "I've been down in the pit but I'm out—hooray! I will testify to the gift. I know what it's like to be down. Come to me, I understand." There is none of the closed serenity of the figure on the left.

Note how the three figures are connected by very fluid lines, representing perhaps, as Walter Brueggemann suggests, that we are always on the move in the life of faith. The figures of orientation and disorientation are not connected. Why? Once you've been disoriented, you can't easily return to your former orientation. In fact, Brueggemann changed his original label from "reorientation" to "new orientation" for this season of life. The "Seasons of Faith" quilt (on the next page) made by the Reverend Glenda Condon[44] makes this point very well. We put ourselves back together in new ways after our pit experience.

Brueggemann argues that the life of faith expressed in the psalms shows two important movements: the move out of orientation to disorientation, and the move out of disorientation into new orientation. When something happens to shatter our security and sense of order, such as the death of a loved one, a divorce, or the loss of a job, we tumble into the pit of disorientation because the order of our known world is destroyed. This move is accompanied by a rush of what society terms "negative" emotions: anger, resentment, guilt, shame, isolation, grief, despair, hatred, denial, fear. Laments can help us as individuals or as a group to bring this new, painful situation to speech and acknowledge the reality of our experience. The other move we make is out of disorientation to new orientation. This move is accompanied by a rush of "positive" emotions: surprise, gratitude, delight, wonder, awe. Thanksgiving psalms and enthronement psalms tell of God's

rescue, deliverance, healing, and reversal of the situations of distress. For Christians, the first move is embodied in the crucifixion of Jesus, and the second in his resurrection. That is why enthronement psalms belong in our Easter services.

We are regularly surprised by and resistant to these movements of faith. Think about that the next time you ask someone, "How are you?" Do you really want to know, or has this become just another social greeting? How comfortable would you be if someone responded by telling you exactly how she or he felt, either miserable in the pit of disorientation or wonderingly thankful in her or his new orientation, with all the corresponding details.

Powerful emotions accompany our movement in and out of the seasons of life. American society has traditionally urged us to curb any excess of emotion, either positive or negative. "Poker face" and "keep a stiff upper lip" used to be words to live by; women in particular suffered from stereotypes of being too "emotional." But things are changing. Talk shows regularly showcase ordinary people spilling their guts before millions, either on TV or radio. "Reality TV" has become very popular, from "Road Rules" for the MTV set to "Survivor" to "Temptation Island." Road rage makes headlines daily. People complain about the loss of civility in everyday life. Robert Hughes even speaks of our "culture of complaint" fueled by "emotional bribery" and a denial of personal responsibility.[45] How do the psalms fit in such a changing world? Primarily by giving voice to what is happening *outside* church and worship *inside* church and worship, within the supportive community of faith and before God, where these emotions can be acknowledged, worked through, and shepherded in the direction of healing and wholeness.

Look at the "Three Figures at Prayer" sketch again. Think about when in your life you have experienced what each figure is expressing. Which figure best expresses your season of life right now? How might you change or redraw each figure?

CHAPTER THREE

Your Hallelujahs Don't Have to Be Hollow Anymore

Praise Psalms

What is it that we do when we praise God in a psalm hymn? How does our praise function? What does it mean? We cannot answer these questions by merely insisting that the content of the psalm hymn is praise and that the function of the hymn form is to express praise of God in a situation that calls for such praise. Consider this comment about our praise in worship: "Often, in listening to the prayers presented publicly in churches, it seems as if the form of praise is merely a preamble—a suitable introduction to the real business of asking for things which are bound to follow!"[1]

In this connection, think about how our Sunday liturgies are constructed. We usually begin with a call to worship that praises God (often in the form of an excerpt from or pastiche of psalms), followed by a song from our hymnals praising God, followed by confession of sin and then the assurance of pardon. Only then can we hear the scripture lessons read and proclaimed and raise our petitionary and intercessory prayers. It does seem that praise functions as a preamble for the real business of asking for things!

Is our praise of God in worship simply a tool for buttering up God, a means to an end? Have we become so mechanical and unthinking in our praise that our hallelujahs have become hollow? Furthermore, in our culture of immediacies with its hype, sports, and constant entertainment, can we distinguish between feeling and deep emotion? In our church praises, can our ecstasy lack substance? Have we come to expect that one worship service will be more exciting than another?[2]

A study of psalm hymns can show us just how unbiblical our hollow hallelujahs are. In praising, Israel learned about God and was given a model for its response to God. As Patrick Miller puts it: "Praise is language to God and about God, elicited out of the human experience of God."[3] In praise we learn about God as well as about ourselves and our place in the world. In praise we both acknowledge the infinite possibilities that God has set before us and confess our dependence on God, who created us. It is this discovery and acknowledgment of who we are as dependent creatures of the Creator that is, I think, especially missing in our hollow hallelujahs. As Bruce Birch argues, "Much of our worship in the U.S. churches…has been lacking in any sense of recognition of dependency on God. The church has been affected by our national ideal of self-sufficiency. Thus, many worship services speak more of self-congratulation than of praise."[4]

The community of faith exists to praise God. This is part of Second Isaiah's message to the community of exiles: "I will make a way in the wilderness and rivers in the desert…to give drink to my chosen people, the people whom I formed for myself so that they might declare my praise"(Isa. 43:19b, 20b, 21, NRSV). This praise of the faith community is humbled when it joins with the praise of the whole created order: "Praise Adonai, all you stars of light! Praise Adonai you heights of heaven!" (Ps. 148:3, 4a).

Some psalm laments use the recognition of the creature's duty to praise the Creator as a motivation for God to act to end the present distress; if the psalmist dies, praise of God will come to an end. One's inability to praise is God's loss; "the speaker is *valued by God as one who praises*."[5] For example, Psalm 30:9 pleads: "What profit is there if I go down to the Pit? Can dust praise you? Can it declare your faithfulness?" (Compare with Pss. 6:5; 9:13–14; 88:10).

Vows of praise in psalm laments function similarly in their anticipation of the deliverance that has not yet occurred. The psalmist pledges, "I will sing praise to the name of Adonai, the Most High" (Ps. 7:17) with the understanding, "I will do this *if* you deliver me" (compare with 13:6; 22:22; 26:12; 35:28; 71:16, 22–24). Here we have the idea that the psalmist acts through praise as God's "public relations agent" or "press agent" in the world.

Our praises can help us to define ourselves in the world; they can shape our self-identification. As Bruce Birch suggests, praise marks us as the people of God in that our offering of praise is an acknowledgment of dependency on God, an act of community, and a reminder of the power of symbols, especially in a time of crisis.[6] In praise we know who and whose we are. This is the message of Psalm 100:3: "Know that Adonai is God. It is Adonai who made us and we are God's. We are God's people and the sheep of God's pasture." This recognition undergirds black worship. James Cone argues that the black congregation is an eschatological community with a changed identity because the Spirit of Jesus is there, renaming the people. "Black worship demands involvement," in song, preaching, praying, testifying, or shouting, which is nothing short of "a conversion experience."[7]

We are reminded in praise that our relationship with God is not private, but a shared experience with the people of God of all times. Amidst confusion and crisis, the praise of God in worship provides a focused center that demands the recovery of our historical symbols and language. In and through praise, then, we can become fully human, fully whole, and firmly anchored in community. Praise is a communal act. Think about this for a minute. In what ways do you share your praise with one another in your Sunday worship service? In what other ways does your church praise God—through community service, music programs, social events?

This praise of ours is never static; instead, it speaks of our dynamic relationship with God. It makes sense, then, that Claus Westermann views responsive praise to God as one pole along the continuum of prayer between supplication and praise.[8] Miller suggests that rather than swinging back and forth like a pendulum between supplication and praise, one is always "moving *toward* praise...Praise and thanks are in a sense the *final word*, the direction one is headed, in the relationship with God."[9] Although we may begin our worship services with praise, praise is also the final goal of worship. The New Testament expresses this movement toward praise in Philippians 2:10–11: "that at the name of Jesus every knee should bow...and every tongue confess that Jesus Christ is Lord." A later confessional understanding of this goal is found in the first question of the Westminster Shorter Catechism: What is the chief end of human life? "to glorify God and enjoy [God] forever." C. S. Lewis, who initially struggled with the command to praise God, points out that these "are the same thing. Fully to enjoy is to glorify," since "all enjoyment spontaneously flows into praise...praise almost seems to be inner health made audible."[10] Do you feel yourself moving toward praise in your own life? Why or why not?

The Psalter shows this movement toward praise, not only within individual psalms, but throughout the whole collection, as discussed in chapter 1. A shift from petition to praise can also be seen outside the book of Psalms in the story of slavery overturned by God (Ex. 1—15), in Hannah's lament over barrenness turned to thanksgiving for the God who gives her a child (1 Sam. 1—2), and in the praise of the Creator who is about to create anew and bring comfort to the Israelites in exile (Isa. 40—55).[11] It is this experience of and response to the God of reversals that erupts into praise. Thus, we can see that "the praise of God in the Old Testament is always devotion that tells us about God, that is, *theology,* and proclamation that seeks to draw others into the circle of those who worship this God, that is, *testimony for conversion.*"[12] The New Testament call to discipleship embraces these elements of devotion and proclamation found in the Hebrew Bible.

Dare we open our mouths with hollow hallelujahs when so much is at stake? We are no less than theologians when we take up a psalm of praise as our own, no less than missionaries when we testify to our experience of God in the praise that we offer. We take our stand within the community of the faithful, inviting others to join us because of who God is and what God has done. Our praise speaks the universal language of our shared experiences.

There is no better way to illustrate this than to engage in a group psalm-praying exercise.[13] Take a few minutes to skim through the psalms; start anywhere you'd like. Skim quickly and identify several psalms of praise or praise verses in other types of psalms. As you skim, jot down one or two verses of praise that express most closely your own feelings and thoughts. Focus on these verses by reading them prayerfully again and again. After five minutes, have the person previously designated start to read out loud the verse(s) of praise chosen and have the group respond in unison with the following (in the classroom, write this down on newsprint before beginning the exercise): "O God, receive our praise and bless us with your presence." When each one who wishes to share his or her verse(s) has had a chance to do so, and the group has responded with the refrain, say "Amen! And let all the people say Amen!" You will discover how infectious praise is and how animated the refrain becomes the more often it is repeated, as well as hear the wide range of actions and attributes for which God can be praised.

There is another aspect of our praise that we must consider. Brueggemann argues that a hymn of praise is an articulation of orientation that affirms a well-ordered, no-surprise, reliable world. As such, it is an expression of creation faith; trust in God's order emerges from the daily workings of the world and leads to an affirmation of God's faithfulness. Such hymns give testimony to and proclaim the nature of God. They say simply that "this is the way things are" rather than "this is what happened."

Hymn praise can function in two ways sociologically, one positive and one negative. First, it can create and keep in place a "sacred canopy." This kind of hymn praise celebrates a relied-upon givenness guaranteed by God, "under which the community of faith can live out its life with freedom from anxiety."[14] Brueggemann warns us, however, that we must ask who experiences life as ordered, reliable, and good? What wants to make these kind of assertions, and why? One could say that it is the well-off, the economically secure, and the powerful who experience life as ordered and good. If these secure ones pray hymns of praise, they convert no one, because they testify to oriented persons like themselves who celebrate the status quo. This is the negative dimension of hymn praise. Creation faith expressed in hymn praise can grant self-approval and serve "as a form of social control." We must watch for "the slippery ways in which creation faith easily becomes social conservatism, which basks in our own well-offness."[15]

The church will be a "speaker of orientation" in the negative sense through its psalms of praise unless it acknowledges that not everyone experiences life as good and ordered and that orientation for some comes at the expense of others. A quick look at the television or the newspaper ought to confirm this. "The fact is: the world is not an easy place in which to live doxologically."[16] We must ask if our own praise embraces the pain of the world and its injustice or ignores it. Do we view those who are not secure and well-off as outside of God's creation blessing? Do we undergird structures of injustice with our status quo praise that keep the powerless in line?

If we do, we need to recognize and affirm a second sociological function for hymns of praise, one that focuses on the eschatological nature of praise. Wainwright speaks of the "eschatological tension" that marks Christian living and is focused in Christian ritual. This tension marks the church as it is in the world, a "pilgrim community," struggling to become the church as it is meant to be, the people of God's final realm. Christian rituals do not usually maintain a once-given world order, but are "predominantly transformative in character," helping to shape the church into what it is to become.[17]

In the same way, this tension can be found within psalm hymns of praise in that they anticipate an ordered and oriented life that is not yet experienced. Psalm hymns point to God's good purposes and intention for the world, to creation that is not yet completed. With this eschatological reading, psalm hymns can give hope to the oppressed, for order is lifted up as God's intention for *all* creation, and we are tapped as cocreators with God of that order-in-the-making. If we are aware of how we use a psalm hymn, we can promote social criticism and transformation instead of social control.[18] We have seen above how James Cone points to the transforming eschatological element in American black worship as a source of the radical change in black identity. This is a liberating experience. "It is this experience of being radically transformed by the power of the Spirit that defines the primary style of black worship."[19]

Brueggemann argues that though ancient Israel's praise grew out of its experiences of rescue and transformation by God, this praise became distorted as it was linked closely with the royal palace and the temple complex. Praise came to serve the interests of the king and those in control, legitimating the royal social system. This was idolatrous praise. In order to recover its genuine praise, Israel had to return again and again to its concrete memories and experiences of transformation that overturned such distortions.[20] In the same way today, the church as a speaker of orientation needs to turn to its concrete and transforming memories in order to overcome its distortions and to recapture genuine praise. Lifting up the eschatological element in psalm hymns can help the church in its crucial task of becoming inclusive, that is, of embracing all persons as the body of Christ in the world.

Similarly, David Pleins suggests that the psalm hymns of praise "take the perspective of eternity to jar the worshiper into rethinking all that is earthly," redefining the human, and reexamining military power (Ps. 33:13–16), poverty (146:7–9; 113:7–8), idolatry (135), and Earth's resources (8; 104).[21] In worship, praise hymns help us to encounter God, not as an "escape" from earth, says Pleins, but as a way to glimpse God's creative spirit and to link creation and justice as a springboard for action that will shape the world as God intends it to be. I would suggest that issues such as Proclaim Jubilee, sponsored by Bread for the World and its coalition partners, which proposes debt relief for the world's poorest countries, take on a new urgency in light of hymns of praise. So, too, does the fact that one out of every eight people in the United States (34.5 million), lived in poverty in 1998 according to the U.S. Census Bureau, with children experiencing the highest poverty rate (18.9 percent) of the age groups. Sit down with a newspaper and generate your own list of pressing international, national, or local injustices or incidents of suffering. Then think about how Psalms 8, 33, 104, 135, and 146 provide us with a different perspective on each of these problems.

The Structure of the Hymn Psalm

When we say "hallelujah!" we are actually speaking Hebrew. *Hallelujah* is a transliteration of the Hebrew word, which can be broken down into two parts: *hallelu*, a command meaning "praise!" and *jah*, the German spelling for the shortened *Yah* of the divine name Yahweh, Israel's special name for God (vocalized by pious Jews as Adonai, translated in our English

Bibles as LORD). Hallelujah means literally "praise Yahweh," or "praise Adonai," or "praise the LORD." Many other praises are found outside of the book of Psalms, such as the Song of the Sea in Exodus 15:1–18, the Song of Deborah in Judges 5:1–31, the Song of Hannah in 1 Samuel 2:1–10, and hymns in Isaiah.

The Hebrew title of the Psalter is *tehillim,* "praises." Calling the whole psalm collection "praises" means that Israel considered everything in the psalms—the laments as well as the hymns, thanksgivings, and wisdom psalms—to be praise of God. This inclusive sense of praise can help Christian liturgy, the public worship of the church, to retain its meaning as the work of the people, in the sense that Geoffrey Wainwright intends. Wainwright argues that people bring the whole of their existence into the liturgy so that the liturgy may envelop it in praise, and Don Saliers similarly defines liturgy as "the whole of life"; what Jesus said and did then is said and done now in worship.[22] Since the psalms articulate the varied experiences of human existence, they provide ready vehicles for our liturgy, for the gathering up of our lives in praise. Our liturgy, then, ought to embrace the full range of psalm prayer as "praises."

From the liturgy, people depart with a "renewed vision" of God's realm.[23] Liturgy imagines an alternative community that is in tension with the way things are. In this sense it is very close to the understanding of worship found in the Hebrew word *'abodah,* which comes from a root that means "to serve." Just as in the New Testament, liturgy and service *(diakonia)* are connected. The religion of the heart cannot be divorced from the religion of the hands; the Israelite prophets proclaimed this message over and over again. So, too, John Wesley spoke of worship that led to conversion and to practical charity.

A hymn is specifically in the form-critical sense a song of praise to God, with a special form and content. There are several subgroups of hymns—hymns to God as creator of the world (Pss. 8, 33, 104, 145, 148) and creator of Israel as a nation (95, 105, 114, 135, 136), hymns to the God of Zion (46, 48, 84, 87, 122), and hymns to God the Sovereign (29, 47, 93, 96—99, the so-called enthronement psalms)—each subgroup emphasizing a particular characteristic, or aspect, of God in praise.

In this chapter we will consider in detail Psalms 150, 104, and 46. Psalm 150 cannot readily be classified in one of the subgroups of hymns. It is a great summary hymn, a psalm of praise for the entire book of Psalms, and gives us a glimpse of how powerful (and noisy!) our praise can be. Psalm 104 is an example of a hymn to God as creator, which reminds us of God's continuing creative activity in the world and our partnership with God in that activity. As a hymn to the God of Zion, Psalm 46 presents us with a picture of the future that God intends for us, a picture that judges our present.

Brueggemann argues that hymns to God the Creator express the faith theme of orientation, that is, of security, well-being, and trust in God's order, while hymns to God the Sovereign articulate new orientation, or the surprise of a new situation when one's orderly world has fallen apart. In this way, Brueggemann's themes of the life of faith cut across form-critical lines, bringing together "the gains of critical study...and the realities of human life."[24]

Because the themes of our faith journeys guide this book, hymns to God the Sovereign will not be discussed until chapter 6, with other psalms of new orientation. When classifying a psalm, remember that there exists no master computer printout making clear which psalms belong to which theme or form-critical category. The same psalm may express more than one theme, depending on the intention of its speaker and the use to which it is put.

Both the form and content of the hymn of praise in the Psalter bear witness to Israel's experience of God. They also invite us to join in the praise. Hymns usually unfold in three parts: (1) the summons to praise, (2) the motive or reason for praise, and (3) the closing call to praise. The summons to praise is normally a plural command; the plural suggests a setting within communal worship. We are thus reminded by the hymn language that praise is not a private matter. We call others to hear what we have to say about God, and we ought, therefore, to give careful and earnest voice to our words.

One of the oldest hymns in the Hebrew Bible, the Song of Miriam in Exodus 15:21, begins with the plural command "Sing to Adonai" and is followed by the reason for this summons: "for [because] Adonai has triumphed gloriously; the horse and his rider [Adonai] has thrown into the sea." There is no closing summons, which is true of several psalm hymns. The opening summons to sing is thus connected in the Song of Miriam with Israel's experience of deliverance by Adonai in the exodus. The praise is real and joyous.

Patrick Miller cautions that though this praise may even be exuberant, it is "never irrational...To the contrary, praise is a making glad that makes sense."[25] This is the case even when Israel is called to praise God in a general way for God's majesty or creative power, instead of for a concrete act of deliverance as, for example, in Psalm 104 or 148. Often the active participle "one who does" communicates God's majesty or creative power; the participle suggests the general nature and activity of God, God's ongoing processes, what God does regularly and everywhere, rather than "an intrusive eventfulness."[26]

Miller suggests that one acknowledges God's glory in this general way as one acknowledges the beauty of a flower.[27] In fleshing out his analogy, I imagine myself (because I am a gardener) on a walk alongside a stream when I discover an exquisite wildflower nestled among the rocks. As soon as I see it, before I can think about why it is beautiful, I suck in my breath with an "Oh!" of delight and appreciation simply because I have encountered it. In the same way, praise of God is, as Miller puts it, "unavoidable" simply because God is, simply because of our relationship with God. In this light, one could say that the opening summons of the three-part hymn structure is pre-reflective, pre-theological in mood.

The body of the hymn giving the motive for praise would be analogous to my lingering to consider the color of the flower, the arrangement of its petals, the shape of its leaves, the way the sunlight plays upon it. The flower has not actively done anything, but I consider why it is beautiful. My consideration of its beauty is analogous to the body of the hymn, which is a deliberate theological effort. The closing summons to praise would be built on my examination of the flower and my desire to have everyone else see it; it would be "a making glad that makes sense." I take one last look at it before I walk away.

Psalm 117 offers a compact example of the hymn structure. Verse 1 erupts with "Hallelujah [praise Adonai] all nations! Extol Adonai, all peoples!" Beneath this command rests the belief that God rules the world, and therefore, God's congregation must be universal; see the same situation in Psalms 47:1; 96:1, 7, 9, 11–12; 97:1; 98:4, 7–8; 99:1–3; 100:1),[28] and in Paul, who picks up this psalm as part of his argument that the gospel is for Jews and Gentiles (Rom. 15:11). This sweeping summons to praise is followed by the reason for praise, customarily introduced by the Hebrew particle *kî* (because, for). Why are nations and peoples called to praise Adonai? "For [because] great is Adonai's *hesed* towards us, and the reliability of Adonai is forever" (117:2, cf. Ex. 34:6). *Hesed* is usually translated as "lovingkindness" or "steadfast love" but also speaks directly of God's covenant loyalty. Because God's faithfulness in covenant has been experienced in Israel's past, God's faithfulness can be counted on in Israel's future.[29] To live under God's rule is to anticipate the eschatological unity of the whole creation. Note how God is referred to in the third person; this praise motive tells *about* God rather than addresses God. The closing "Hallelujah!" illustrates how often the opening call to praise is repeated (compare Pss. 104—106, 113, 115, and 116, which have the same ending).

Sometimes the summons to praise is not directed to others. In Psalm 103:1, for example, the self is addressed, but others are also encouraged by this address: "Bless Adonai, O my self,[30] and all my being, Adonai's holy name!"(cf. Ps. 146:1). The plural of self-address is found in 95:1: "O come let us sing to Adonai!" In 145:1, God is addressed directly: "I will extol you my God and Sovereign and bless your name forever!"so that we are caught up in the psalmist's enthusiasm. In 118:2, after the opening command, comes, "Let Israel say 'Adonai's *hesed* endures forever!'" Sometimes a simple declaration is voiced: "the heavens are telling the glory of God" (19:1), and "Great is Adonai and greatly to be praised" (48:1). The notion of blessing God is uncomfortable for some, especially if they hold to the image of an all-powerful, unchangeable God who has no need of our blessing. Yet Pentecostals regularly declare in worship "let us minister to the Lord." Psalm hymn praise points to the fundamentally dialogic relationship we have with God and with one another in worship.

Not only are nations addressed and the psalmist encouraged by the summons to praise, but often all of creation is called to praise God, the Creator. "Make a joyful noise to God, all the earth" (66:1). "Praise Adonai, all the angels! Praise Adonai, all the host!" (Ps. 148:2); compare with Psalm 29. Here we see that the language of praise "is truly primal and universal. All existence is capable of praising God and does so."[31] This humbling perspective reminds us that the whole cosmos depends on this Creator God and that the whole cosmos is united with this dependence. But even more than this is at stake, as David Pleins urges. We have polluted and mismanaged God's handiwork and this problem "will take on a radically different character if we regard nature, as the psalmists do, as an active, responsive partner in an intimate relationship with the human community and God."[32] Nature can shape us if we stop controlling it as object and listen to it.

Psalm 33 summons Israel to praise its Creator with five commands: rejoice, praise, make melody, sing, play. The reason for this "new song" is given in the body, verses 4–19: "For the word of Adonai is upright and all Adonai's work is done in faithfulness…By the word of Adonai the heavens were made"; Genesis 1 and creation by the word echoes here. God's word and work are the creation of the universe. From this "vantage point of the eternal," human war making and military arrogance are futile:[33] "A king is not saved by his great army…The war horse is a vain hope for victory, and by its great might it cannot save" (vv. 16–17, NRSV). Those who are not able to "read creation" as Brueggemann puts it, who are not able to see in its order the loyalty of God, will not be able to trust; they will lead hopeless lives. Unless one is obedient (the "upright" and "righteous" of v. 1), one "may look and never see. Even creation is rightly read only through covenantal response, discerned through believing eyes."[34]

Hymns of praise lift up God the creator of heaven and Earth, who is also the God of history. Israel offered praise for the story, or history, of

God's mighty deeds on its behalf, as in narrative Psalms 78, 105, 106, 114, 135, and 136. All these deeds of God testify to God's ongoing faithfulness. The story told in these psalms "is not related with detachment but is told as a drama that is true 'for me' or 'for us'"[35] in the same way that the Christian story is told; Christians incorporate Israel's story of deliverance, out of which emerges the story of Jesus Christ.

Psalm 136 forges a clear link between creation and Israel's story in history by tracing God's mighty deeds all the way back to primordial creation. In a litany of praise set in motion by the opening verse, "O give thanks to Adonai, for Adonai is good, for Adonai's *hesed* endures forever," Israel praises God, whose first act was the making of the heavens and the Earth and who brought Israel out from Egypt, led them through the wilderness, and settled them in the land. Just as God created the heavens and the Earth, God created Israel "out of the historical nothingness of slavery and gave them a future and a vocation."[36] That God "remembered us in our low estate...and rescued us" (vv. 23–24) could refer to the return from exile and an extension of God's *hesed* into the present, for "faith never lives in the past";[37] so Deuteronomy 5:3: "Not with our ancestors did Adonai make this covenant, but with us, who are all of us here alive today." Psalm 136 ends with the declaration that "God gives bread (Hebrew: *lehem;* NRSV translates "food") to all flesh." The psalm moves from God's creation of the cosmos to God's provision of daily bread, "both part of the continuum of God's mighty works," as they are in the Lord's Prayer.[38]

Psalm 136 offers what David Pleins calls a "competing" positive memory of Israel's history, rather than the negative memory of the Deuteronomistic History (Deuteronomy—Kings) which sees God at work punishing and destroying rebellious Israel for its sins (as in 78 and 106). He suggests that 136, with its "history of kindness," can lead us to new paths of liberation, compassion, and empowerment.[39] In this light, it is no surprise that 136 came to be known in Jewish tradition as the "Great Hallel" and was associated with Passover; in contemporary Jewish liturgy it is recited standing at the morning service for Sabbath and festivals. Christians use it in the Easter Vigil, affirming that God's *hesed* continues in the life, death, and resurrection of Jesus.

These hymns of narrative praise of the God of history prompt us to look for evidence of God at work in our history. Where do we see God's order in the world and in our experience? Where do we see signs of God's concrete action in the world today, action that elicits our praise? Perhaps God's loyal action on our behalf can be seen in the dismantling of the Berlin Wall and the reunification of the two Germanies, in the talks between North and South Korea, in the freeing of Nelson Mandela from a South

African prison and his ensuing presidency, and in the open worship of Christians in the former Soviet Union. God is at work in the world, overcoming the barriers that divide peoples from one another. As one pastor puts it, "God is up to something good."[40]

We can also ask how God is at work closer to home, in the United States. Pro-choice and anti-abortion supporters, advocates of the homeless, and supporters of Jubilee year for debt relief marching on Washington, the Million Man marchers, the Million Mom marchers, all witness to God's work here in America. Local churches throughout America act as the instruments of God's work through the homeless shelters, soup kitchens, and day-care centers they operate, through Alcoholics Anonymous, Cub Scouts, and other groups that are invited to use their buildings, and through the lobbying they do for affordable housing in their communities. How does your church support God's ordering activity?

It may be difficult for us to acknowledge that these all are ways in which God is working through us to shape the world into what God intends. Sometimes we prefer to limit God to spiritual activity: God comes to us in Sunday worship; we say hello; and then we go about business as usual for the rest of the week. Church becomes in this way an escape from the world and its problems rather than an embrace of the world; Sunday liturgy no longer functions as "the work of the people." Jesus' life and ministry, however, call us to confront the reality of the world. Jesus lived among us on Earth and took our problems on himself; he is "the Word made flesh." If we are to be the body of Christ in the world, then we need to stop resisting seeing God at work in certain actions and people.

We might prefer a God we can control and be comfortable with to a God who challenges us. We would like to say, "God is on my side, not yours," but such a God would not be the creator of the world and all its people. Such a God would be our personal puppet. In the wake of 9/11, bumper stickers and banners hanging from highway overpasses scream at us: God Bless America. Does God not bless any other nation? Perhaps we restrict God in this way because we think that we are in control, that we are the center of life. We do not want to give up our power and acknowledge that all of life is a gift from God the Creator. Perhaps we resist because we are afraid of the changes that must come when we give ourselves and our world over to the God who made us and who controls history.

If we took seriously the words of Psalm 100, "It is Adonai who made us, and we are Adonai's. We are God's people, and the sheep of God's pasture," we would reflect God's character in the way we live our lives as God's creatures. We would perhaps more readily offer ourselves as instruments for God's work in the world and more readily recognize God at work in the world through one another. In this way our praise of God would become a shared praise and not our private activity. We would learn how to listen to the praise of others whose experiences are different from ours. We would come to see that there is no national or economic or cultural litmus test for praise of the creator of us all. To claim membership in God's people would mean that we acknowledge our mutual dependence on God and our unity in that dependence.

Psalm 150: "The Great Hallelujah"

Creating a communal torn paper collage in form and color can help us to make the praise of Psalm 150 our own. This exercise is not as easy as it sounds. We are more accustomed to offering up personal, individual praise or to joining together in unison praise in the responses that are already given to us in worship. This exercise is different because it requires creating praise together at the same time using only colored construction paper and a glue stick (no scissors!). You will need to put up a long horizontal piece of butcher block paper on the wall or the chalkboard. Have two people in the group read alternate verses of Ps. 150. Concentrate on what you see and feel when you hear the words, on the images and colors that come to mind. Image the psalm in your head.

Verse by verse, tear pieces of construction paper into shapes that express each verse. You may have two or more people who are drawn to the same verse; work out your image together, or perhaps produce a series of images for that particular verse. Avoid images that are too literal. For instance, because I'm a gardener, when I hear "Praise God in God's sanctuary" (v. 1), I think of Earth as God's sanctuary in warm, brown tones, and of structures on Earth in which we gather to give praise, that is, our churches. So I will tear paper to create something akin to a spire, using brown construction paper. When I hear "Praise God in God's mighty firmament," I think of the sun and God's creative power, a domed shape in yellow. When you are finished, step back and look at Psalm 150, which you have now expressed in form and color. One of my students introduced this exercise to her Sunday school class, and they were so delighted with what they had done that they had it laminated and hung in the Sunday school hallway as a permanent display!

Psalm 150 is often called "The Great Hallelujah" because it offers a fitting general doxology for the end of the Psalter. The opening imperative call to praise in verse 1 begins with "Hallelujah!" Praise is to come from God's sanctuary, or holy place, and from God's mighty firmament. What is suggested by these words in verse 1 is that praise unites two spheres of the cosmos: heaven (God's mighty firmament) and earth (God's sanctuary).

The whole creation is one in praise of the Creator. As Artur Weiser argues: "in praising God, the meaning of the world is fulfilled. To praise the abundance of God's power is the purpose which links together the most diverse voices in heaven and on earth in a tremendous symphonic hymn of praise."[41]

The shortest section of this hymn is the body, in verse 2. The motive for praise is not introduced by "because" or an active participle; we are simply called to praise God for mighty deeds and exceeding greatness. The closing, verses 3–6, constitutes a renewed and expanded call to praise. The stress is on how one is to praise, with the entire temple orchestra: trumpet, lute, harp, timbrel (like a tambourine), dance, strings, pipe, cymbals (loud, clashing cymbals). Everything that breathes must praise God.

Two observations emerge out of this structure. First of all, and quite obviously, Psalm 150 reminds us that Israel's praise was not always subdued or reflective but sometimes raucous and exuberant. The "joyful noise" of Psalm 150 recalls the Song of Miriam in Exodus 15:21 and the dance of the rejoicing women. Worship can involve the whole person—mind, body, and heart—as the Israelites experienced and exemplified. The black church tradition is more comfortable with this kind of praise than many white, mainline churches, which hustle children off to Sunday school sometime before the scripture reading, whisk crying babies hurriedly out of the sanctuary, resist sacred dance as somehow not dignified enough, and generally show discomfort with praise shouts punctuating sermons or bodies swaying to hymn music. The black embrace of what might be called *becoming* rather than *being* welcomes the joyful noise; perhaps it is the mainline embrace of *being* rather than *becoming* that shuns it.

A second observation about the hymn's structure is that the truncated body of the hymn forces us to look twice at the nature of praise. Most scholars explain the fact that the motive for praise in Psalm 150 is the shortest part of the psalm by pointing to its placement at the end of the collection; all the preceding psalms have given every possible reason for praising God, so no repetition is necessary. Such reasoning underscores the point that hymn praise is solely a response to God, that is, one must praise God because of what God is or has done.

I see in the hymn, however, more than a straight line between divine act and human response. The situation is more circular, more dialogical. The relative silence of Psalm 150 regarding the motive for praise points to this circular situation. When God is praised, and praised properly, God is the better for it. God's power becomes more focused; God's power is magnified because God allows and equips the entire universe to sing the divine praises. We praise, not just for the sake of spreading God's name among the world and among ourselves, but for God's sake as well. If our praise makes a difference for the world, then it also makes a difference for God. Those related in worship—God, human beings, and the rest of creation—are all now different from how they were before this worship of praise.

As mentioned earlier, the lamenting psalmists knew this when they reminded God of the "public relations" value of their praise. This view of praise points to the power of worship. All comes from God; we use God's power to sing God's praises, and all goes back to God. Pentecostals glimpse the power of their praise at the point in their service when they announce, "Now let us minister to the LORD." How does a community of faith minister to God? Through its praise. The hymn titled "Stand Up and Bless the Lord" (no. 662 in *The United Methodist Hymnal*) reflects the same understanding in its first stanza: "Stand up and bless the Lord, ye people of [God's] choice; stand up and bless the Lord your God with heart and soul and voice." In stanza 2, however, the hymn pulls back from asserting that blessing, or praise, has any power over God, for God is "high above all praise, above all blessing high." Only the KINGAFAP God that Brian Wren sees in our hymns would be unmoved, unchanged by such praise. Perhaps an omnipotent God cannot love God-self back so that we must.

Psalm 150 prompts us to take a careful look at our own praise. If our hallelujahs are hollow, it is perhaps because we go though the motions of praise without realizing how much is at stake for us and for God. Perhaps we are unwilling to see God at work concretely in the world and to praise and help in that work. Perhaps we fear throwing our whole selves into worship and revealing too much about ourselves and our dependence on God. We could avoid hollow hallelujahs if we dared to acknowledge the power of our praise in worship. Praise as an expression of our relationship with God would not allow us simply to butter God up so we could ask for things or to limit the praiseworthy actions of God to the familiar and comfortable. Praise emerging from the circle of relationship that embraces God, human beings, and the created order is praise that can make new, unify, create, and empower. This kind of praise is not tired or routine; it almost bursts out of us. It testifies about God in the presence of other people and focuses God's power. This kind of praise puts us in right relationship with others and with God. How powerful and empowering it is!

Psalm 104: A Hymn to God the Creator

"O Adonai, how many are your works! In wisdom you have made them all!" (v. 24). Psalm 104 offers up sweeping praises to God the Creator. Think for a minute about moments in your life when you have been overcome by a sense of the awesome creative power of God. Where do you see God's creativity today in your life? Jot down a short list of praiseworthy aspects of creation. Using the three-part hymn structure described above, write your own hymn of praise to God the Creator. Read it out loud; share it with a partner. Once you have done this, read over other psalm hymns that praise God the Creator, especially Psalms 8, 19, 29, 33, and 148. Does your praise hymn overlap with any of these psalms?

Psalm 104 is related in form and content to the Egyptian "Hymn to the Aton." This hymn was discovered in a tomb at el-Amarna, the capital of the Egyptian pharaoh Akhenaton (Amenhotep IV, 1380–1362 B.C.E.), who worshiped the universal care and recreating power of the sun disk (the Aton).[42] This hymn probably came to Israel through wisdom circles (see chapter 4 on wisdom psalms). The major difference between the two hymns is that, for Israel, the sun is not divine itself, but is one of God's creations.

The opening summons to praise in Psalm 104 is directed to the self: "Bless Adonai, O my being!" The Hebrew word *nephesh* is translated "being"; it does not mean "soul" in the Christian sense, as it is often translated. In Israelite thought there is no dualism of body and soul, of an indestructible core of being that can be distinguished from physical life. One does not have a *nephesh* but is a *nephesh*. In Psalm 104, the psalmist calls on his or her whole person, or self, to praise God. Do we throw our whole selves into our praise of God, or are we tepid and timid? The opening of Psalm 104 can serve to remind us not to hold anything back in our praise of God.

The reasons for this self-encouragement to bless are given in the body of the hymn, beginning in verse 1b and continuing though verse 30. The psalmist addresses God directly, using the second person "you" rather than the customary third person: Verse 1 says, "O Adonai my God, you are very great" (cf. Pss. 47:2; 48:1; 95:3; 96:4). "You are clothed with honor and majesty," the aspects of royalty (see Pss. 21:5; 45:3; 96:6; 145:5). Following this is a series of descriptive phrases for God's majesty and continuous activity in creation as the maintainer of world order: "The one who covers yourself with light as with a garment," (cf. Habakkuk 3:4; see Pss. 4:6; 27:1; 43:3; 44:3 for associations of light with God's presence) "who stretches out the heavens like a tent, who sets the beams of [God's] chambers on the waters, who makes the clouds [God's] chariot." God's "tent" refers to the curtain of the tent or tabernacle; the psalm suggests that God's dwelling place is not the temple, but the universe, the whole created order.

The closing, verses 31–35, returns to the initial theme of God's power. The psalmist prays that God's power may "endure forever" and vows to praise "while I have being." Verse 35c repeats exactly the opening call to praise. The verb *'asah*, which means "to do, make, create," ties the hymn together, since it occurs at the beginning and end of succinct sections of the psalm: verses 4, 13, 19, 24 (twice), and 31; this distribution lifts up God as creator and sustainer of the world. It also ties this psalm into Psalm 103, which begins with the same line; together, these psalms ground the enthronement psalms in book 4 theologically as a response to the theological issues raised in book 3.[43]

In verses 1b–4, God's power is described in the language of theophany (God's becoming visible to humans), that is, God appears in the world in terms of the storm imagery used for ancient Near Eastern deities: clouds, wind, fire, and flame. In the Canaanite pantheon, Baal is the god of fertility, rain, and thunderstorm. One of his titles is "the Rider of the Clouds," and he is imaged carrying a thunder club and a lightning spear. In Israel, God is not equated with the wind or the clouds or the fire; these are God's creations rather than personifications of God. The clouds and wind are God's winged chariot; fire and flame are God's ministers. God came down to the people at Mount Sinai to enter into covenant with them: "There were thunders and lightnings, and a thick cloud upon the mountain…And all of Mount Sinai was in smoke, because Adonai descended upon it in fire" (Ex. 19:16, 18). Although God's appearance at Sinai is cloaked in the image of volcano and storm, Israel was clear that these phenomena are not God, as in the prophet Elijah's encounter with God at Sinai as he flees the wrath of queen Jezebel: "Adonai was not in the wind…Adonai was not in the earthquake…Adonai was not in the fire; and after the fire a sound of sheer silence" (1 Kings 19:11–12). In the divine wisdom, God has made them all (Ps. 104:24); God is sovereign over all these works of creation.

God's first act, creation, is treated in verses 5–9, a section that calls to mind Genesis 1, Job 38, and Psalm 77:16. A narrative of the world's origin and continued existence is one of the characteristics common to the religions of Israel and its neighbors in the ancient Near East.[44] Such narratives that express a worldview of a people are called myths. The word *myth* does not characterize a narrative as untrue. A myth is not history, strictly speaking, but myths do portray a people's understanding of their identity and origins as well as those of their gods. One function of myth is to personify the forces and tensions of life and name them so that one can petition and praise them.

In Psalm 104:5–9, Israel returns to primordial time, to the first act, creation, when Adonai imposed order upon chaos. For Israel the chaos is represented by "the deep" *(tehom),* verse 6. Note the correspondence between *tehom* and Tiamat, the goddess of the salt sea representing the power of chaos in the Babylonian creation myth. Tiamat is vanquished by the young storm god Marduk, who becomes the head of the divine assembly of the gods. The battle between them results in the creation of the world out of Tiamat's body. In many myths of creation, water is seen as an enemy, as destructive flood. Water could, through inundation or drought-causing withdrawal, reduce order and life to chaos and death; compare the gentle and life-giving picture of water in verses 10–13, 16, 25–26 later in the psalm. In verse 7, God "rebukes" the waters, and they flee; God's voice is like "thunder." This reference to God's voice draws out the association with "God said" in Genesis 1, creation by the word. Together with God's building of the divine chambers on the waters in verse 3, verse 7 suggests God's defeat of the chaos waters as sovereign of the universe (see Pss. 74:12–15; 93:3–4).

In verse 9, God sets for the waters "a boundary that they may not pass, so that they might not again cover the earth" (NRSV). The "boundary" is the firmament in the heavens, literally, the hammered out part, or dome (*raqi'a*, as in Gen 1:6–8), in which slits allow the chaos waters to fall beneficently to earth as rain. Here the psalmist asserts that the order of the world will endure, that it is not subject to disorder. This is meant to evoke our trust and the no-surprise world of orientation. The picture of the cosmos in verses 5–9 as a three-tiered universe also supports the assertion of orientation. Earth is a kind of circular disk floating on the ocean, anchored by pillars: "You set earth on its foundations, so that it should never be shaken or totter" (v. 5). Leslie Allen calls this assertion about not being shaken or moved the "motto" of orientation.[45] It challenges the shaking of the earth's foundations by the rule of the gods set forth in Psalm 82:5. God the Sovereign holds the world together (see Pss. 24:1–2; 93:1; 96:10).

The "boundary" for the waters points up a difference between Israel and its neighbors in thinking about the world. In the ancient Near East, life was a constant struggle with death; the earth was a copy of heaven, in which the divine personalities, each of whom personified some aspect of creation, struggled with one another in a cosmic drama. The people of these societies retold and acted out the divine drama, the primordial act of creation, to ensure order in the cosmos. In Israelite worship, however, God is not a force in nature. Nature is God's creation and is under God's control. God has set "bounds" for it; order does not depend on human worship each year. In verse 25, for example, the "sea" is not dreaded as chaos water, but viewed as teeming with playful creatures and with ships. Leviathan, the great sea monster, "sports" in it as God's "rubber ducky." Yet the positive order of things associated with creation is not irreversible. Continuation of the positive order is a corollary of God's faithfulness; creation is a corollary of covenant. God did not eliminate chaos in creation in Genesis 1, but rather confined it to two places, the sea and the sky. This theme of confined chaos[46] presents itself here in Psalm 104 as well as in Proverbs 8:29 and Job 38:8–11. God's mastery is even more challenged in Psalms 82:8 and 74:12–17, in which Israel's core testimony about God's control and confinement of chaos is juxtaposed with Israel's countertestimony out of its present experience of chaos and abandonment. This tension draws Israel closer to its ancient Near Eastern neighbors than is initially apparent.

In verses 10–13, the poet lists the different aspects of God's orderly creation; this description of nature praises God as sustainer. Springs, trees, and animals are all connected and in harmony. The center section of the psalm, verses 14–23, begins and ends with human beings (*'adam*) at work. Though the focal point of creation, they share the world; beasts of prey prowl the night, while humans work during the day. This too is part of the order of things. Recognition of this order erupts into a mini-hymn of praise in verses 24–26. The whole created order participates in God's rhythm of life. God brings forth bread *(lehem)* and wine to strengthen and gladden. Humans require both the necessities for life and the means for enjoyment and relaxation. The hymn "Bless the Lord, My Soul and Being" expresses this: "Food you bring forth from our labor, wine for joy and bread for plate."[47] Bread and wine are the basic elements of life that are products of both nature and culture, requiring divine origination and human cultivation. No wonder, then, that the church has used bread and wine for its sacramental life.[48]

The dependence of all creation on the Sustainer is made clear in verse 27: "These all look to you to give them their food in due season" (NRSV). God did not create and withdraw, but is still intimately involved in creation, which cannot exist on its own no matter how well-ordered it is. When God hides the divine face or takes away their breath, "they die and return to their dust" (v. 29). This verse recalls the creation story in Genesis 2:7, in which God gives divine CPR to the earth creature, *'adam,* with the breath of life. The Hebrew here is different, however; the same word, *ruah,* which can be translated as "breath, wind, spirit" is used in both verses 29 and 30, but it is translated as two different words in the NRSV. It is the same word used in Genesis 1:2 for what was sweeping over the face of the waters when the universe was created. The whole created order depends on God's grace for its life: "in wisdom you have made them *all*" (v. 24); "these *all* look to you to give them their food in due season" (v. 27, NRSV); the hymn "All Things Bright and Beautiful" captures this sense.[49]

God's creatures "gather" their food (v. 28); this is the same verb *(laqat)* used to describe the gathering of manna in the wilderness in Exodus 16:4. When God gives, creatures are "filled" or "satisfied." Again, this is the same verb *(saba')* used in Exodus 16:8. In creation and in history, God is constantly satisfying, renewing, filling. No wonder that verse 30 is prayed in the Walk to Emmaus and that Psalm 104 is traditionally used on the Day of Pentecost to celebrate the gift of God's spirit to the disheartened disciples (Acts 2); the church, as well as all creation, is renewed by God's spirit. "O Worship the King" eloquently sings about this renewing spirit, but with a difference.[50] Stanza 5 speaks of "frail children of dust, and feeble as frail," which counters the psalm image of the blessed and contented farmer who delights in the world God has made, nourished by bread and wine.

What it means to be totally dependent on God is amplified in the closing verses, 31–35, in which there is a return to the God of power and the theophany language of the beginning of the psalm. Just a look from this mighty Creator God, and the earth "trembles"; just a touch, and the mountains "smoke." There is a hint here that all is not well with God's order. The prayer in verse 35, "Let sinners be consumed from the earth, and the wicked be no more!" is addressed to God the Judge. God's careful order is challenged and disrupted by human actions, and this will not be tolerated; this is anticipated by the hiding of the divine face in verse 29. As Brueggemann puts it, "The world is a free gift from God, but with it comes an expectation and a cost. It cannot be otherwise."[51] Fabric artist Catherine Kapikian's work in wool captures the drama of Psalm 104.[52]

Psalm 104 prompts us to look around our world for signs of God's continuing creative activity. We can perhaps point most easily to the birth of babies, beautiful sunsets, and the change of seasons as signs of God the Creator at work. Yet even these are not unambiguous signs. In our technological age, we can create babies in test tubes, clone sheep, and contribute to global warming that modifies the weather. Some even claim that creation can exist on its own without God. Psalm 104 raises an ominous challenge to our sense of self-sufficiency, by asserting our ultimate dependence on God, who created us. When God hides the divine face, we are "terrified"; God takes away the divine breath, and we mortals die, no matter how long science can prolong our life on Earth.

There are many signs today that not all is well with God's order: the homeless, drug abuse, oil spills, sexism, endangered species, tribal warfare, racism, children living in poverty. "Sinners" and "the wicked" challenge God's intentions and authority. God the Creator is also God the Judge, who intervenes to uphold God's good intentions for creation. The look and the touch of this God can make the earth tremble and the mountains smoke. Some people do not want to see this aspect of God within Psalm 104; they claim that verses 29 and 35 "spoil" the beauty of the psalm! These verses, however, remind us that God's intentions for the created order override any of our attempts at control of the world. If we exercise a cocreatorship with

God, it is because God allows us to. Verse 31b prays: "May Adonai rejoice in what Adonai makes [or has made]." This prayer recalls the assessment of each creative act in Genesis 1: "and God saw that it was good." We are God's creatures, part of what God has made and is constantly renewing, and our activity ought to bring God joy. The expectation of Psalm 104 is that what we do on Earth matters to God; this is our empowering challenge.

Psalm 46: A Hymn to the God of Zion

Zion, "the city of God," "the holy habitation of the most High," is one of the hills in Jerusalem on which the temple was built; eventually all of Jerusalem came to be called Zion. In the hymns to the God of Zion, Zion is seen as the center, or navel, of the universe, chosen by God as the earthly center of the divine presence in the midst of the people. God's temple and the king's palace stand on Zion. Hymns to the God of Zion form a subgroup of the form-critical category of hymn; they include Psalms 46, 48, 76, 84, 87, and 122. *The Presbyterian Hymnal* offers no fewer than six hymns based on 26; the *United Methodist Hymnal,* two. The most famous hymn based on 46 is, of course, Martin Luther's "A Mighty Fortress Is Our God."[53]

In the Hebrew Bible, Zion becomes the focus for God's eschatological work for Israel and all the nations. The mythological, primeval mountain Zion will become the highest mountain to which all the nations will go up, back to the source of life, blessing, and peace. This view is expressed eloquently in Isaiah 2:1–4 and Micah 4:1–5: "It shall happen in the latter days that the mountain of the house of Adonai shall be established as the highest of the mountains...and peoples shall flow to it...For out of Zion shall go forth the Torah, and the word of Adonai from Jerusalem" (Mic. 4:1–2).

The significance of a central, sacred place at which contact between the divine and the human worlds is made is another of the characteristics common to every culture in the ancient Near East.[54] The songs of Zion in the Psalter show how Israel adapted this common cultural idea to its own unique view of God. The basic social and political unity in the ancient Near East was the city-kingdom. The city was the center of order, and the farther one moved away from it to fields and then to wilderness and desert, the more chaos threatened. How ironic that in America, the city is often viewed as the center of decay and chaos rather than of blessing, so that the farther one moves from the city, the more secure one can be.

The highest point within the city, the central, sacred mountain of God, was the order core, the place within which order originated and from which it emanated to the surrounding areas. Upon this sacred mountain were situated the king's palace and the god's or goddess' temple, copies of those in heaven. Each city had it own particular god or goddess who dwelt in its temple in the city center on the sacred mountain. This god had conquered his or her chaos enemies and exercised sovereignty over all the other gods and goddesses by ordering the city and lands of the city-state. The king was the deity's ordering agent on Earth.

This myth of the central, sacred place helped to explain the institutions of society and the role of the city from which dominion over a certain territory was exercised. As Joseph Campbell puts it, myth has a sociological function of "supporting and validating a certain social order"; myth is in this sense "the public dream" with which one's private dream or myth must coincide in order for one to live healthily in society.[55] When myth supports an oppressive social order that denies the private dreams of racial groups or other minorities, then it becomes, as Brueggemann warns, a tool for social control and the status quo. We can see the same dynamic at work in what Cain Hope Felder argues is one of two processes related to racism in the Bible: sacralization, in which national political ideology becomes religious belief in order to serve the interests of a particular ethnic group. The reversal of order of Noah's three sons, putting Shem last in the Table of Nations in Genesis 10, gives emphasis to the Shemites, who see salvation history in terms favorable to them rather than others; this is sacralization that supports the oppressive status quo.[56]

King David was the key to Israel's adaptation of this ancient Near Eastern myth of the temple city as center of the universe to support Adonai's rule in the world and Israel's hope for the future. Israel's story claimed that David had conquered Israel's Canaanite enemies and made Jerusalem his political and religious capital. By depositing in Zion the ark of the covenant, a kind of portable throne or sanctuary that symbolized God's presence, David declared Adonai head of the pantheon of deities, conqueror of chaos enemies, who reigned in Jerusalem. Jerusalem was the point at which contact was made between the divine and human realms, the place in which Israel's God was in control.

Some interpreters do not classify Psalm 46 as a Zion hymn because it contains no explicit references to Zion or Jerusalem, but rather speaks of the "city of God," and then only in the middle section (unlike 48, which refers to Zion and temple in all three parts of the psalm, verses 1, 8–9, 11, 12). It is not the city but the word *earth* that ties Psalm 46 together (verses 2, 6, 8, 9, 10). Some do not consider Psalm 46 to be a hymn, but rather a psalm of confidence or trust like Psalm 23. Though Psalm 46 can be broken down into three sections, these sections do not correspond to the typical hymn structure of opening praise summons, motive for praise, and concluding praise summons. Psalm 46 holds together in its own way as a hymn to the God of Zion, most obviously through use of the refrain in verses 7 and 11: "Adonai of hosts is with us; the God of Jacob is our refuge." Most agree that this refrain should also conclude section one, after verse 3; some English translations do include it there. It is this idea of God as refuge, refuge in the chaotic cosmos, refuge from the hostile nations of the world, and refuge in the future of peace that ties the psalm together. The liturgical term *selah* also punctuates each section.

The first section of Psalm 46, verses 1–3, inspired Martin Luther's great Reformation hymn "A Mighty Fortress Is Our God." Take a minute to compare the text of hymn and psalm. How are they alike or different? Luther's hymn moves beyond the sovereign God of the psalm who has power over all creation and all of history to a hostile world "with devils filled" whom Jesus Christ must fight. The psalmist sees the enemies as human and earthly, while Luther identifies the enemy as evil itself, personified in the Prince of Darkness. The psalmist sees the world as the place where God dwells in the midst of God's people, and looks toward the time when all nations will exalt God. Luther sees a devil-filled world and calls on us not to be tied to earthly possessions, family, or our bodily existence, anticipating a fulfillment beyond this world. Luther's hymn is very much a product of his sixteenth-century European world. He was deeply pessimistic about the depravity of humankind and exterior religion, and urged the German princes to wage war against rebellious peasants, a stance that cost him support from the populace.

Verses 1–3 of the psalm do not open with the customary call to praise, but rather with a declaration about God: "God is our refuge and strength, a constant help in trouble." The word *refuge (mahseh)* is first introduced in Psalm 2:12 and occurs twenty-three more times in Books 1 and 2 of the Psalter to emphasize God's trustworthiness. The word *strength ('oz)* occurs in psalms that declare God's reign (29:1; 93:1; 96:7; 99:4). God's strength is not neutral or malevolent but "for us." God as "helper" is a frequent image in the psalms (10:14; 22:19; 28:7; 30:10; 33:20; 37:40; 40:17).[57] With the language of the primordial chaos battle, verses 2 and 3 seem to describe a coming cataclysm at the end of days: "Though the earth should change, and the mountains totter into the heart of the sea." What is described is much like our modern fears of global nuclear war or global warming and the destruction of the ozone layer resulting in complete annihilation of the planet.[58] According to ancient Near Eastern conceptions, the world was a three-tiered universe in which mountains anchored the dry land in the watery chaos and acted as pillars to hold up the dome of the sky. If the mountains were to shake and tremble, the structure of the world could collapse, unleashing chaos waters from above and below. Though it is not possible for it to happen, given who Adonai is, the mythological language here asserts that if it did, "we will not fear" because God "is a help in trouble." One can trust this God; one can feel secure in God as refuge, because God will again confine the chaos waters, just as God did in the primordial creation act. This language of confidence is rooted in the Genesis 1 creation story.

Section two, verses 4–7, seems to focus on history and the nations rather than nature and the cosmos; the God of creation is the God of history. The city of God, rather than God the divine self, offers protection and refuge. Look at the transition from the roaring and foaming chaos waters of verse 3 to the "river whose streams make glad God's city" in verse 4; the scene and mood change recalls the river that "goes forth from Eden to water the garden, and from there is divided and becomes four rivers" in Genesis 2:10. This is a river of blessing and life, not the water of death and chaos. No river, in fact, flows through Jerusalem; the psalm river symbolizes God's presence as it flows from the temple in Ezekiel 47:1–12 and from the throne of God in Revelation 22:1–12.

Even though Zion and Jerusalem are not named, "the city of God" and "the holy dwelling of the Most High *[El Elyon]*" suggest Jerusalem, God's city, where orderly contact is made between the great chaos water and the earth, so that the watery chaos "makes glad" the city of God, that is, serves life and order. This city, because "God is in the midst of it," "shall not totter, shall not be shaken" (46:5). It remains stable in the midst of the chaos and motion. Here again is the motto of the oriented life; the same idea is expressed in Psalm 125:1. But we must heed this caution: to identify this city with Jerusalem or any human institution would be to co-opt God who "is with us" into "the God who is on our side, who exists to prop up our human power structures. The 'city of God' stands over against all such earthly power as a rock in the midst of the shifting sands of human history."[59] Similarly, David Pleins argues that psalms such as 46 and 48 ask worshipers "to critically reflect on the realities of security."[60] Without God, there can be no peace.

In Robert Alter's discussion of Psalm 48, which is applicable as well to Psalm 46, he notes the paradox of the belief in one god over all the Earth who yet chooses one people and one place as the medium of revelation. This paradox has a major geographical corollary; Jerusalem is "the city of our God who is also the God of all the nations (46:10). It is the poetry that interlocks these disparate elements and highlights the tensions."[61]

This city, Zion, is secure knowing that "God will help it by daybreak" (46:5). Even if the nations roar, Israel can trust in God as refuge. The poet uses the same words used in verse 2 of the mountains and in verse 3 of the chaos waters, to describe the nations who attack Jerusalem in verse 6:

"mountains totter, waters roar" in verses 2 and 3, while "nations roar, kingdoms totter" in verse 6. All it takes is God's voice, and the nations, like waves, collapse. "God utters the divine voice; the earth melts" (v. 6), just as in Psalm 104:7 the waters fled at God's rebuke (compare with Ps. 29:3; Ex. 15:15; Josh. 2:9, 24; Jer. 49:23). This "assault of the nations" theme is a familiar one in Israelite eschatology, as for example, in Ezekiel 38, in which King Gog of the land of Magog is warned of his coming defeat in his battle against God's people, Israel, so that all the nations will know Adonai. Historical events take on cosmic significance for Israel. In Psalm 46, Jerusalem, or Zion, remains secure through it all because God is "refuge" (v. 7), a different Hebrew word from that used in verse 1, but synonymous. God as "the LORD of hosts" in verse 7 recalls the association with the ark of the covenant (1 Sam. 4:3–4) and with armies (Num. 10:35–36; 1 Sam. 17:45). These military overtones not only provide comfort but also prepare the way for the overturning of military might in part 3 of the psalm.

The eschatological picture in section 3, verses 8–11, ties the two preceding sections together. Here the psalmist looks forward to the realization of God's realm on Earth with the invitation, "Come! behold the works of Adonai," reaching back to creation and through history. Verse 8 takes a cosmic look at what happens when humans and creation oppose God— "desolations," which recall the chilling picture of uncreation Jeremiah describes in Jeremiah 4:23–26. Behind the "desolations" is God, who is working for the end of war. God is "exalted" (v. 10, *rûm,* cf. the exalted God as sovereign in Pss. 99:5, 9; 145:1) not because God perpetuates war, but because God ends it, destroying the instruments of war—bow, spear, shield.

In verse 10 God declares, "Stop! Realize that I am God"; once the nations acknowledge God's sovereignty over the whole Earth, wars will end. NRSV translates "Be still" for the first word of verse 10, but the Hebrew means more precisely ceasing a behavior and not simply being quiet. This is not just war fatigue or longing for peace and rest; there is something more decisive and positive meant here. Faith in the realm of God is faith that overcomes the world and its wars and divisions. McCann argues that in light of what God does in verse 9, verse 8b may be sarcastic. God's "desolations" are the end of war and the destruction of the weapons of war. The military imagery of the refrain is reoriented because "God the warrior" fights for peace; only God gives security.[62]

Psalm 46 moves from the story of the beginning of the world to the story of the Earth's consummation in peace. That movement is supported by the reversal of imagery within the psalm. We begin with God standing still as refuge and move to the middle section, in which the city of God does not totter or shake while the waters foam and roar and the nations roar and totter. The psalm moves in its final section to a very active God who "breaks the bow and shatters the spear," while now it is the nations who cease activity, who are still.

Peter Craigie sees the importance of the poetry in tying the three sections of Psalm 46 together.[63] The first two sections are connected by the use of the verb *roar* in verses 3 and 6; the verb *totter* or *shake* in verses, 2, 5, and 6; and the noun *help* in verse 1 with the verb from the same root *will help* in verse 5. The second and third sections are tied together by the repeated use of *nations* in verses 6 and 10 and the refrain in verses 7 and 11. The whole psalm is woven together by the word *earth* in verses 2, 6, 8, 9, and 10; the use of this word points to God's universal power. Unfortunately, most English translations rob us of the poetic repetition; contemporary editors view repetition as monotonous and scramble to find synonyms to substitute for repeated words.

Psalm 46 raises for us the issue of what Walter Harrelson calls "worship and the end."[64] Harrelson suggests that it is wrong to view the eschatology of Psalm 46 or any part of the Bible as a hope in the future that has no contact with present history. Neither is eschatology Israel's hope in the ideal spiritual condition of the faithful in the present. "The Bible speaks of an End which moves into the present, of a present that stretches forth toward the consummation."[65] In worship and in faith, all of us live out of the future and are judged by the future, by God's intention for us. Life is not a return to a primordial time, but a meeting with the future that attracts us.

The picture of the end in Psalm 46 judged Israel's present and judges the church's present today. To worship the God who puts an end to war and brings peace is to condemn humanity's engagement in war and racism and economic injustice. If we do not do so, God will. You may argue that this notion seems hopelessly naive for us today. But as Harrelson rightly insists, "There is a lure, a fascination with the image of a world set right. Believing, as we are enabled to believe in acts of worship, that this day comes to meet and greet us, we are propelled forward to meet the living Lord."[66] No wonder, then, that the church associates Psalms 46 and 48 with the first Pentecost in Jerusalem (Acts 2:1–42), during which pilgrims from all over the world were able to understand the apostles by the power of the Holy Spirit. All the world can become citizens of God's holy city and anticipate God's realm, even now.

What would it mean for America today if we allowed the eschatological picture of Psalm 46 to judge our present? What would it mean especially for our cities blighted by poverty, crime, drugs, violence, and despair to recover the sense of the city as the point of contact between the divine and human realms through which God's blessing is mediated and in which God is especially present? It would mean a reversal of our whole attitude toward the city. Instead of our witnessing the flight of the church from the city to the suburbs, we would see churches witnessing in the inner city to the God who intends blessing for us all. Order would once again flow from the city center to the surrounding areas instead of in the reverse direction, as it does now. We would perhaps discover that it is not "us" against "them," but that we are all "refugees" seeking the "refuge" of the God of Jacob; all of humanity is a "refugee."[67] In that discovery awaits our humanity and wholeness and God's realm.

CHAPTER FOUR

You Get What You Deserve, Don't You?

The Torah and Wisdom Psalms

One of the most prominent themes in wisdom thought is the theme of the "two ways": the way of the wicked leads to punishment and death; the way of the righteous, to reward and life. The wise choose the righteous way, for its natural outcome is blessing; only a fool would choose the wicked way, for it leads naturally and inevitably to disaster. This theme of the two ways is also called divine retribution, act/consequence, or "you get what you deserve." Proverbs 11:21 states it succinctly: "Be assured, an evil person will not go unpunished, but the children of the righteous will be safe" (cf. Prov. 10:3; 12:7; 13:9; 13:21; 14:11; 15:16; 15:29; 24:16; 26:27).

We don't think about this idea all the time in the ordinary run of things, especially when things are going well for us. However, as soon as something goes wrong and we are confronted by a tragedy, it is very likely that our first thoughts will be "Why me?" which is a way of asking "What have I done to deserve this?" Though questioning of this type is clearly expressed by the wisdom literature, it also permeates the entire Bible and even our liturgies.

For example, we find Moses in Deuteronomy 30:15–20 exhorting the Israelites to choose the right way: "I have set before you life and death, blessing and curse; therefore choose life, that you and your descendants may live" (v. 19, RSV). Choose life by keeping covenant, by obeying the commandments. The choice rests with us, and we must suffer the consequences of choosing wrongly.

The Israelite prophets offer their prophecies of disaster based on the same principle of act/consequence. For example, Amos warns: "Woe to those who lie upon beds of ivory…but are not grieved over the ruin of Joseph! Therefore they shall now be the first of those to go into exile" (Amos 6:4–7, RSV). Similar passages are found in Isaiah 3:16–17 and 5:8–10; Jeremiah 6:8–12 and 14:10; and Micah 2:1–5. The prophetic social analysis connects the disobedience of the people with their coming punishment; prophecies give the reasons for the announced coming disaster. In the same way, Deutero Isaiah preaches "comfort, comfort" to the people Israel in exile, for they have received from Adonai's hand double for all their sins. Jerry Falwell and Pat Robertson tried to make similar prophetic connections between act and consequence shortly after 9/11 by arguing that gays, feminists, abortionists, and the A.C.L.U. had "helped this happen" and that God was allowing the enemies of America to give us "probably what we deserve." Unfortunately, there are few audible voices offering any social/political analysis to counter their divisive assessment. To criticize America is to be perceived as anti-American.

The Deuteronomistic history (Joshua, Judges, 1 and 2 Samuel, and 1 and 2 Kings), which was probably brought together and edited in exile, views Israel's entire history as an articulation of "you get what you deserve." The cycle in Judges 3:7–12 is typical: apostasy ("the Israelites did what was evil…forgetting Adonai their God and worshiping the Baals"), punishment ("therefore the anger of Adonai was kindled against Israel, and Adonai sold them into the hand of…"), repentance ("but when the Israelites cried out to Adonai"), and forgiveness as deliverance ("Adonai raised up a deliverer for the Israelites, who delivered them"). This cycle gives hope to the exiles. History may not be over; if they repent, God may deliver them.

In the New Testament, Galatians 6:7–10 declares: "Do not be deceived; God is not mocked, for whatever one sows, that one will also reap." In Matthew 7:13–14, many enter the wide gate to destruction, while few enter the narrow gate to life. The winnowing fork separates the wheat from the chaff in Matthew 3:12 (cf. Luke 3:17), and the Son of Man separates the weeds from the righteous in Matthew 13:36–43 (cf. John 3:36). This is a theme also found in the parable of the wise and foolish virgins in Matthew 25:1–13. In Romans 1:18, God's wrath is revealed against the ungodly and the wicked. Paul asserts that "to set the mind on the flesh is death, but to set the mind on the Spirit is life and peace" (Rom. 8:6, NRSV). Act/consequence permeates the letter of James. The Beatitudes (Mt. 5:1–12) affirm that the meek, the merciful, and the mourners all deserve God's blessing, an affirmation of "you get what you deserve" that reverses society's judgments about who is blessed. In the apocalyptic framework of the book of Revelation, in which a persecuted, righteous minority hopes for God's intervention for justice, the "new heaven and new earth" will be the inheritance of those who worship God, while the faithless will be burned with fire and sulfur (Rev. 21:1–8). In our liturgies, we assume that repentance, in the form of our confession of sin, will bring God's forgiveness. It is only after that forgiveness that we dare to offer petitionary prayers.

Think about the many ways in which we affirm the theory of act/ consequence in our daily lives. The American legal system upholds act/ consequence, at least for some: if you break the law, you are punished. Debate centers on whether or not the punishment "fits" the crime; that is, did this person get what she or he deserved? We evaluate illness and tragedy, success and wealth according to the reward/punishment idea: "How could Mrs. Simms get cancer? She's such a nice person, always helping everybody; it's not fair"; "Why should Mr. White drive such a fancy car and get such a long vacation? He's so mean at work, a real back-stabber; he doesn't deserve it"; "Why should Ann get better grades than I do when I work so hard and she never studies?" Often we seek at least a balancing out of the good and the bad in our lives. How many times have you heard someone say, "My kids have been sick on and off for a year with ear infections and strep throat; the roof leaks; my husband didn't get his raise—everything seems to come at once. I'm due for a good year now." Psalm 90 expresses the same idea in a petition to God in verse 15: "Make us glad as many days as you have made us miserable, as many years as we have seen misfortune."

The problem with the theory of act/consequence is that it can very easily become a way in which we victimize the victim. Working backward from the theory of act/consequence, that is, from sickness or material success or whatever, we place more emphasis on the result than on the act itself and what caused it. This is what Job's friends did; they saw Job sick on the dung heap, bereft of family and wealth, and they automatically assumed that he had done something wrong to "deserve" that kind of "punishment." Because their minds were made up about it, they could not listen sympathetically to Job's protestations; and, more important, they did not hear Job's pain. They acted as district attorneys rather than as friends and comforters and were thus unable to do anything to affect the act or the consequence. Churches that do not hold God's grace in tension with God's judgment but overemphasize the harsh nature of a God who calls us to account reinforce the belief that we get what we deserve in this negative way. On the other hand, churches that offer Dietrich Bonhoeffer's "cheap grace" let us off the hook too easily to do whatever we want.

This distorted, backward application of "you get what you deserve" has alarming social implications. There are some in America who view the statistics on the number of African Americans and Latinos in jail as a confirmation of the inferiority of races. They "deserve" to be in jail, because they are lazy or unintelligent or evil. The social conditions of poverty and substandard education that contribute to minority crime, as well as racism and discrimination within the criminal justice system, are dismissed. On the other hand, those in control, who are successful, attribute their success to their own goodness and superiority. If "those" people cannot "make it" as we did, then it's their fault. Not only do we see this in relation to American society, but also on a global scale. The United States basks in its world power and pats itself on the back for its industriousness and virtue. If countries in the Two Thirds World are poor, it's their fault. This argument is a factor in the resistance to Jubilee Year debt relief for the Two Thirds World. American self-congratulation also blocks our understanding of how other countries see us, especially in light of 9/11. Ileana Rosas, a UM pastor in northern Virginia, argues that the Two Thirds World is David with a slingshot, dwarfed and threatened by the giant.

In what ways do we affirm an act/consequence way of thinking in our daily lives? In what ways does the church reinforce the belief that we get what we deserve? How might our affirmation of act/consequence serve to critique and transform our society and promote justice instead of contribute to the status quo and social control? We could focus on the action and what causes it rather than on the consequence, so that new behavior can have positive, life-enhancing outcomes. Many churches have begun to lobby for affordable housing in their communities; to provide decent day-care programs for working mothers, especially those in one-parent households; to operate homeless shelters and soup kitchens; and to educate against drug abuse. This approach to act/consequence can empower rather than doom people. It takes seriously the dignity of every person and our responsibility to one another, as well as God's good intention for us all. When act/consequence becomes a private yardstick for an individual or a specific nation, it can become a whipping stick rather than a shepherd's crook to draw us closer together as the people of God. Act/consequence can be a way for us all to live in the way God intends. The charge that Moses in Deuteronomy 30:19 put to the Israelites as they were about to enter into the promised land of Canaan is one that we also must heed today: "Life and death I have set before you, blessing and curse; choose life, that you and your descendants may live."

The psalms called wisdom and the Torah psalms help us to think about this notion of choice and act/consequence. We can say that wisdom and Torah psalms articulate the season of orientation and orderliness, just like the hymn psalms we considered in chapter 3. Unlike the hymn psalms, they do not constitute a recognizable literary type or form, but rather distinguish themselves by their content and worldview. Psalms 1, 19, and 119 can be classified as Torah psalms. Scholars disagree about what they mean by wisdom and which psalms should be included in the categories of wisdom and Torah psalms. James Crenshaw, for example, questions whether there should be a category of wisdom psalms at all, since wisdom concerns "exercised the minds of all thoughtful people."[1] He does affirm, however, that some psalms resemble wisdom literature by focusing on teaching/learning, searching for life's meaning, and using proverbs.

The Septuagint (Greek translation of Hebrew Bible) translates Torah as "law," but the word means much more than that. Torah means god's "instruction" or "guidance" for Israel, which includes law but also poetry, story, saga, and genealogy. Jews call the first five books of the Hebrew Bible the Torah. In Israel, Torah and creation are understood together, for Torah is the way by which Israel responds to God's well-ordered creation. As Walter Brueggemann argues, "The good order of creation is concretely experienced in Israel as the *torah.*"[2] Psalm 19 makes this connection explicit. The first six verses are a hymn to God the Creator: God's handiwork, the heavens, "tell the glory of God," while verses 7–14 meditate upon the Torah of Adonai. The heavens may reveal God in general, but Torah reveals Adonai, the one who redeemed Israel from slavery and entered into covenant with them. The sun may give light and heat (v. 6), but Torah is "radiant" and "enlightens the eyes" (v. 8). Just as the sun's circuit is all-encompassing, so too, is Torah; they both give life.[3] The psalm moves from the cosmic to the national to the personal level; the cosmic god El (v. 1) becomes the national God Adonai (vv. 7–9), who becomes "my rock and my redeemer" (v. 14). The praise of God in creation and in Torah leads to an awareness of the psalmist's own place in creation and relation to God, which leads to a prayer for forgiveness: "Clear me from hidden faults" (v. 12). In this sense, Psalm 19 can be called a psalm of new orientation, for embracing Torah prompts self-examination and a critique of the status quo.

Verses 10 and 11 declare that the ordinances of Adonai's Torah are sweeter than honey and "in keeping them there is great reward." Psalm 19 defines the reward that results from keeping Torah in terms of the simple being made wise, the heart rejoicing, and the eyes being enlightened, rather than in terms of material aggrandizement. This is what happens when one lives in harmony with God's intentions. Certain actions have certain consequences.

In Hebrew, the word for wisdom is *hokmah,* and the Greek equivalent is *sophia,* both feminine nouns. In the Hebrew Bible, wisdom means many things: skill, as in the artistic or technical skill of the farmer, the sailor, the artisan, the diplomat, and the king; cleverness or cunning, in terms of being able to seize the moment and make the best of every situation; the art of living, in terms of behavior and attitudes toward life; religion or faith, for "the fear of Adonai is the beginning of wisdom" (Prov. 9:10; Job 28:28; Ps. 111:10).

In Proverbs 1, 8, and 9, wisdom is personified as Woman Wisdom who is preacher, friend, hostess, lover; there are some similarities between Woman Wisdom and the woman of worth of Proverbs 31. Ultimately, however, wisdom cannot be defined; it is hidden. As Job 28:12 asks, "But where can wisdom be found?" "It is hidden from the eyes of all living" (v. 21). "God understands the way to it and knows its place" (v. 23). In this sense, wisdom is the principle that holds the world together, the order given by God to the world. God alone has access to it; it is beyond human limitations.

In the Hebrew Bible, the books of Proverbs, Job, Qoheleth (Ecclesiastes), and some psalms are considered to be wisdom literature. Sirach (Ecclesiasticus) and the Wisdom of Solomon in the Apocrypha or deuterocanonical books are also wisdom works. Other cultures in the ancient Near East, especially Mesopotamia and Egypt, produced an extensive wisdom literature. Wisdom thinking was not unique to Israel, but an international movement.

Wisdom literature articulates a particular worldview, or way of looking at things.[4] Wisdom is (1) anthropocentric. This means that it is centered on human beings rather than on God. Wisdom asks, "What is good for us?"

Wisdom is (2) pragmatic. Thought and behavior are evaluated according to whether or not they yield practical, life-enhancing results. What enhances life is good; what detracts from life is bad.

Wisdom is (3) experiential. Wisdom is a human search; it does not talk about the will of God. The answers to life's questions can be learned from experience and discovered by human reason; the parable is undergirded by this understanding. The sage, or wise person who teaches wisdom, makes no claim to divine authority. The validity of the sage's teaching stands or falls on whether or not human experience confirms it.

Wisdom is (4) universal. Wisdom is open to all; it can be discovered by human intelligence. Wisdom is not the property of an elite, but assumes a oneness and order from God about the world. A search for wisdom is a search for order and the effort to live in harmony with that order. Wisdom in its universal sense can lead the church away from narrow concerns of denomination to broader human problems.

Wisdom is (5) optimistic. Successful living is within everyone's grasp; just follow the sage's advice. A modern distortion of the optimism of wisdom can be seen in "the power of positive thinking" and "success through prayer"; if you don't succeed, it's all your fault—you just haven't prayed or thought hard enough. "Thought conditioner" no. 24 from Norman Vincent Peale's prayer pamphlet from the 1950s puts it this way: "If you hold the faith thought, the positive thought, you will create about yourself an atmosphere propitious to success, health and well-being." Thought conditioner no. 39 insists: "If you are not getting answers to your prayers, check yourself very thoroughly and honestly as to whether you have resentments in your mind. Spiritual power cannot pass through a personality where resentment exists."[5] This "change your thoughts and you can change anything" optimism has been picked up more recently by Robert Schuller and his Crystal Cathedral in California.

A good way to illustrate the five aspects of the wisdom worldview is to create a wisdom wall in your Sunday school room. Post the five aspects on newsprint. Then put up a long piece of butcher paper on the wall or chalkboard, and have participants collect pictures from magazines and newspapers or downloads from the Internet that articulate these aspects of the wisdom worldview. Tape the pictures to the butcher paper and label each one with one of the five aspects. After the class has had the chance to view the collection, people can pair up and discuss where they see order in their own lives and when and how they have experienced God's order. Based on that experience of order, each person jots down a brief piece of advice for others or for themselves. Those who are willing might want to share their advice with the larger group.

In order to articulate the wisdom way of looking at things, the sage uses riddles, debate, didactic narratives, and the proverb or *mashal,* a short, pithy saying that sums up some observed truth or fact of human experience, as for example, Proverbs 12:19: "Truthful lips endure forever, but a lying tongue is but for a moment." Wisdom themes range from concern about table manners, laziness, proper speech, drunkenness, and anger, to God's justice and the inescapability of death. Many express the theme of the Two Ways or act/consequence. Think for a moment about the proverbs that govern your life, either those handed down in your family or modern proverbs that have found their way onto bumper stickers. Today we, too, try to sum up life and make sense of it. Create a proverb wall with a fresh piece of butcher paper. Buttons, bumper stickers, or proverbs written with markers are encouraged. What pithy sayings sum up life in America? Has our consumptive lifestyle obliterated Ben Franklin's "a penny saved is a penny earned," or does it still sum up life for us? Many of our recent bumper stickers reflect a profound pessimism and cynicism that would make the ancient sage very uncomfortable, for example, "The one who dies with the most toys wins," or "Life is a b— and then you die." Similarly, an ad in an in-flight magazine declares: "In business, you don't get what you deserve, you get what you negotiate." Later on the class can bring in pictures and headlines that challenge these proverbs and the wisdom wall collection.

Psalm 1: Gateway to the Psalter

Psalm 1 can be called both a Torah psalm and a wisdom psalm. It is a wisdom psalm in that the theme of the Two Ways is clearly articulated by the contrast between the righteous and the wicked. Also, act/consequence is encapsulated in the proverb on which the psalm is built in verse 6: "For Adonai knows the way of the righteous, but the way of the wicked will perish." It is a Torah psalm in that delighting in and meditating on the Torah of Adonai marks the way of the righteous person. The choices one makes can lead to life or death. The poetry reinforces the comprehensive nature of this choice. "Happy," the first word of the psalm, begins with the first letter of the Hebrew alphabet, while "perish," the last word of the psalm, begins with the last letter of the Hebrew alphabet.[6]

Why did the editor of the Psalter recognize the appropriateness of placing Psalm 1 at the head of the collection? The context for praying, singing, or preaching the rest of the psalms is set by Psalm 1 and its declaration of the Two Ways and the joy of Torah. Psalm 1 serves as our guidepost at the entrance to the Psalter; it helps us to keep our bearings through life's journey because it tells us that Torah articulates God's intentions for us. As Brueggemann argues, Psalm 1 "announces that the primary agenda for Israel's worship life is obedience"; how we choose to live our life matters in terms of God's purpose for creation. Furthermore, the beginning and end of the Psalter, Psalms 1 and 150, are connected in that "a life grounded in obedience leads precisely to doxology."[7]

The book of Psalms "begins with a beatitude"; "happy," "blessed," or "fortunate" *('ashre)* occurs twenty-five times in Psalms and eight times in Proverbs.[8] In its Greek form *(makarios),* it is the word used in the Beatitudes in Jesus' Sermon on the Mount in Matthew 5:3–12. Fred Craddock argues that "happy" in the Beatitudes conveys God's favor in both present and future. Pronouncing them so actually conveys blessing. This language is not hortatory, something we ought to do. It is pronounced before a single instruction is given, before there is time to obey or not. Occurring at the beginning of the Sermon on the Mount without conditions, "happy" says that "God's favor precedes all our endeavors."[9] That is also the assurance of the beginning of the Decalogue, Exodus 20:2: "I am Adonai your God, who brought you out of the land of Egypt, out of the house of slavery." God's initiative and blessing give the context for all our behavior. This is also the assurance at the beginning of Psalm 1 and of the whole book of Psalms; the righteous are pronounced blessed before they make their way through the Psalter. God's favor gives the context for our journey of faith. Are we able to accept this blessing? As Craddock observes, "It is more difficult to hear and receive a blessing than to attempt to achieve one."

The first half of the proverb in verse 6 of Psalm 1, the part concerning the righteous, is taken up in verses 1–3. The righteous are defined negatively, which also introduces their contrast with the wicked. The righteous are those who do not walk, stand, or sit with sinners; in short, they have nothing to do with those whose way is wicked, for the three verbs encompass all human activity. Many of us are uncomfortable with the either/or contrast between the righteous and the wicked in Psalm 1. Most of us would like to see a bit more ambiguity than the psalm allows, for we don't seem to be completely either one or the other, either wicked or righteous. The real problem is that we cannot accept the blessing God holds out to us up front as pure grace. That became clear to me when I visited a terminal cancer patient in the hospital. I was surprised by the fact that Psalm 1 was her favorite psalm: "God knows I am trying to be righteous, and that's enough" she said. What a humble acceptance of God's blessing! From all the psalms that follow Psalm 1 in the Psalter, we know and God knows how difficult the life of faith is, yet we are blessed as we begin our faith journey.

Negatively, the righteous one avoids the wicked; positively, she or he delights in and meditates on Adonai's Torah (cf. Ps. 119:16, 24, 35, 97, 103), and in that activity discovers the meaning of life. Joshua also is to "meditate" on this Torah day and night (Josh 1:8; cf. Deut 17:18–19). The righteous one is "like a tree planted by streams of water," deeply rooted and nourished. Just as a tree planted by a stream will flourish because of its constant water supply, so a person rooted in Torah will "prosper" because of her or his constant instruction from God. Torah is our human water source. Jeremiah 17:7–8 presents a similar picture.

"Prosper" is an unfortunate word choice of the NRSV; many people think immediately of material success and wealth. The righteous have the Midas touch! There are texts in the Hebrew Bible that suggest this concrete understanding on both a national and a personal level. In Joshua 1:8, a prosperous way includes crossing the Jordan, defeating enemies, and settling in the promised land. On an individual level, those who "fear Adonai" will have a large family (Ps. 128:3; 144:12). But there are other ways to understand "prosper." The JPS of the Jewish Publication Society translates the word more appropriately as "thrive." To "thrive" is to live within guidelines set by God as outlined in the Torah, to be "known" (v. 6) by God in the sense of "embraced," "looked after," "cherished." This means that one is able to sustain relationship with God, even when in the pit of disorientation, even when, and especially when, one is troubled.

To be prosperous and to delight in Torah does not mean that one is sheltered from the problems of the world; the guidance of Torah helps one through problems. The tree planted by the stream is not necessarily protected from strong winds, flood, or drought, but its deep roots help it survive them. Neither does it yield fruit all the time or any time it wants to, but "in its season," that is, at the proper time. As one parishioner on the eastern shore of Maryland told his pastor, "I'm prosperous, like the person in Psalm 1." This was an old man who had been a fisherman all his life, who was not rich at all and, in fact, just made enough to get by. But he was weathered and solid; he'd been through it all and prevailed, survived, just like the deeply rooted tree by the stream. I think Peter Craigie is right when he argues that blessedness is not a reward but rather the natural result of a particular type of life.[10] Torah is the way one should naturally go; that way is not a burden but a delight.

The antithetical idea of righteous/wicked is sharpened in verse 4: "Not so the wicked." This abrupt declaration denies any rootedness to the wicked at all; they do not thrive. Instead, they are "like chaff that the wind drives away." They are winnowed out of the "congregation of the righteous" (v. 5); they are too unstable, worthless, and light to "stand in the judgment." The wicked just can't compare with the kernel of grain that is too heavy for the wind to blow away; the wicked cannot endure (cf. Job 21:7–9). This point is emphasized by the fact that it takes only three lines of poetry to dismiss the wicked, but six lines of poetry to plant the righteous.

The poetic language of Psalm 1 actually makes the idea of act/consequence seem built into the very structure of reality. As Robert Alter points out, indicators clue us in to the transition between righteous and wicked at the beginning of verse 2 ("but," or "rather"), verse 4 ("not so"), verse 5 ("thus" or "therefore"), and verse 6 ("for").[11] The verbs in the poem depict the wicked in constant motion, restless, without direction, carried away as objects by forces over which they have no control. The righteous, however, are "planted," a passive participle, as they meditate. The envelope structure of the psalm, in which the end formally echoes the beginning, also anchors this idea that you get what you deserve. The psalm begins and ends with the wicked, *resha'im*. Into their midst, but not associating with them, come the righteous. The way of sinners, which the righteous avoid (v. 1), leads nowhere; it perishes (v. 6) because it is not connected to God. The righteous are in intimate connection with God, who "knows" or "watches over" them; the verb *yada'* is used in the Bible for sexual relationships.

Psalm 1 makes it clear that how we choose to live our lives matters to God. When we choose the right path and obey God, God embraces us and we thrive. This is not to say that we will never experience hardship or pain, but if we do, God is with us and cares for us. Eli Ezry, a recovering addict, recognizes how crucial our choosing is. In his correlation of the psalms with the Twelve Steps in a powerful little book of meditations, he reflects on the contrast between righteous and wicked in Psalm 1 in connection with step 2, recognizing a power greater than ourselves. He speaks of his insanity as an addict, that is, "doing the same thing over and over while expecting different results," thinking he "could live comfortably in two radically different worlds." Having become sane, he admits that "my two worlds can no longer coexist...there really are two distinct paths for me."[12]

Psalm 1 shows us a God who is a powerful judge ("the way of the wicked will perish") but also a loyal caregiver who blesses us on our journey through life. This is a confession of faith rather than a description of life.[13] This psalm holds up Torah, God's instruction, as a standard against which we can judge our behavior toward one another. There is a right way to live life, and it does matter, not only to God, but to those with whom we live in community. Do we walk, stand, or sit with those who trivialize God by straying from the right path God has set out for us? If we do, then our community is harmed. We don't want to make trouble or get involved, so we look the other way when someone does something wrong and excuse it by arguing that "it was a little infraction" or "it won't really hurt anyone." Do we let our standards of human conduct slide when it's to our advantage or when it's just the easier thing to do? In a world in which it seems that "anything goes," Psalm 1 calls us back to God as our center and standard and to faithful conduct toward one another.

Psalm 37: Success of the Wicked?

Psalm 37 is also a wisdom psalm, but it does not declare so boldly that "you get what you deserve." Rather, it appends a qualifier: "Don't you?" This is clear from verse 1 (and verses 7 and 8): "Do not fret because of the wicked; do not be envious of wrongdoers." Obviously, the wicked are not getting what they deserve; they are doing well enough to be envied. This psalm struggles with the painful picture of the wicked prospering while the righteous suffer. According to the theme of the Two Ways, this is not how it is supposed to be.

Many have dismissed this as a forced struggle, because the psalm unfolds in the form of an acrostic; the first letter of every verse or every other verse is a successive letter of the Hebrew alphabet. This acrostic form is impossible to detect in English translations. Psalm 37 is dismissed as a mere hodgepodge of proverbs strung together in this artificial way. But Brueggemann reminds us about the pedagogical purpose of an acrostic: "The carefully ordered arrangement corresponds to the claim made for the substance of the psalm; that is, the world is exceedingly well ordered, and virtue is indeed rewarded."[14] The theme of act/consequence permeates the psalm and ties it together. To understand the powerful ordering effect of an acrostic psalm, try to compose one. Let each member of your Sunday school class take a successive letter of the alphabet and write a verse that expresses a wisdom theme or the wisdom worldview, for example, the "Two Ways," God in control, moderation, and so forth. Have each person put her or his verse on newsprint in alphabetical order so that the class can pray the psalm together.

In order to deal with the apparent breakdown in the wisdom claim that you get what you deserve, the sage gives advice to those who are fretting. In keeping with the wisdom worldview, the sage's advice is practical, experiential, and human-centered. See how many pieces of advice you can identify within Psalm 37. You have probably given similar advice to your friends and family many times. Psalm 37 begins with advice: "Do not fret" (vv. 1, 7, 8). Why not? "For like the grass they soon wither" (v. 2; compare with v. 20); the apparent success of the wicked is temporary. Verse 10, "Yet a little while and the wicked will be no more," repeats this observation. All you need to do is "wait patiently" (vv. 7, 34), and things will work out as they should. While you wait for the wicked to vanish, "trust in Adonai" (vv. 3, 5) and "delight in Adonai" (v. 4).

To trust means that you must "commit your way to Adonai" (v. 5), "be patient" (v. 7), and "refrain from anger" (v. 8). Wisdom thinking holds up control and silence as proper behavior that leads to successful living; passion and an unbridled tongue mark the way of the fool. In a similar way, our patriarchal society today values "the poker face" and the "stiff upper lip" as marks of control and authority. Against this standard, women are often seen as too emotional and therefore weak and not worthy of trust. Compare this minimizing of women's abilities and capacities to the very positive view of Woman Wisdom in Proverbs 1—9 and of the woman of worth in Proverbs 31.

Why fret when even Adonai "laughs at the wicked" because "their day is coming" (Ps. 37:13)? The wicked will not be able to escape the consequences of their actions. The sage shares some proverbs in verses 16, 18, and 21 to undergird the advice given. The sage counsels not only refraining from certain behavior and thoughts but also acting positively in order to deal with the situation: "Turn from evil and do good" (v. 27; also v. 3). One cannot just sit back and let God do it all; one needs vision and purposeful activity to live through and beyond the present painful situation. One must keep to God's way (vv. 5, 23, 34), and that requires very positive action.

What personal testimony does the sage offer up to support the advice given? "I have been young and now have grown old; yet I have not seen the righteous forsaken or their children begging bread" (v. 25). How many times have you heard from someone older than you, your parents or grandparents, that they've lived longer and can tell you a thing or two? A second time the sage insists: "I have seen the wicked oppressing…Again I passed by, and they were no more" (vv. 35–36, NRSV). What is your reaction to this testimony?

Your first response might be, where has this person been? Is this a hermit who has been hiding in a cave? Just open the newspaper and turn on the TV and see how these statements are contradicted. Walk down the street and see the homeless, the addicted, the abused. At first glance these testimonies of the sage seem grossly out of step with reality. Our experiences just don't confirm them. Besides, nowadays old age just does not guarantee that one is more experienced than someone else; children grow up fast. On one level, then, Psalm 37 underscores the dangers of an unreflected faith, of closing one's eyes to the reality of the world and its brokenness. Psalm 37 can be used in this way for social control and the perpetuation of injustice.

On another level, however, Psalm 37 can be used very positively for social critique and transformation. It speaks of God's purposes for our lives, of behavior that is in harmony with God's intention for order. The sage asserts that "God loves justice" (v. 28), and the psalm seems to say that this justice involves our doing good (vv. 3 and 27), being generous and giving (v. 21), giving liberally and lending (v. 26), and uttering wisdom and speaking justice (v. 30). We must ask ourselves if we are doing that; only then may we be counted among the righteous.

The sage does not ignore the fact that God's justice is not evidenced in the world. The sage acknowledges that "the wicked plot against the righteous" (v. 12), and that "the wicked draw the sword…to bring down the poor and the needy" (v. 14). The life of faith is not easy; if it were, the sage would not have to repeat so often the advice to have patience, wait for God, trust.

This kind of faith motivates the psalmist to accept and endure the tensions of this life, tensions between what cannot be seen and yet what must be believed. The psalmist believes that "the meek shall inherit the land and enjoy themselves with great well-being" (v. 11); Jesus in the Sermon on the Mount knew this type of faith (Mt. 5:5). Psalm 37's insistence on the meek's inheriting in the face of the wicked raises the issue of how long an oppressed people can wait for that to happen and what to do in the meantime. In the face of the continued suffering of the black community, womanist (black feminist) theologians are beginning to fashion a new paradigm of redemptive suffering; black suffering has meaning and redemptive power because it confronts institutional evils such as racism and sexism. Only the oppressed can develop this paradigm, however. The oppressors have no right, for redemptive suffering too quickly can become a support for oppression—"suffering is good for you."

Psalm 37 makes it clear that it is more important to behave in positive ways than it is to worry about those who are doing well and not getting what they deserve. This psalm makes it difficult to blame somebody else for our problems and pushes us to take responsibility for our own part in the world. Psalm 37 does not claim that life is easy and that the sage's advice is easily followed. Rather, it observes that energy wasted in envy could better be spent doing good, being generous, lending, and speaking justly. We must ask ourselves whether this observation can be applied to our lives today, whether at work or at home. Do we spend more time complaining about a colleague at work than doing better at our own job? Do we waste time comparing our children to other children and wonder why ours don't do as well at school or at sports, when we could be spending more time with them playing ball or going over homework or just talking? Do we lament the crime and drug abuse in our neighborhoods but fail to volunteer our time and energy to address their root causes?

All the wisdom psalms point beyond ourselves to a reality that endures and gives us direction: God. Wisdom psalms focus on our behavior as central to God's blessing: "Adonai embraces the way of the righteous, but the way of the wicked will perish" (Ps. 1:6). How we define who the righteous and the wicked are in the wisdom psalms says a great deal about how these psalms speak to our own lives. It is dangerous to claim that the righteous are only those who are just like us, and the wicked are those who are "different." If wisdom is truly universal, and not the possession of an elite, then there are practical, life-enhancing things we can do, not only for ourselves and those like us, but also for others not like us. This is the way of wisdom; this is justice, and "Adonai loves justice" (Ps. 37:28). Do we?

Psalm 73: God's Goodness?

"Some things are best communicated by personal testimony."[15] The psalmist in Psalm 73 struggles with theodicy, that is, justifying God's ways when God's justice is not evident in the world. The psalmist's experience resonates with our own as we struggle with traditional teachings of act/consequence that we see contradicted every day; we search desperately for evidence of God's goodness. Verse 1 opens with the declaration: "Truly, El is good to Israel, Elohim to those who are pure in heart." The psalm ends with a redefinition of "good" in terms of God's presence rather than in terms of traditional expectations of more concrete rewards, such as long life, children, or wealth. The psalmist affirms traditional views "while simultaneously raising the discussion to another level."[16] God who is good to Israel in verse 1 turns out to be good to the individual also in verse 28; "good" and "God" in these two verses create an envelope or *inclusio* frame for the whole psalm. Verses 1 and 28 reverse the order of the words "good" *(tob)* and God *('elohim);* the word in the middle of the phrase is changed from "Israel" to "me."[17] Echoing this movement in the psalm is the shift in the use of divine names. Elohim may be the keeper of justice and act/consequence in verse 1, but it is Adonai (LORD), Israel's personal name for God, who is refuge in verse 28. The universal becomes personal. What has brought about this transformation?

Psalm 73 begins Book 3 of the Psalter, and its superscription links it to Asaph; all but one of the eleven other psalms linked to Asaph are found in Book 3, and all deal with theodicy issues. Perhaps the canonical editor of the book of Psalms intended to contrast Psalms 72 and 73. Psalm 72, linked to Solomon, makes eschatological promises of peace and justice, while Psalm 73 expresses the reality of present oppression; the psalms are contrasted by means of parallelisms and repetition of key words.[18] Miller and Brueggemann suggest that the speaker of Psalm 73 is the king and that Psalm 73 provides an alternative "script" for a monarchy that needed to be rethought after Solomon's reign.[19] The script is not heeded, since book 3 ends with the disaster of monarchy in Psalm 89, and enthronement psalms of God outnumber royal psalms in book 4. Psalm 73 is also tied to introductory Psalms 1 and 2, echoing the first half of the Psalter. The wicked are the focus in Psalm 1:5–6 and in Psalm 73:3–12. The conclusion of Psalm 73 speaks of those far from God who "perish" (73:27), just as the wicked "perish" in 1:6. God is "refuge" in 2:12 and 73:28. In this way, Psalm 73 stands at the theological and canonical center of the book of Psalms.[20]

The opening verse is often translated "Truly God is good to the upright" by redividing the Hebrew words and creating different spellings. This is not necessary. This verse expresses a traditional affirmation of Israel's experience of God. Psalm 73 divides into three parts marked by the Hebrew adverb *'ak,* which is translated "truly" in verses 1 and 18, and "all" or "entirely" in verse 13; the structure of the psalm marks the psalmist's journey of transformation. Crenshaw notes that the exclamation/affirmation of *'ak* occurs in three different contexts: in the motto that has come into question about God's goodness; in the false assertion that the psalmist's innocence is a waste of time; and in the closing assurance that the wicked slip, which is the flip side of the belief in God's goodness.[21] These two assertions about God bracket the psalmist's wavering in verses 13–14. McCann sees the three parts of the psalm as an outline of the problem, the turning point, and the solution.[22] The psalm structure communicates the reversal of the situation.

Verses 3–12 offer an extended description of the wicked. But their situation will be overturned, as verses 18–20, 27 declare. This results in the goodness experienced by the psalmist in verse 28. The problem is that the psalmist envied these wicked and almost slipped to their level. These wicked prosper without any fear of divine retribution: "How can God know? Is there knowledge in the Most High?" (v. 11). God is too far away (*'El Elyon*, God Most High) to care about what they do, and they do not care about God. In the meantime, they continue to enjoy an easy life while they bad-mouth God: "Their tongues range over the earth" (v. 9). Body parts personified lend power to the arrogant attitude of the wicked. So does the imagery of pride as a "necklace" and violence covering them "like a garment" in verse 6. Their way of operating in the world is as much a part of them as their clothing. Their reward is more security and riches (v. 12). David Pleins argues that one of the most "strident" biblical critiques of wealth occurs in these verses. Verse 12, especially, draws the connection between the amassing of wealth and social injustice. Like Psalm 49:10–11, 17–20 and skeptical Ecclesiastes 2:11–12, 18, 22, Psalm 73 embraces the prophetic critique. Pleins argues that Psalms 49 and 73 do not simply echo traditional wisdom views of wealth, but reevaluate them. As such, they serve as a model, "compelling worship and catechesis to be proactive in challenging prevailing views of poverty and wealth"[23] rather than accepting the status quo.

Karen Cassedy argues that from the viewpoint of one who has been overweight most of her life, verse 4, "their bodies are whole and well nourished," and verse 7, "their eyes swell out with fatness" (NRSV), or "their fat oozes out malice" (NJB), or "fat shuts out their eyes" (JPS), do not provide a "positive portrayal of fat," despite the fact that fat was a sign of success and reward in biblical times. She suggests that the psalmist makes a direct connection between the "over-consumption" of these "immorally obese" people "and the violence and oppression they perpetrate against others." She shares that "I feel that my extra poundage reveals to all that I am following the way of the wicked. This is both a personal shaming and a societal indictment. For I live in a society that takes more than its share of the earth's resources in many ways, including food. Being overweight is an option that most Two-Thirds World people do not have. In fact, our society's over-consumption prevents many from even satisfying their hunger. My self-indulgence is therefore an act of violence and oppression against others." She sees redemption in her choice to follow a Twelve Step program such as Overeaters Anonymous, and suggests that Psalm 73 may be helpful to use with a Lenten discipline of fasting. "God helps us to hunger creatively" and becomes our "portion" (v. 26), so that we can "provide space for God in time for an Easter resurrection."[24]

The second section of the psalm begins with verse 13: "All (or "entirely," Hebrew: *'ak*) in vain I have kept my heart clean." The psalmist's envy creates a crisis; what's the point of not being like the wicked since the end result is punishment (v. 14)? Martin Buber notes the repetition of the key word "heart" *(leb)* in Psalm 73 six times (vv. 1, 7, 13, 21, 26 [twice]). Note how in verse 13 the internal attitude expressed by keeping the heart clean is linked to the external act of washing the hands; the whole person is involved with God. For Buber, however, "the state of the heart determines."[25] It determines if one lives in the truth in which God's good is experienced or in the semblance of truth where tough times are confused with God's not being good.

McCann is right to argue that verse 15 marks a turning point in the psalm as significant as that in verse 17, since verse 15 addresses God directly for the first time. Loyalty to God's people ("circle of your children") kept the psalmist from giving up and becoming like the wicked. If the psalmist shared publicly the thoughts of verses 13–14, God's family (Israel) would be betrayed. "What brings the psalmist through the crisis of faith, then, is apparently his or her identity as a member of God's people,"[26] an identity that is then solidified in worship (vv. 16–17). But the psalmist would never have gotten to the sanctuary or temple if the prior decision to remain faithful hadn't been made in verse 15.

The experience in the temple as part of the community of faith leads the psalmist to proclaim new understandings. The third part of the psalm begins with verse 18, "truly *('ak),* you set them in slippery places" (NRSV). The wicked now occupy the slippery slope that the psalmist almost experienced in verse 2. The security of the wicked outlined in verses 4–12 has vanished; the psalmist is now secure and can address God directly (vv. 21–28). The situation is reversed because the psalmist understands it differently; the heart determines. The psalmist now sees that the prosperity of the wicked is unreal. Crenshaw is right to suggest that, just as in verse 1, the adverb "truly" *('ak)* "takes us to the world of confession. This I believe: God will place sinners' feet where not even a toehold can be found."[27] The envied will become the pitied. The hands that had been washed in vain (v. 13) are now grasped by God (v. 23). The heart that earlier was "pricked" (v. 21) will now find God as its strength ("rock") and its portion (v. 26). The word for "portion," *(heleq)* usually means the piece of land that each Israelite possesses as a sign of the covenant and life, passed on to future generations. God is now "portion" for the psalmist. Envy had transformed the psalmist into the "brute beast" referenced in verse 22, but identity with the community of faith and worship have enabled the psalmist to be taken by the hand by God and to acknowledge God's continual presence (v. 23). "Now in worship he discovers that faith depends not on his fragile, often vulnerable grasp of God, but on God's grasp of him."[28]

Does verse 24b promise a life after death? It says, "and afterward you will receive me with honor (to glory?)." The three Hebrew words that make up this phrase can be translated in very different ways. Does "afterward" *('ahar)* mean after death or during the psalmist's lifetime? Does the word "honor" or "glory" *(kabod)* refer to the psalmist's reputation in the community or to the majesty of God or to the psalmist's being with God beyond death? Does the verb "receive" or "take" refer to the "translation" of Enoch in Genesis 5:24: Enoch "walked with God and was not, for God took him" (cf. Elijah in 2 Kings 2:1). Or does "receive" mean simply "welcome" or "accept" me? The same verb used in Psalm 49:15 raises the same questions. This verse probably does not point to a developed doctrine of resurrection.

In verses 27–28 it becomes clear what "God is good to Israel" means in verse 1. It is not what the wicked experienced in their ease in verses 4–12. "Good" means nearness to God, who is refuge. Out of this security of God's presence, the psalmist tells of all God's works, not holding back as in verse 15, which uses the same verb. Out of crisis and self-pity in verses 13–14, the psalmist moves toward praise. This movement does not wipe away the questions, but it does make the psalmist aware of God's presence in the midst of those questions.

CHAPTER FIVE

Complaining in Faith to God
Psalm Laments

There are times in our lives when our acknowledgment of sin rightly moves us to confession and petition for God's forgiveness, but there are other times when we honestly do not understand why we suffer, and we question angrily rather than confess. In light of these other times, we must ask with Roland Murphy whether "we have lost the art of complaining *in faith* to God in favor of a stoic concept of what obedience or resignation to the divine will really means."[1] Many Christians think that "complaining in faith" is a contradiction in terms; if one complains, one is not faithful. This view comes to the fore in a comment I heard recently from a pastor: "I deal with a lot of widows trying to cope with the change in their situation. Of course once they've asked the question 'why me?' they've already lost their faith, so a lot of rebuilding has to be done."

This seems to be a harsh comment, doesn't it? Have you ever said anything like that? Your response is probably no, but think about how this view emerges in other things that we say and do when someone is hurting. When my twenty-three-year-old brother, Brian, drowned, many well-meaning people came to the funeral home and said to my sobbing mother, "Have faith, Rose." Their comments suggested that her sobs and anger and questions of "why?" were unfaithful responses to the pain of her loss. She certainly took the comments that way, which added more anger and also guilt to her pain; she sobbed all the more.

The following poem by the Reverend David G. Bowen[2] speaks of the necessity for reverential silence in the presence of suffering. It was written a year after the death of his daughter Lesley Ayn, at age 16, while he was on a Wesley Theological Seminary immersion to Poland and the Holocaust sites. This poem was produced after his visit to Auschwitz and the buildings there that hold thousands of personal effects of the Jews, as well as canisters of Cyclon B gas, which was sold, billed, and delivered as disinfectant; 20 percent less Cyclon B was used in the summer.

There Should Be a Silence in Some Museums
MAY 21, 1997

Lesley would have graduated from high school
This month.
Instead, they took her
Suitcase
Prosthesis
Crutches
Comb
Hairbrush
Toothbrush
Shoes
Doll
Dress
Pig tails
Gold fillings
Prayer shawl
Thimble
Glasses
And when they were finished,
She was de-liced, numbered, and later
Disinfected with CYCLON B.
But they used a smaller quantity.
Because of the warmer weather
Not as much is required.
Think of the savings.
These buildings, now museums,
Are the hardest for me.
Perhaps, the only conversation
Allowed should be these silent tears.

The question "why me?" (Or "why my brother?") is undergirded by the theory of act/consequence discussed in chapter 4. "Why me?" means "what did I do to deserve this?" Parents who have lost a child in an accident or to a disease such as cancer will review their efforts on the child's behalf and wonder, "What good does any of it do? We've done all the right things all our lives; everything was planned out carefully. We thought that if we lived the way we should, things would work out the way we wanted. It just doesn't seem fair." In their assessment, they and their child did not get what was deserved.

The failure of act/consequence in our experience of death or prolonged illness is exacerbated by cultural values and assumptions about health. We operate under the illusion that we can control our lives if we exercise, eat right, wear the right clothes, and manage stress. We expect to stay young and avoid death if we do all these things. Think of all the TV and newspaper advertisements for instant pain relief, health spas, and food that showcase this theme. When a child dies, however, or an elderly parent succumbs after a long and painful illness, our sense is that things are no longer under our control. Life is not supposed to be this way if we play by all the rules. The ordering of our lives according to the idea that we get what we deserve is challenged by our experience of inexplicable disorientation.

Cultural values about health are just a slice of what Walter Brueggemann calls the dominant American cultural ideology of success, continuity, and the avoidance of anything messy, such as pain and loss in all areas of life. Again, TV and radio advertisements that would have us believe the right bank or life insurance policy is the key to success, sitcoms that resolve gut-wrenching problems in thirty minutes, and the difficulty of attracting and holding people in the caring professions—all are symptomatic of our cultural unwillingness to deal with the painful reality of our human situation.

Despite the illusion of success, we experience repeated challenges to the order and reliability of life that shake our confidence in the One who keeps order. These challenges move us out of orientation into disorientation. In this move, which the laments enable us to articulate in a way that matches our experiences, "we engage in a countercultural activity,"[3] because our disorientating experiences fly in the face of the dominant cultural ideology of success. Laments offer countertestimony to Israel's core testimony about who God is and how God acts most of the time.

Many different kinds of losses, in addition to the death or illness of a loved one, can push us into disorientation and challenge our cultural illusions. Divorce, loss of a job, a partner's adultery, substance abuse by a member of one's family, AIDS, chronic illness, child abuse, spouse abuse, rape—all confront our individual perceptions or orientations, the security of a well-ordered world, and the notion that we are in control or that God oversees the running of a well-ordered world. We also experience communal losses and disorientation; toxic waste dumps threaten the health of whole communities; racism in our schools and work places divides blacks, whites, Latinos, and Asian Americans; stock market plunges and international terrorism threaten our national pride and place in the world.

Whatever our experiences of loss, our movement out of orientation into the pit of disorientation is one that society does not acknowledge or support. This lack of support is evidenced in many ways, because society evaluates different pits of disorientation differently. Even minimal support levels vary depending on whether a personal loss is from accidental death, divorce, mental illness, substance addiction, or AIDS. Societal evaluation of communal losses is even more complex; communities are fragmented and diverse today, and we are not often willing to become involved unless we are directly affected.

When my brother died, my father was allowed only three days off from his blue-collar job for his grief process. Yet even though this timetable seemed insensitive, his coworkers almost tiptoed around him deferentially; his son was a good boy, Phi Beta Kappa, top 10 percent of his class at the University of Michigan Law School, not a drug addict or homosexual with AIDS. If that had not been the case, would his coworkers have kept their awkward, respectful silence, or would they have said something purposefully hurtful, implying that he got what he deserved?

How can we deal with disorientation if our culture will not acknowledge our questions as we make the painful move into disorientation? Will the church listen? The fact that the angry laments have been so little used in our liturgies suggests not. Our pastor may meet with us to help us work though the pain, but without the larger support of the community of faith that is the church, this isolated care, though helpful, will be incomplete. Does the community of mutual caring that is the church care enough about the pain of its members to make room for the lament in its liturgical life, teaching, and counseling?

Nearly one-third of the 150 psalms in the Psalter are laments that articulate the experience of disorientation in the life of an individual or in the corporate life of the community Israel. Most of the laments are the so-called angry, or imprecatory, laments that find the present situation of distress unfair and inexplicable, and complain about it to God. Only the seven penitential laments (Pss. 6, 32, 38, 51, 102, 130, and 143) accept the experience of suffering as deserved punishment for sin. Among the corporate (in contrast to the individual) laments, those that mention the people's sin do not see the people's suffering as just punishment, but as excessive and thus undeserved.

Despite the fact that laments are so numerous, they are seldom used in Christian worship. People are often surprised to find laments in the Bible at all, considering them to be "unchristian." Occasionally we find an angry lament as a responsive reading in the back of our hymnals, but with all the angry parts cut out. At best, the church uses the seven penitential laments during the Lenten season, for these psalms articulate repentance. Psalm 51, for example, poignantly pleads: "Grace me, O God, according to your *hesed,* according to your abundant womb-love, blot out my transgressions. Wash me thoroughly from my iniquity and cleanse me from my sin" (vv. 1–2).

Lament language can help the church speak the truth about human experience and the life of faith. By ignoring or suppressing the laments, the church turns its back on a canonical witness to the struggle for faith in God. Why does the church cut itself off from a valuable resource for healing and wholeness within the brokenness and suffering of our world? In order to recognize the truth of lived experience, have your Sunday school class create a communal lament collage. On a long sheet of butcher paper, glue pictures and headlines from magazines and newspapers that challenge the optimistic wisdom worldview of order. Have everyone work at once so that the result is a truly random arrangement. When you are finished, discuss how society and the church respond to the disorientation depicted in the collage. How does your church deal within its worship services with this kind of pain? within its ministry?

A form-critical analysis of the lament structure can help to show why the lament can be called a legitimate complaint in faith to God and how the lament can contribute to healing and wholeness. I will illustrate the parts of the lament structure with verses taken from different laments, then treat selected individual and communal laments in their entirety. The structure outlined below is an ideal structure only; not every lament will correspond to this form in every detail. In fact, it is the deviation from the conventional, the move away from the norm, that often contributes to the meaning of a psalm. One can identify all the parts of a lament, but the investigation of a lament psalm should be a new way of seeing both the psalm and ourselves whole. In this way, lamenting can be a healing process. (Outline items 1, 2, 3, and 4 appear in this chapter and items 5 and 6 in chapter 6).

The Structure of the Lament

1. Address
   a. Short, emotion-packed
   b. Why? How long?

2. Complaint proper
   a. The psalmist's suffering (I/we)
   b. The enemies (they)
   c. God accused of not caring/doing (You)
3. Petition
4. Motivations
   a. Confession of sin
   b. Protestation of innocence
   c. Public relations value of psalmist
   — — — — — — — — — — — — — — — — —
5. Confession of trust
   a. Usually introduced by *but*
   b. Faith that knows what it is talking about
6. Vow of praise

As can be seen from its structure, a lament does not merely bemoan hardship, but rather, seeks change. It means to get something from God and thus "is primarily an appeal."[4] A lament psalm describes a distress, interprets it, and appeals to God based on that interpretation. The psalmist's intention is to motivate God's intervention. In order to motivate, lament language is vivid and metaphorical, evocative and provocative. It seeks God's involvement to change the situation of distress. Lament language is intense, because it is language at the extremities of life, language in the pit of disorientation.

If we are to enter the world of the lament, we must enter into the intensity and emotion of lament poetry, rather than judge it or be shocked by it. How ironic that there is very little that seems to shock us in the secular world anymore. Hollywood stars and "ordinary" people share the most intimate details of their lives with millions of people on the TV and radio talk shows. Just let people say exactly what's on their mind to God in prayer, however, and shock and pious censure are our immediate response. What a wedge we drive between the secular and sacred in our lives! How can we possibly be whole before God when we split our lives in this way?

Address

The lament address is usually very short and packed with emotion as, for example, in Psalm 22: 1: "My God, my God, why have you forsaken me?" Jesus also takes up these words as his last ones on the cross (Mt. 27:46, Mk. 15:34). Jesus' lament on the cross signals that Lent can be a way into our pain and the pain of the world, a way to acknowledge and articulate that pain, a way that may not always begin with repentance, but sometimes with questions and doubts. The address is actually a mini-faith statement, clearly identifying the One to whom the psalmist prays. The address suggests that this One matters to the psalmist; if not, why would she or he bother to pray to God in the first place? By naming God, the psalmist asserts that God is the source of healing, the One who can overcome the present distress.

The use of the possessive adjective "my" in the address of Psalm 22 claims an intimate past relationship with God, which underscores the present distress and undergirds the later petition for intervention. The psalmist, in effect, reminds God of their relationship and the expectations surrounding that relationship. This verse also shows how often an exclamation or a rhetorical question is interwoven with the identification of God in the lament. These questions actually belong to the complaint proper.

The Hebrew question *lamah* ("why") is the most frequently occurring question in the psalms. It is not simply a question of information, as if God could explain the pain away. The why indicates that something is very wrong and that the psalmist does not understand what is happening and feels totally helpless; otherwise the following petitions for God to intervene would not make any sense.

As Harold Kushner points out about Job's friends, their first mistake was to think that when Job asked, "Why is God doing this to me?" he was asking a question that they could answer and that their answer would be helpful. "In reality, Job's words were not a theological question at all, but a cry of pain,"[5] requiring an exclamation point rather than a question mark. Job's friends were so busy doing theology (talking about God) that they almost forgot about Job; they did not show any sympathy to the one on the dung heap. Their authoritarian use of scripture was meant to convict Job of sin and change his unrepentant behavior; they were not interested in really listening to him and thereby comforting him. One of them, Zophar, even goes so far as to say that Job is not getting as much as he deserved (11:6b). The pastoral sensitivity of the friends was strongest when they sat with Job in silence for seven days and seven nights. Whereas the "Why?" in laments is full of reproach and accusation of God, the also frequent "How long?" expresses the urgency of the painful situation. Both are rhetorical questions.

"How long?" is also not a question for information, as if knowing that the pain would end in six weeks or three months or one year would satisfy the psalmist and make everything all right. Rather, the psalmist asks, "how long?" in order to assert, "This has gone on long enough![6] I can't take it any more!"

Complaint Proper

The largest part of the lament psalm is usually the description of the distress, a setting forth of what is wrong. Language in this section is highly metaphorical and figurative. It is meant to be provocative and evocative, to draw us into sympathy and outrage.

Both God and the community of faith that hears the psalm must be convinced of the intensity of the suffering and the need for God to act. The complaint may contain one, two, or three foci: (1) the one lamenting and her or his suffering, or the community's suffering (I/we); (2) the enemies (they); and (3) God, who is accused of not caring or of not doing or of acting in the wrong way (you).

The Psalmist's Suffering (I/We)

One cannot remain unmoved by the very emotional language describing the sufferer's distress. In Psalm 22:14–15, for example, the psalmist cries out: "I am poured out like water, and all my bones are out of joint; my heart is like wax, it is melted within my breast; my [strength] is dried up like a potsherd, and my tongue sticks to my jaws; you lay me in the dust of death" (NRSV, a potsherd is a piece of a broken pottery jug or jar). Bracketing out for now the fact that Jesus, according to the gospels of Matthew and Mark, used the first verse of Psalm 22 from the cross and that these words of suffering can be applied to him, what do you think the psalmist is suffering from? What is wrong?

To be "poured out like water" may suggest fatigue and exhaustion, either physical or spiritual. People with arthritis have pointed to the "bones out of joint" as an indication of their condition. The "tongue sticking to the jaws" always reminds me of the cancer patients I have visited in the hospital who had just come back from their chemotherapy treatments and could not drink anything. All they could do was suck on an ice cube to reduce the terrible dryness in their mouths. Note how the *I/we* of the complaint moves into the *you* of complaint, to God, in the last part of verse 15. God is seen as the source of the psalmist's pain. The psalmist's suffering is the result of God's action: "*You* lay me in the dust of death" (italics added).

Although scholars have tried to uncover the specific circumstances that evoked this description of suffering, most agree that to do so is impossible. If five people were asked to write down what they thought the psalmist's distress was in Psalm 22, they would probably give five different answers. This illustrates the beauty and staying power of stylized psalm language, which describes in a vivid way shared situations of suffering. Thus, the same psalm can be used by different people in varied circumstances. Today we can plug into psalm descriptions of suffering at many different points in our lives and particularize them with our own personal experiences. The image of suffering suggested to us today in Psalm 22:14–15 may be different six months from now, depending on what has happened in our lives. In the same way, we can understand how the early church used psalms such as this one to talk about the life, death, and significance of Jesus of Nazareth.

In many laments, the psalmist's distress is likened to death, or to being overcome by the powers of darkness, or to going down to Sheol (pronounced shay-ole), also called the Pit. The Israelites believed that Sheol was a region deep down in the bowels of the earth where the dead, whether they were good or bad in life, existed as shades of their former selves. The Hebrew Bible reveals no belief in the afterlife in a Christian or later Jewish sense (except in the case of Dan. 12:2–3, which is a late book, from the second century B.C.E.). The famous story of King Saul and the medium of Endor (1 Sam. 28) illustrates Israelite thinking about Sheol. Saul asks the medium to "bring up" from Sheol the prophet and judge Samuel, who had anointed Saul king. Samuel comes up as "an old man…wrapped in a robe," none too happy about being disturbed, and gives Saul bad news, reaffirming Adonai's rejection of Saul as king.

The psalms themselves are not all in agreement about whether or not one maintains communion with God when one dies and goes to Sheol. Some laments attempt to persuade God to act to end the psalmist's distress by reminding God: "What profit is there in my death, if I go down to the Pit? Will the dust praise you? Will it tell of your faithfulness?" (Ps. 30:9, NRSV; also Pss. 6:5; 88:6; Job 10:21–22; 17:12–16; Isa. 38:18). Death means the end of the relationship and of the psalmist's praise of God. On the other hand, Psalm 139:7–8 insists: "Where can I go from your spirit? Where can I flee from your presence? If I ascend to heaven, there you are; if I make my bed in Sheol, you are there" (cf. Pss. 22:29; 49:15).

This psalm suggests God's omnipresence, but more than that is meant here. Psalm 139 testifies to the intimacy of relationship with God in Sheol or anywhere else, an intimacy that is rooted in God's "knowing" the psalmist. "Know/knowledge" is used seven times in this psalm (vv. 1, 2, 4, 6, 14, and 23 twice). The calligrapher Michael Podesta has created a visual image of this knowledge and intimacy in his drawing "The Alexander," which was designed as a birth announcement for his son.[7]

Psalm 88:3–6 offers an example of suffering described in terms of Sheol and death. "For I am sated with troubles; I have reached Sheol. I am numbered with those who go down to the Pit; I have become like one without strength abandoned among the dead, like bodies lying in the grave of whom You are mindful no more, and who are cut off from Your hand." Is the psalmist actually dying? Perhaps not, since we hear words such as "*like* bodies lying in the grave," and "I am *numbered with* those who go down to the Pit." Though the psalmist may not be on her or his deathbed, anything that threatens one's shalom (wholeness, integrity, relationship with God and people) is likened to death, and makes one feel as good as dead. The rhetorical questions of verses 10–12 draw a negative picture of life in Sheol, where everything associated with a God-centered life is lacking: "praise," *hesed,* "faithfulness," "darkness," "forgetfulness." This is the place of the "shades" (*repa'im,* cf. Isa. 14:9; 26:14), the dead who point to "that weak, ghost-like existence from which all real life has been drained." This is Abaddon (Job 26:6; 28:22), related to the verbal root "to perish, destroy"; this is personified destruction; no surprise that in Revelation 9:11, Abaddon is the angel of the bottomless pit.[8]

Pastoral counselor Wayne Oates hears in the language of Psalm 88 the isolation of being trapped in an "iron cage of despair." Feeling helpless in relation to God and other people, the psalmist is trapped in a "can't do" mode and will not or cannot hear the good news of God's presence.[9] The psalmist feels cut off from God's presence and from the understanding of friends and family. The psalm ends literally and figuratively in darkness. Eli Ezry meditates on Psalm 88:7, 9 to express his isolation as an addict: "I feel utterly alone. My shame is so great that I cannot share my secret life as an addict with anyone…I suppose I am lying in the bed I made. And it feels as narrow as the grave."[10]

Psalm 88: 6–7 moves into the *you* of lament language: "You have put me at the bottom of the Pit, in the darkest places, in the depths. Your wrath lies heavy upon me; you make me miserable with all your breakers." God is accused of causing the psalmist's present distress. That distress is described not only in terms of the Pit, or Sheol, but in terms of chaos waters ("breakers," "waves") overwhelming the psalmist. As Psalm 104 asserted (chap. 3), God has set boundaries for the chaos waters in creation. The psalmist of Psalm 88, however, feels as if those boundaries have been removed: she or he is experiencing the terror of the waters of creation out of control.

Walter Brueggemann declares that Psalm 88 "is an embarrassment to conventional faith."[11] It portrays the terror of a God who does not answer. Yet God's silence does not lead to rejection of God, but to more intense address, couched in urgent anger and rhetorical questions. Why is a psalm like this in our Bible? Because "life is like that," and sometimes "easy words" cannot comfort.[12] The distress of the psalmist is deep in Psalm 88, and for this reason I used it in a memorial service for a young woman who had committed suicide. Those who had known her glimpsed the depths of her despair through the vivid metaphorical language of the psalm. Her parents wanted people to understand how deeply isolated and afraid their daughter had been; they told me they were comforted by Psalm 88's being proclaimed publicly in that way.

Psalm 88 offers truthful, and therefore comforting, countertestimony about God's hiddenness, ambiguity, and negativity to Israel's core testimony about what is generally believed to be true of God over time, that God is a God of covenant, doxology, and presence.[13] My son Brian has experienced the reality of this countertestimony about God. The one named after my dead brother, freshly 19 last summer, has just returned to college after a year-long leave of absence devoted to the dark night of the soul, bursting with what he called "so many questions that won't go away, that don't have any answers." Why aren't more people asking these questions, he wants to know?

The Enemies (They)

The enemies in the laments are always vicious, and usually compared to mad dogs, bulls, or lions. The modern equivalent might be the pit bull. Psalm 17:10–12 describes them in this way: "They close their hearts to pity; with their mouths they speak arrogantly. They track me down; now they surround me; they set their eyes to cast me to the ground. They are like a lion eager to tear, like a young lion lurking in ambush" (NRSV). Who are these enemies in Psalm 17? Some scholars argue that they are false accusers in a law court or sorcerers or Israel's national enemies, but, again, most interpreters agree that we can't say who these enemies are. They are faceless enemies found in any typically human struggle, either national or personal.

When I posed this question about who the enemies are in this psalm to an intergenerational group at a church Bible study, parents were shocked to hear their teenagers say that the parents were the enemies in this psalm! Our parents, the youth felt, "don't really understand us"; they "close their hearts to pity." "They track me down, lurking in ambush," always waiting for me to mess up, to make a mistake so that they can ground me or say, "You see, I told you you weren't a responsible person." Some elderly people saw in this language a description of their adult children who were watching them closely for the first signs of senility. "They're just waiting for me to leave the stove on when I go out or forget my keys one more time, then, one, two, three, I'll be put in the nursing home."

Hospital patients saw doctors as the enemy in this psalm: "Just when I'm feeling a bit better, they order more tests and jab me for more blood; they hurry into my room, talk medical jargon and leave, never asking how I really feel or if I understand what's happening to me." Many people thought that their supervisors or bosses were like "lions eager to tear," waiting in ambush to deny them a promotion or a raise. At a pastor's retreat, the pastors chuckled with relief to hear that their colleagues thought of the pastor-parish committee or the church council or the consistory in this role—just waiting for the pastor to do something that they could complain about!

The description of enemies in Psalm 17 is one that most of us can concretize easily from our own experience. But what happens when we encounter the violent language of revenge against enemies in Psalm 58:6–8? "O God, break the teeth in their mouths; tear out the fangs of the young lions, Adonai! Let them vanish like water that runs away; like grass let them be trodden down and wither. Let them be like the snail that dissolves into slime, like the untimely birth that never sees the sun" (modified NRSV).

Many people are disturbed by this negativism and violence. Brueggemann argues that in these psalms people speak unguardedly about life as it really is, and that these psalms show Israel refusing to ignore this unguardedness, but instead seeing it as honest communication with God. The metaphors are strong and bold. If any of you garden, you are familiar, perhaps, with "the snail dissolving into slime." My garden in the D.C. area is plagued by slugs; an old remedy I use is to flick on the lights after dark and rush out with a salt shaker and sprinkle them, which causes their membranes to burst so that they literally dissolve into a pool of slime.

True, the psalmist does not ask for the personal power to punish enemies in this way; that is left to God, as is the case for all the laments except Psalm 41. Also, the psalmist asks that God take away from the enemies only what they use to hurt, that is, fangs, teeth. But these observations do little to diffuse shock over the hatred-of-enemies language in the psalms. Some Christians believe that the God of the New Testament is a God of love, grace, and forgiveness and not the God of anger, law, and judgment in the Hebrew Bible; this hatred-of-enemy language, they hold, is not "Christian." But they draw an inaccurate dichotomy between the two parts of the Christian Bible, both of which show grace and judgment. A paradigmatic example of grace in the Hebrew Bible is in the prologue to the Ten Commandments in Exodus 20:2: "I am Adonai, your God, who brought you out of the land of Egypt, out of the house of bondage." God's free and graceful act of the exodus preceded God's giving of the law (the Torah, the Ten Commandments). In Genesis, God forgives the matriarchs and patriarchs again and again, and works through their mistakes and doubts to keep the promise of land and descendants alive.

In separating the God of wrath from the God of grace, Christians point also to Jesus' Sermon on the Mount: "Blessed are those who mourn, … the merciful, … the peacemakers, … those who are persecuted for righteousness' sake" (Mt. 5:4–10). How can one hate enemies given this teaching of Jesus? In Mark 12:28–34, Jesus names the two great commandments: love God with all your heart, soul, mind, and strength and your neighbor as yourself. Where is there room for hatred of enemies if we are commanded to love God and our neighbor? Yet the Jews of Jesus' time knew these commandments too. The first is found in Deuteronomy 6:4–5: "Hear, O Israel, Adonai our God, Adonai is one, and you shall love Adonai your God with all your heart, and with all your being, and with all your might." This is the first part of the Shema, the supreme affirmation of God's unity. The second is found in Leviticus 19:17–18: "You shall not hate your brother [or sister] in your heart, but you shall reason with your neighbor, lest you bear sin because of him [or her]. You shall not take vengeance or bear any grudge against the children of your own people, but you shall love your neighbor as yourself; I am Adonai." These two commandments stood in the Hebrew Bible along with the angry lament language about enemies.

Jesus is also quoted twice in the gospels as saying "love your enemies" (as an antithesis to "hate your enemies," which is nowhere commanded in the Hebrew Bible) and "turn the other cheek" (Lk. 6:27–31; Mt. 5:43–46). How can one be commanded to love? Even Jesus becomes angry; he curses a fig tree and overturns the tables of the money changers in the royal portico of the temple mount. Perhaps the angry-enemy language in the psalms recognizes the difficulty of commanded love and speaks to the process of loving. Can we love someone before we acknowledge our hatred of him or her? Can such an acknowledgment of hatred be cathartic and defuse a hateful action, especially if it is offered up in the context of worship within the community of faith?

Given these Christian protests against the enemy language of Psalm 58 and other laments, we must ask who the enemies in Psalm 58 are. Again, we cannot say for sure, but in a real sense they seem more than human. They represent all that is opposed to shalom and wholeness, all that threatens life and order in the world. Since God intends life and order for God's creation, the psalmist's enemies become God's enemies as well. The enemies threaten not only the psalmist but also her or his God. The urgency and vehemence of the enemy language in Psalm 58 come, in part, from this identification that the psalmist makes between personal enemies, or the people's enemies, and God's enemies. Not only is the psalmist's future at stake, but God's reputation is too. Will God allow the enemies to triumph over the righteous ones who follow God? If God does give the wicked what they deserve, then, as Psalm 58:11 puts it: "People will say, 'Surely there is a reward for the righteous; surely there is a God who judges on earth'" (NRSV). When President Bush declared war on terrorism from the pulpit of the National Cathedral after 9/11, he in effect, equated America's enemies with God's enemies. His attorney general, John Ashcroft, has similarly spoken of "the way of the terrorists." Are we so certain that God is on *our* side?

The violence of the enemy language in laments also emerges out of the this-worldly focus of the Hebrew Bible. Because there was no life after death aside from Sheol until later in Second Temple Judaism (second century B.C.E. on, with the rise of apocalyptic literature, such as the book of Daniel), injustices had to be put right here and now in this life. This was a matter of great urgency. Such a worldview can, in the words of Roland Murphy, "serve to correct an exaggerated eschatologism [focus on the end time] which fails to meet squarely the realities of this life, such as issues of social justice, or the sacramental and wholesome nature of all God's creation."[14]

Erhard Gerstenberger also argues that the theme of enemies and evildoers in the laments can help us to name social enemies, and thus relates to crucial social issues of our times. We must, in our impersonal world, be able to ask who is responsible for societal suffering, and identify those who are guilty of destruction and dehumanization in our communities. We must show solidarity with the poor against existing power structures. The enemies in the psalm laments thus can become for us, as they were for ancient Israel, the structural enemies of our own society, supra-individual representatives of the chaos opposing God's good order for the world.[15] Similarly, Erich Zenger insists that a society without justice points to an absent, nonfunctioning god. Enemy language takes God's justice and integrity seriously; it begs God to have the last word. "Ultimately, this is the question of theodicy; where the righteous find no justice, God has forfeited existence."[16]

In a similar way, Gerald Sheppard suggests that "enemies" are part of the "politics of prayer" in the Psalms. Since psalm prayers were spoken out loud in worship, they were intended to be overheard by friends and enemies. They were not simply resources for private and individualized catharsis, but were "shared with an audience to which the enemies belong."[17] Such a prayer becomes "a significant alternative to gossip" because God is listening. The assumption undergirding the use of laments with enemy language is that those who overhear should discern a "fit" between the words of the prayer and specific persons and events. In this way, these laments "become a unique political event that tests the loyalty of friends who must choose to stand either near or afar off."[18] In Psalm 55:12–14, for example, a friend who has become an enemy is present and should be convicted by the rhetoric of the psalm: "It is not enemies who taunt me...but it is you." This formula of accusation is found in prophetic parables, such as the parable of the ewe lamb delivered to David by Nathan the prophet (2 Sam. 12:7; cf. Isa. 3:13–14 and the Song of the Vineyard in Isa. 5:7). A side benefit of public prayer is that the enemy may learn from the prayer and change, as in Psalm 51:13: "I will teach transgressors your ways, that sinners may return to you."

Rather than leave all our human problems to God to resolve in the end time (eschatology), or when we die, the lament-enemy language urges us to work with God now to transform and make new. We cannot dismiss wrongdoing in our life with a glib "Why should I worry? God will give them what they deserve when they die. She'll get hers; he'll get his." Rather than turn our backs on the world, the lament-enemy language pushes us to face the world and its pain now. Although many Christians put this world's justice issues off until the next life, others do not even believe in a final reckoning when they die. In a recent newspaper article, Martin Marty, a church historian from the University of Chicago, is quoted as saying that before 1952 about half of Americans believed in hell. More recent surveys show that only 8 to 13 percent of Americans "thought of hell as in any way a possibility for them." Most, however, still think they are going to heaven when they die.[19] If not in this life or the next, then when will the wicked be called to account? What hope is there for the oppressed? Why bother to be "good" at all?

The psalm laments insist on an embrace of this life and a push to justice. Given what is at stake in the laments, it is no wonder that we hear angry and anguished calls for revenge such as we find in Psalm 137. Given lament urgency, we ought to shun any allegorical interpretation of this psalm that avoids its harsh enemy language. Many of us have been drawn into Psalm 137 by the haunting beauty of the opening words: "By the rivers of Babylon, there we sat down and wept when we remembered Zion"; the captors of the Jews in exile in Babylon taunt them to sing their songs of Zion in an unclean land. Sweet Honey in the Rock, a female African American a capella group, sings about this beautifully. Lee Porter's quilt "By the Waters of Babylon,"[20] shown on the next page, combines Psalm 137:1–4 with the text of Jeremiah's letter to the exiles in Jeremiah 29:5–7. She wants to show the different reactions to the same event. Psalm 137 focuses on the past and present; Jeremiah focuses on the present and future.

We have been repelled by the closing verses of Psalm 137, which are often omitted in responsive readings: "Fair Babylon, you plunderer, a blessing on [the one] who repays you what you have done to us; a blessing on [the one] who seizes your babies and dashes them against the rocks!" In order to avoid this bloodthirsty language, some have read the psalm allegorically, seeing another and "higher" level of meaning beyond the literal one. Read allegorically, the psalm speaks of enemies in our lives that come to us at first as "babies," such as indulgences that are initially small, attractive, and harmless. Just as the infants of the enemy must be killed before they grow up to attack, so too must our "harmless" indulgences be destroyed before

they destroy us. What is most distressing about this allegorical interpretation is that it refuses to acknowledge the very real pain of the Israelites in exile. All the symbol systems of Israelite life had been shattered by the Babylonians: The temple had been leveled; Jerusalem had been burned; the king and the leaders, artisans, merchants, and teachers had been led away to captivity in Babylon. Those left behind to live amidst the devastation of Jerusalem and its environs were starving and homeless (see the book of Lamentations). Yet despite this staggering blow at the hands of Israel's enemy, all that the allegorical interpretation acknowledges in the way of an "enemy" is our personal, little excesses that may grow to make us stumble. What an insult to the grief of the people and the depth of their pain!

Allegorical interpretation of Psalm 137 is a dishonest response, given the reality of the Holocaust and the oppression of whole peoples throughout the world today. Do we dare ask them in their suffering to deny their true feelings of pain and revenge? As Dorothee Soelle argues: "The more people anticipate the elimination of suffering the less strength they have actually to oppose it. Whoever deals with [their] personal suffering only in the way our society has taught [them]—through illusion, minimization, suppression, apathy—will deal with societal suffering in the same way."[21] We in the West erect walls between ourselves and the reality of suffering. We cultivate numbness, and so we are outraged by the intensity of pain in the enemy language of the psalms. The psalm laments do not bid us to share the sufferer's hate, but rather, the sufferer's pain by allowing that pain to be expressed.

Those who would suppress that pain forget the reaction to the attacks of September 11, 2001. Although we did not specifically call for the dashing of the heads of Afghani babies against the rocks, the net result of our bombing of Afghanistan has been the same—dead women and children. How easy it is for us to condemn ancient Israel's cry for revenge and support our own, hiding behind our more impersonal methods of warfare! How many other times in recent history has America called for national retaliation in this way?

A pastor of a very conservative church in Pennsylvania decided to embrace the anger and anguish of the enemy language in Psalm 137 during the Tehran hostage crisis, a time at which many called for the bombing of Iran. He used this psalm as the scripture reading and sermon focus on the Sunday after the storming of the American embassy. He told me that he felt he was taking the biggest risk of his ministry by doing that, but that he could not conduct a worship service pretending his congregation was not angry. He did not believe that worship should force us to leave our real feelings, whatever they are, outside the church doors; that would not be an honest way to come before God. The pastor preached his sermon on Psalm 137, pointing out how many of us felt like the Israelites, wishing for vengeance on the Iranians. He called on his congregation to acknowledge and express their anger before God and then give it up on the altar to God. His hope was that through this communal cleansing, the congregation could redirect its energies to a different solution to the crisis. The vast majority of the congregation felt relief and thanked him for allowing them to wrestle with their feelings before God. They left the service with their anger acknowledged and defused. How powerful a moment that was for them all. How striking that we missed opportunities for similar communal cleansing through our liturgies after 9/11!

This experience and the angry enemy language of laments such as Psalms 58 and 137 raise the issue of the nature of spirituality. If we define spirituality as Brueggemann does, that is, "genuine communion with God," then the psalms remind us that "communion with God cannot be celebrated without attention to the nature of community, both among human persons and with God."[22] Psalm spirituality raises questions about the nature of the community, questions about theodicy. Theodicy is never simply a religious question about the character of God; it is also a social question about life and the way we live it, about the struggle of the oppressed against the unjust, about a "fair deal." The old "consensus about theodicy"[23] in Western society, which legitimated social structures as blessed and approved by God, is in crisis. It is being challenged both by Christian environmental awareness and by black, feminist, and Latino liberation theologies, which suggest different social arrangements in the name of the God of the exodus.

In this light, the psalms cannot be the private possession of those who pray them; they cannot be the stuff of romantic spirituality cut off from the world and the issues of justice. Psalm spirituality is all about the righteous and the wicked and the faithfulness and trustworthiness of God. The enemy language in laments articulates disorientation and the crisis in the ordering of life, not with violent acts but with violent speech, for "a new system of meaning will not come without abrasion, and that is what these psalms offer."[24]

The spirituality of Psalms 58 and 137 is passionate, but the psalmist does not take action and break the teeth of the enemy or crush babies' heads against the rocks. Because Israel leaves the vengeance to God, it can hope for a new Jerusalem. Brueggemann suggests that Psalm 137 might fit into Christian faith in the way it asks about how we endure and maintain identity. "This psalm poses some questions: Can there be a claim that overrides forgiveness for the sake of constancy? Can forgiveness be a mode of coming to terms too easily? Could it be that genuine forgiveness is possible only when there has been a genuine articulation of hatred?"[25]

Brueggemann's questions recall Dietrich Bonhoeffer's discussion of "cheap grace," that is, grace that lays no demand on us for obedience to Christ and moral behavior. This is "grace sold on the market like cheapjack wares,"[26] grace without cost. Christian oversimplification of the sweeping grace of the New Testament tends to excuse our lack of moral outrage and acceptance of the status quo. Cheap grace asks no questions and sets no limits; all we have to do is leave the world and show up in church for an hour or two on Sunday morning, and we are assured that our sins are forgiven. This is as false a reading of New Testament grace as is understanding Torah demands in the Hebrew Bible as excessive. Torah calls for covenant loyalty, for keeping God's commandments, for loving God and neighbor. Brueggemann's question puts both false readings in proper perspective: Can forgiveness be a mode of coming to terms too easily?

The Accusation of God (You)

In this part of the complaint, the psalmist accuses God of negligence or hostility, often by means of a string of harsh rhetorical questions. When enemy language and accusation of God are found within the same psalm, it is clear that the enemies are not the cause of the psalmist's distress; God is. The enemies simply make the situation worse. As Brueggemann argues, psalm spirituality calls the world into question in conversation with God, a conversation that is honest and daring. Far from being unchangeable, "God assumes different roles in these conversations."[27] In hymns of orientation, God guarantees the old order and is praised for that. In thanksgivings of new orientation, God establishes a new justice. But in laments of disorientation, God is in the disorientation, absent or acting unjustly. This can be seen in Psalm 77:7–9, which talks about God in the third person rather than addressing God directly, perhaps indicating how painful the psalmist feels it is to express these questions about God: "Will Adonai reject forever, and never again be kind? Has God's *hesed* disappeared forever? Are God's promises at an end for all time? Has God forgotten to be gracious? Has God in anger shut up the divine womb-love?"

The verb "to forget" (Hebrew, *shakach*) occurs always as a question in the laments (Pss. 42:9; 44:24; 77:9; Lam. 5:20). Psalm 44 contrasts the people's not forgetting the covenant with God's forgetting the people. In lament petitions, the psalmists ask God not to forget the one(s) praying. In the prophetic writings, God's forgetting is sometimes interpreted as God's judgment on the people for their idolatry and social injustice; God purposely ignores them (Hos. 4:6). In other prophetic passages, God's salvation is proclaimed as God's not forgetting (Isa. 49:14–15). In the laments, God's forgetting is usually not associated with God's punishment, but with the worry that the psalmist's problem has actually slipped the divine mind.[28] That worry probably also undergirds the petition in Psalm 44:23, a communal lament: "Rouse yourself! Why do you sleep, Adonai? Awake! Do not reject us forever!"

Psalm 77 mentions God's anger or wrath, but one should not assume that this divine anger is a deliberate response to the psalmist's sin. Often in the Hebrew Bible, God's wrath is not readily understood. In many lament psalms, no motivation for God's anger is given (see, for example, Pss. 6, 74, 88, and 102). Even in Psalm 79, which petitions God to forgive sins and deliver the people from their enemies, God's anger seems excessive—"How long?" (v. 5). Also, in the psalms "God's anger is never associated with beneficial chastisement";[29] suffering is not good for you. God's anger and punishment can be separated (Pss. 6:1; 38:1).

Many Christians are disturbed by such harsh questions as are hurled at God in Psalm 77; some call them blasphemous. Perhaps such Christians react this way because we all tend to want to pretty up our prayers before God, and we want other people to do so as well. We want to hide from God our true feelings of anger and doubt. We don't think that those emotions have any place in our prayers or in our relationships with God. Thus, when we voice our questions, we take on an extra burden of shame and guilt. Our theology tells us that the things we fear—God's forgetfulness, inconsistency, or lack of caring—simply can't be true of God. Must we get our theology straight before we pray? There is a growing push today to allow our prayer to inform our theology: Begin with honest prayer and let it help us talk about God. As Pierre Wolff warns in *May I Hate God?* we tend to approach God "selectively" in prayer and reveal to God only what we think God can handle; whereas, psalm prayer does not limit the relationship with God to "pious moments or sentimental hours."[30] If hate is our only channel of communication to God left open, then we ought to accept it and use it as Job did. God comes in the whirlwind, not despite but because of Job's angry words. The angry psalm laments were certainly my only connection to God while I was dealing with my brother's death; without them, I would not be teaching in a seminary today.

The psalmists risk encounter in order to keep up relationship with God. There is no false reticence in Israelite piety. The psalmists dare to speak to God directly and honestly. They think out loud in God's hearing. This thinking out loud may even involve angry enemy language and accusations toward God. This is intense prayer. God is not "boxed in" by this kind of prayer. If our relationship with God is real, "then God is open and vulnerable to being hurt, moved, and even changed by what [God's] children say and do."[31] This is deep and real relationship that dignifies both parties in the relationship.

Robert McAfee Brown suggests that denouncing God in prayer is perhaps "a sign of how much we care, that we dare to express our outrage even toward the One who created us."[32] To be angry with God is not impious, but an acknowledgment that God matters to us. The supreme insult would be to behave as if God did not exist by refusing any response. Though seemingly a strange affirmation of faith, the angry response, Brown insists, is part of being truly human. This is expressed by one of Elie Wiesel's characters in his semiautobiographical novel of the Holocaust, *Night*, as he responds to the question "Why do you pray?" "A strange question. Why did I live? Why did I breathe?"[33] Wiesel sees us raising ourselves toward God by the questions we ask God. In a similar way, Wolff argues that our angry prayer moves us toward greater intimacy with God. Harold Kushner evaluates anger toward God quite differently in *When Bad Things Happen to Good People*. He acknowledges that anger in situations of disorientation seems to be instinctive, but that the important question is what do we do with our anger. Sometimes we turn our anger toward the person responsible—the one who fired us from our job, the spouse who walked out, the doctor who misdiagnosed an illness. Sometimes we find someone to blame, whether or not the person is guilty. Sometimes the anger is turned inward as depression, and sometimes we are angry at God.

Kushner agrees that being angry at God won't hurt God; and if it makes us feel better, "we are free to do it." But our goal should be "to be angry at the situation, rather than at ourselves, or at those who might have prevented it, ...or at God who let it happen."[34] Self-directed anger makes us depressed, anger at others scares them away from helping us, and anger at God "erects a barrier" between us and the resources of religion.

In Kushner's view, there seems to be little room for the angry psalm laments, even though for some people, the laments are the only way left to God. This is because in reconstructing his theology in the aftermath of his son's death from a rare disease, Kushner relied heavily on the book of Job and its discussion of suffering. Kushner argues that in Job three premises are laid out, which most of us would like to believe and which hold together when all goes well for us:

1. God is all-powerful (omnipotent) and causes everything that happens.
2. God is good, just, fair, and gives people what they deserve.
3. Job (substitute your own name here) is good.[35]

When we fall into the pit of disorientation, one of these premises has to go in order for us to hold on to the other two. Job's friends wanted to throw out number 3; Job got what he deserved, but he just didn't want to admit it. The friends blamed the victim. Job wanted to throw out number 2; he protests his own innocence in chapter 31 and acknowledges God's power in chapter 42—what a blustering God assails him from the whirlwind in chapters 38—41! Kushner wants to throw out premise number 1; our suffering is not really God's fault. Kushner claims that this is what the author of the book of Job believes, based almost exclusively on one passage, 40:9–14: If you think it's so easy running the world, Job, you try it. In other words, God is still trying to overcome pockets of chaos in the world and is not all-powerful. In this light, Kushner's son's genetic defect was a random remnant of the chaos God has not yet overcome.

This theology brings relief to Kushner because if God does not do bad things to us, God can still be on our side when they happen and can help us. This view frees God from our unrealistic expectations and allows us to be angry at what happened rather than at God, our enemies, or ourselves. We can feel God's own anger and compassion in the situation. This is close to the stance that William Sloane Coffin adopted when his twenty-four-year-old son, Alex, died. His car slid off a dark road without guardrails into Boston Harbor. Angry over those who would claim that this was God's will, Coffin asserted in a sermon two weeks after his son's death that no one knows enough to say that: "My own consolation lies in knowing that it was not the will of God that Alex die; that when the waves closed over the sinking car, God's heart was the first of all our hearts to break."[36] One cannot shake one's fist at this suffering God who is not omnipotent; one cannot pray the angry psalm laments. What happens to Jesus' last words on the cross in this theological view: "My God, my God, why have you forsaken me?" Such a prayer cannot really be prayed.

Both Kushner's and Coffin's responses can be located within Richard Vieth's categories of twelve theological responses to the problem of evil in the world.[37] If omnipotence and goodness define God, then the presence of evil in the world forces us to choose between arguing that a good God does not exist or that evil is not real, since good and evil have meaning only as they stand opposite each other. If we reject both conclusions, then we may wish to attack the three premises listed above from which the conclusions are drawn, either rejecting or revising one of the premises to dissolve the contradiction.

Four positions reject or redefine the first premise of God's omnipotence: that the world is dualistic and evil forces vie with good ones; that Satan (leader of a domain of evil) exists; that natural order explains many events (thus, evil is a by-product of natural forces in an ordered universe; Kushner's view fits here); and that free choice—which includes choices made out of error, sin, and fallenness—is responsible for some events (Coffin's view probably fits here: his son "blew it" by driving too fast, although he may also argue from the perspective of natural order with Kushner).

Four positions reject or redefine the second premise of God's goodness: despotism (God is indifferent or malicious), judgment (God punishes us for our sinful ways), testing (God tries our faith), personal growth (suffering leads to maturity, and, therefore, God wills it or allows it). Two positions explain suffering by denying or redefining evil: illusion (evil is not truly evil)and partial perspective (evil is real, but contributes to a larger, harmonious whole that we cannot see). Vieth lists as "additional positions" atheism (the reality of evil makes belief in God impossible) and mystery (we cannot solve the problem).

Jürgen Moltmann's notion of the crucified God[38] can be seen as a fifth modification of premise number 1, God's omnipotence. Drawing on Anson

Laytner's investigation of the theology of protest in Jewish tradition,[39] as well as on his work with survivors of child abuse, David Blumenthal modifies premise number 2, God's goodness. He argues that "in a post-holocaust, abuse-sensitive world, we must: (1) acknowledge the awful truth of God's abusing behavior; (2) adopt a theology of protest and sustained suspicion;…(5) resist all evil mightily…(6) open ourselves to the good side of God…and (7) we must turn to address God, face to Face, presence to Presence."[40]

What do you think about accusations of God in the laments? Where would you place your own response to suffering and evil on Vieth's twelve-point chart? Where would you place the angry laments as a response to suffering and evil?

Petition

Petition is actually implied in the entire act of lamenting. The petition is a call or plea to God to intervene, to change the situation of distress and save the sufferer. The petition often uses strong anthropomorphic (using human characteristics) language, such as "Arise! Awake! Give ear! Answer me!" Implicit in these petitions are accusations of God: God is not doing what God is expected to do, and the petition, in effect, reminds God of this expectation. The petition is thus a call to both God's justice and mercy; these divine qualities are interwoven.

The intense distress of prolonged duration in laments calls into question individual and communal beliefs, or traditions, about God. The petitions name these beliefs about God and reflect how God has contravened them by permitting the distress.[41] In many communal laments, such as Psalms 44, 60, 80, and 89, God has not lived up to the traditional expectation that God is a God of holy war and conquest who goes out with Israel's armies for victory and upholds the Davidic king. In each of these psalms, a foreign nation has victimized God's people. Psalms 74 and 79 lament the destruction of God's holy place, the temple. Here, the Zion tradition (compare with Psalms 46 and 48) is called into question because God has not defended the temple in which God is thought to be especially present with the people.

Thus, the concluding petition of Psalm 44 pleads: "Rise up, help us! Deliver us for the sake of your *hesed!*" God is called upon to do what the tradition says God has done in the past (that is, deliver the people from their enemies in covenant loyalty), but that God is not doing now. In the same way Psalm 60 calls on God: "O grant us help against the enemy, for human help is worthless. With God we shall do valiantly; it is God who will trample our foes" (vv. 11–12). Psalm 74 holds up the assaulted Zion tradition in this plea: "Direct your steps to the perpetual ruins; the enemy has destroyed everything in the sanctuary" (v. 3). In the individual laments, the complaints and petitions are more general pointers to the traditions being called into question by the distress. Usually the tradition most applicable is that God hears when called on in prayer.[42] Prolonged distress calls this tradition into question and prompts anguished declarations such as that in Psalm 22:2: "O my God, I cry daily, but you do not answer; and at night, but I find no rest." This state of affairs prompts petitions such as that in Psalm 55:1: "Give ear, O God, to my prayer; do not hide yourself from my entreaty."

If the psalmist confesses sin, as in the penitential laments, the distress is considered to be just punishment from God, so the psalmist petitions God as in Psalm 51:2: "Wash me thoroughly from my iniquity, and cleanse me from my sin" (NRSV). In Psalm 38:4 the psalmist confesses that "my iniquities have gone over my head" (NRSV), and then petitions in verses 21–22: "Do not forsake me, Adonai! … make haste to help me, O Adonai, my salvation!" (modified NRSV). In these penitential laments, God is the just judge who hears confession of sin so that one can be forgiven. Very frequent in laments is the description of enemies who are making the psalmist miserable and of continuous weeping and groaning because of the enemy actions. In these cases, God is called on as deliverer to intervene and save, as in Psalm 80:2, "Stir up your might and come to our help!" or in Psalm 22:21, "Save me from the mouth of the lion" (RSV). God is also called on to punish the enemies, as in Psalm 35:1, 4, "O Adonai, strive against those who strive with me, fight against those who fight against me…Let those who seek my life be put to shame and disappointed."

Motivations

Laments often give God reasons to act to grant the petition, in addition to the very gut-wrenching descriptions of the distress given in the complaint. There are basically three kinds of motivation expressed by the psalmist to prompt God's action: confession of sin, protestation of innocence, or the reminder of the public relations value of the psalmist.

Confession of Sin

Most Christians are familiar and comfortable with the plea for forgiveness. Unison prayers of confession are standard in most Sunday liturgies, and they are lengthy, wordy confessions at that.

In the penitential laments, the psalmist takes the blame for her or his suffering and says, in effect, "I deserve it, forgive and heal me, God," as in Psalm 51:3–4; God is in the right. Lee Porter has created a powerful expression of the psalmist's plea for cleansing in Psalm 51:7 in her quilt entitled "Cleanse Me with Hyssop" (below).[43] In penitential Psalm 143:8, 10, the confession motivation is contained within a petition for instruction: "Teach me the way I should go…Teach me to do your will" (NRSV). Here the implication is that the psalmist hasn't been following God's way and

doing God's will. The psalmist acknowledges this and enters a guilty plea in verse 2: "Do not enter into judgment with your servant; for no one living is righteous before you"(NRSV). If you evaluated me, I'd be guilty, God, so teach me how to do things right.

In the spiritual disorientation of these penitential laments, the psalmist's guilt is part of the suffering, as in Psalm 32:3: "When I kept quiet, my body wasted away." In verse 5, the psalmist confesses, and God forgives; a new relationship is possible. Verse 1 makes that point up front: "Happy is the one whose transgression is forgiven, whose sin is covered over." God is not blamed for the distress, but rather acknowledged for merciful forgiveness. Enemies are often cited, and God is petitioned to punish them. But the enemies are not the cause of the distress; they simply aggravate it, as in Psalm 143:3, 9, 12.

The basis for the confession and plea to forgive in the penitential psalms is God's righteousness and faithfulness, not the psalmist's: "Adonai, hear my prayer; give ear to my supplications! In your faithfulness answer me, in your righteousness!" (Ps. 143:1). In Psalm 130, we have "the miserable cry of a nobody from nowhere. The cry penetrates the veil of heaven! It is heard and received."[44] The good news of the Bible is encapsulated here in that God's ear is especially attuned to cries from the depths. Dr. James D. Siddons has composed powerful music for Psalm 130, known in the Latin liturgy as "De Profundis." His "Psalm 130: Aus tiefer Not" is an anthem for full choir and organ based on the Reformation chorale "Out of the Depths." The text is Catherine Winkworth's translation of Martin Luther's versification of Psalm 130.[45]

The early church and the reformers preferred these penitential laments with their confession of sin to the more numerous angry laments, which do not offer any confession, and, in fact, protest innocence. Because the church does not embrace these other laments, "one can say that in a certain sense the confession of sin has become the Christianized form of the lament."[46] It seems that sin has eclipsed suffering in Christian worship and theology. In this view, Jesus' work of salvation involved forgiving sins and eternal life, not relieving human suffering.

Thus, resistance to laments is undergirded by the belief that we should bear suffering patiently and not complain to God about it, that this world's suffering is insignificant compared to the guilt of sin. What is overlooked in this view is the compassion of Jesus toward the suffering, his hearing of their laments, and his entering into human suffering through his last words of lament on the cross from Psalm 22. In the African American tradition, Jesus acts as intercessor for our laments, reminding God to "remember how I felt on the cross."

Protestation of Innocence

Rather than confess sin and admit that suffering is deserved, psalmists more often will protest their innocence, making it clear that their suffering is not justified and that they are therefore entitled to help. In Psalm 17:3, 5 the psalmist asserts: "You have tested my heart, you have visited me at night, you have refined me, you will not find wickedness in me; my mouth does not transgress…My feet have held fast to your paths, my feet have not slipped"; similar is Psalm 26.

Many take offense at the self-righteousness that seems to be present in such a declaration. This reaction comes in part from our stoic acceptance of suffering without complaint because of our sinful nature (see above) and in part from our belief in act/ consequence: You get what you deserve. We feel constrained to admit all our human sin before we can cry out to God. But the protestation of innocence in the laments tells us that this confession is not always necessary. It is sometimes all right for us to express our pain in words if we do not honestly feel that our suffering is deserved. The lament protestation of innocence gives us a legitimate avenue of approach to God, and without it, we are left like Job, alone and comfortless on the dung heap, feeling wronged by enemies or abandoned by God. Without the lament protestation, we are left alone and isolated from God at a time when we need God most in our lives.[47] This can be extremely dangerous to our spiritual health.

The wider context of these protestations must also be taken into account. The book of Genesis is filled with stories about the matriarchs and patriarchs who doubt God's promise and take matters into their own hands time and time again. Jacob, for example, is a scoundrel and a cheat. Moses in Deuteronomy reminds Israel that Adonai chose them, not because they were "more in number than any other people" (7:7) or because they were more righteous than anyone else (9:5), but simply because of God's gracious love. The prophets relentlessly point out the people's breaking of the covenant. The penitential laments declare, "No one living is righteous before you" (Ps. 143:2) and "If you, O Adonai, kept account of iniquities, Adonai, who could stand?" (Ps. 130:3).

Within this wider context of the Hebrew Bible, the anguished protestation of innocence is the emotional language of people in the pit of disorientation. It is language at the boundaries of life. As Brueggemann puts it, "The speaker has no time for theological niceties."[48] Perhaps, the psalmist says, "Given everyone else, I'm not so bad that I should suffer like this." The psalmist wants God to act quickly to overcome the distress; claiming innocence undergirds the urgency of the emergency call.

Public Relations Value of the Psalmist

Frequent in the laments is a confession of trust (see chap. 6) that maintains that God answers when called upon, as in Psalm 17:6: "I call upon you, for you will answer me, O God." Also, in the thanksgiving psalms (see chap. 7), the psalmist tells the story of how God actually answered, as in Psalm 30:2–3: "O Adonai, my God, I cried to you for help, and you healed me. O Adonai, you have brought me up from Sheol." Most psalms argue that if God allows the psalmist to die and go down to Sheol, then calling on God and God's answering are not possible, and neither is praising God for deliverance, as the psalmist does in Psalm 30:1: "I will extol you, Adonai, for you have lifted me up." Without deliverance God will lose the psalmist's praise; the loss is God's.

Thus, Psalm 6:5 reminds God: "In death there is no remembrance of you; in Sheol who can praise you?" In Psalm 88, in which the psalmist feels very much as good as dead, there are several reminders like this: "Do you work wonders for the dead? Do the shades rise up to praise you?" (v. 10; cf. vv. 11–12). If, as we argued in chapter 3, human beings are always moving toward praise, then God robs them of their human purpose by not saving them from the distress carrying them to Sheol. "The speaker is valued by God as one who praises."[49]

Closely related to the motivation of the psalmist's value as one who praises God is the motivation concerning God's own reputation and prestige. As Psalm 9:16 declares: "Adonai has made the divine self known; Adonai has executed judgment." Similarly, in Psalm 10:13, the psalmist asks: "Why do the wicked despise God, and say in their heart 'You will not call to account'?" Implicit here is the argument that if God allows the wicked to prosper and overcome the poor, then God loses power and respect. The enemies in Psalm 28:5 "do not pay attention to the works of Adonai," the implication being that the psalmist does and that such regard is needed for God's power. The God who keeps order punishes the wicked in the sight of all, as the psalmist in Psalm 31:19 argues: "O how abundant is your goodness that you have laid up for those who fear you, and accomplished for those who take refuge in you, in the sight of everyone!" (NRSV)

A corollary of this concern for God's reputation is the memory of God's salvation in the past, as in Psalm 44:1: "O God, we have heard with our ears, our forebears have told us, what deeds you performed in their days, in the days of old." The psalmist in Psalm 25:11 pleads: "On account of your name, Adonai, pardon my guilt, for it is great." Similar is Psalm 79:9, 10: "Help us, O God of our salvation, for the glory of your name…Why should the nations say, 'Where is their God?'" God's reputation is on the line if those who call on God are not answered. The present distress threatens God's reputation based on past deliverance and present expectation.

The value of the psalmist's praise and the concern for God's reputation seem to some to be prideful human attempts to bribe God to act. Brueggemann acknowledges that "at times the motivation comes peculiarly close to bargaining, bribing, or intimidating. But this also needs to be taken as a kind of parity assumed in the relationship."[50] This parity can be empowering. It maintains implicitly that the psalmist matters to God.

We have now reached the "dotted line" within the lament structure outline. Something happens here. The tone and the language on the other side of the dotted line change from complaint to praise. Chapter 6 will examine that change and discuss the process of the lament. Several lament psalms in their entirety will be analyzed to illustrate the process.

CHAPTER SIX

Life in the Meanwhile

The Process of Lament

The lament begins with address, moves into complaint, voices a petition, and offers motivations for God to grant the petition. At this point, one encounters the "dotted line" of the lament structure. Crossing over to the fifth point (see the outline repeated below), something happens. The mood moves from desperate urgency to trusting joy. The psalmist speaks in a surprising new way about God and the psalmist's relationship to God. Claus Westermann was one of the first to notice this move from plea to praise. Walter Brueggemann declares this move "one of the most startling in all of Old Testament literature."[1] Look at the lament structure outline again to see this shift.

1. Address
2. Complaint proper
   a. The psalmist's suffering (I/we)
   b. The enemies (they)
   c. God accused of not caring/doing (you)
3. Petition
4. Motivations

    a. Confession of sin
    b. Protestation of innocence
    c. Public relations value of psalmist

  5. Confession of trust
    a. Usually introduced by "but"
    b. Faith that knows what it is talking about
  6. Vow of praise

How are these two parts of the lament structure related—that is, 1, 2, 3, and 4 above to 5 and 6 below? How does the psalmist move from one emotion to the other? What is responsible for this move? What does each side of the dotted line tell us about faith?

Confession of Trust

The confession part of the lament psalm can be expanded to become a whole psalm of trust. Psalms 18, 23 ("Adonai is my shepherd"), 27, and 103 are examples. In the lament psalm, the confession of trust is an expression of confidence in God despite or in the midst of the situation of suffering. One participant in a Bible study I led likened the faith in the confession of trust to "the second wind of the runner."

The confession of trust is often introduced by "but," as in Psalm 55:16–18. This psalm opens with a petition, "Give ear to my prayer, O God" (RSV) and then moves into a description of the psalmist's suffering and of the enemies who taunt the psalmist. In verse 16, a shift in attitude is expressed: "As for me ["but"] I call to God, and Adonai will save me. Evening and morning and at noon I complain and murmur, and God will hear my voice." In the midst of the suffering and the enemies, the psalmist asserts the whole basis of offering up the lament in the first place: God hears, cares, and acts. This is faith that knows what it is talking about. It is rather easy to profess trust in God when all is well. It is much more difficult and very painful to do so when the going gets tough and one finds oneself in the pit of disorientation. It takes a strong faith in God to keep talking to God, to keep up the dialogue, when orientation is shattered and we are in despair. That is why the confession of trust is so powerful in the lament.

Even Psalm 23, which is totally given over to a confession of trust, contains echoes of the pit experience. Because it is "an American secular icon"[2] that has been since the Civil War associated with death and funerals, we miss the echoes that are tied to the rigors of daily living. African American artist Tim Ladwig recognizes this in his sketches of a contemporary setting for Psalm 23 centered on an urban family secure in their love amidst the dangers of the city streets.[3] Ladwig's contemporary rendering is supported by tension within the psalm itself; all is not tranquility. The psalm begins with "Adonai is my shepherd." "Shepherd" is often used as a title for the king in Israel, as in Jeremiah 23:1–4 and Ezekiel 34:11–16, where the king fails to carry out his shepherd function to provide for and protect the people, forcing God to step in as shepherd. (See also Gen. 49:24; Jer. 31:10; Mic. 7:14, and Pss. 28:9; 74:1; 79:13; 80:1; 95:7; 100:3 for God as the good shepherd, and in Jn. 10:11, Jesus says, "I am the good shepherd"; Jesus laid down his life for his sheep.)

With God as shepherd, the psalmist can declare: "I lack nothing." The verb for "lack" in verse 1 is the same verb used in Deuteronomy 2:7 in Moses' account of the wilderness wanderings. Verse 2, "he leads me beside still waters," and verse 3, "he leads me in right paths," use the same verb— "lead," "guide"—as Exodus 15:13, the Song of Moses. Isaiah 40:11 speaks of God as the shepherd who "leads" the people home from exile. "Still" or "quiet" waters, or "waters of rest" are cited in Numbers 10:33. Psalm 23 seems to be rooted in agitated memories of the exodus and the wilderness wanderings. The shepherd of Psalm 23 must provide food, drink, and protection to the sheep, that is, must keep them alive, just as God the host/ hostess must do in verses 5–6. It is God's character to provide, so much so that God's goodness and *hesed* will not just "follow" the psalmist but "pursue" *(radaf)* her or him in the presence of the enemies who usually do the pursuing (as in Pss. 7:5; 71:11; 109:16). Structurally, the personal name for God, Adonai, occurs in verses 1 and 6 as an envelope of God's all-surrounding presence.[4] It is this all-encompassing presence, fortified by verse 4: "for you are with me," a shift from third person to direct address, that the psalmist in the confession of trust in the lament longs for and anticipates.

The Reverend Dr. Jan Fuller Carruthers has written a lament entitled "trying to write a sermon in pain," which expresses the anguish of her long, agonizing recovery from brain surgery. A large part of her lament is given over to a confession of trust.

trying to write a sermon in pain
Jan Fuller Carruthers

I sit at my desk weeping,
the brokenness is only a sermon,
a text and title
on a blank page.
Yet my shame, unbidden, bids me
consider how wasted I have been
how lost my days, how silent my voice
how inarticulate my soul.

Is life wasted in illness?
Is nothing to be known from sorrow?
Is the body's brokenness to silence all of me?
I know you have a plan, and that it is
not this.
I know, O Spirit of Life, that You will
make me sometime whole.
I believe that out of this, too, will come
blessing, love, life.
I can only now believe it;
it is to me only unseen.
What is clear is only that I can see
neither end nor beginning exactly, only the
walls of the present moment. And if
it ought to be enough, my heart longs
to know more, to prophesy of more.
But this is all.
Will you make good, O Good One?
Will you recreate, O Creator?
Will you fill me, O Fullness of Grace?
Comfort me, O Comforter?
I believe. Help Thou my unbelief.
Amen.[5]

Vow of Praise

The vow of praise is not always found in the lament, but it follows logically from the preceding confession of trust. The psalmist vows in advance to thank God and declare to the community God's great act of deliverance on the psalmist's behalf, even though the deliverance has not yet occurred. Returning to Psalm 22, with which this study of the lament structure began, we hear the psalmist vow in verse 22: "I will tell of your name to my brothers and sisters; in the midst of the congregation I will praise you" (NRSV).

Some would call this the bargaining of a "foxhole religion"; we turn to God only when we are in trouble in order to strike a deal. "Listen God," we say, "you scratch my back, and I'll scratch yours. Get me out of this mess, and I'll make sure that everyone knows what you have done for me. I'll spread the word." How many times have we found ourselves in that kind of situation? Just let me close this deal at work, or let him recover from this illness, or let my wife come back to me, and I promise I'll go to church regularly and pray every day. We all try to strike these kinds of bargains in our lives of faith, don't we? When we do this, we are, in a sense, betting on God to come through for us. That God will come through for us is the belief that undergirds the whole of the lament and, indeed, all of our prayer.

If we believe that God is omniscient (all-knowing), then God knows what we will pray before we pray it. God knows we are betting on God to come through. Nevertheless, we have a human need to make sure that God gets the details right. Details are important. They help us to come to terms with a situation. That is why those who have just come through an operation are eager to give anyone who will listen (and even those of us who may not want to) a detailed description of that operation: how long it took, what they took out and where, the length of the incision, the time spent in recovery, and so on. We need to hear the details of someone else's pit experience so that we can enter into the experience of the other person as sympathetically, genuinely, and dynamically as possible.

In the same way, God needs to know the details of our prayers so that God can act as sympathetically and as effectively as possible on our behalf. The confession of trust and the vow of praise in anticipation of the deliverance let God know what is at stake for God. In one way, the confession and vow function somewhat like the motivations (which, as we have seen, include confession of sin, protestation of innocence, and public relations value of the psalmist). But they are also declarations of the fact that the psalmist and God matter to each other; this is a statement of faith. What has happened to turn the psalmist's lament into trust and praise in anticipation of the deliverance that has not yet occurred?

Several explanations have been offered by scholars over the years, but we simply cannot know for certain. Perhaps some action took place that is not reported, for example, in Psalm 55 between verses 15 and 16, or between verses 21 and 22 of Psalm 22. Perhaps someone with authority, such as a priest, prophet, or elder at the sanctuary, heard the psalmist's complaint and in God's name declared through a salvation oracle that God had heard; go home and be confident. Perhaps God speaks through a priest after the lament's complaint and petition with words such as those in Psalm 12:5: "Because the poor and needy groan, I will now arise, says Adonai."

Perhaps this certainty of a hearing is more of an inward conviction on the psalmist's part that arises after the complaint has been voiced. The inner catharsis experienced by the psalmist makes the psalmist more receptive to the positive words in the fifth part of the outline, across the dotted line. Whatever happens to signal the change from complaint to praise, the movement within the lament structure expresses the normative belief in Israel that its God is "powerful and accessible" and is characteristically known to intervene to transform situations of distress. Israel's God is faithful to the divine promises; "saving reversal and not tragic reversal is the pattern" of Israel's experience.[6] Thus, a lament is an act of faithfulness.

Brueggemann sees Israel's whole history as a history of trouble and relief, lament and deliverance. This sequence is articulated in the paradigmatic exodus event (slavery to freedom); in the wilderness wanderings (hunger and thirst to manna and water); in the cyclical view of apostasy, oppression, repentance, and deliverance in the book of Judges; in the story of the rise of King David to save Israel from the oppression of the Philistines; and in the public crises of the Assyrian threat in the seventh century B.C.E. and the Babylonian destruction and exile in the sixth century. It is this form of "cry and rescue" "which yields the boldness and conviction which results in gospel, that is, in good news."[7] In the same way, Jesus' actions (feeding, healing, forgiving, raising) are saving responses to situations of distress. The lament structure of cry/response was experienced by the early church as crucifixion/resurrection.

In the same way, Westermann sees the lament as witnessing to God's saving acts and deliverance. The lament is directed to the one who can deliver, and the confession of trust already anticipates that deliverance. The goal of the lament transition is praise of God, as seen in the vow of praise. In the Hebrew Bible, lament and praise are juxtaposed; "it is an illusion to suppose or to postulate that there could be a relationship with God in which there was only praise and never lamentation."[8] Something is therefore wrong if praise of God finds a place in Christian worship while lament does not.

The most important thing about lament is that the distress, whatever it is, is taken before God. God is believed to be the judge and redeemer, the guarantor of shalom (wholeness), the sovereign power over all distress. This belief is the ground for all laments. This means that our anger and doubts need not create a dead end for us in our relationships with God. We need not run around in circles of guilt for our honest feelings.

The basis for praying the lament is that God hears, that God is not defensive even when we lash out in anger. As Psalm 23 affirms, "Even though I walk through the valley of the shadow of death...thou art with me" (RSV). God is with us no matter what we have to say, no matter how difficult the journey. The Reverend Elaine Emeth, recently diagnosed with multiple sclerosis, recognizes this. She writes in this Christmas meditation:

> While I sputter angrily at God in disbelief that this is happening to me, grief at the changes and losses, and frustration with limitations, wishing I could scream—but I'm not there yet, it's churning inside me—I simultaneously rejoice in KNOWING that God wants to know how I feel, is big enough and cares enough to hear it, and

that our relationship is strong enough to bear it...I am humbly thankful to be able to trust our powerful, awesome God with my anger, grief, and frustration, knowing that the commitment is there—on God's side and mine—to work through it. Like an ant standing up to an elephant, trusting the elephant to love it and not step on it.[9]

The laments are thus really expressions of praise and confidence in God when God is felt to be absent. This is the paradox of the lament and of the relationship with God. The very structure of the lament supports this. There is usually a consistent flow from the opening pouring out of troubles to God to a positive statement, from despair to praise. A lament is prayed precisely because there is faith in God's readiness and power to act on behalf of those who appeal to God. A lament, even when it does not move into trust and praise (as in Psalm 88) marks the human struggle never to give up on God, to enter into an ever-deepening relationship with God. A lament, as much as and more than praise, is insistent upon relationship with God as crucial for our lives.

This insistence may give rise to expressions of harshness against enemies and God, but this harshness is really an expression of what Pierre Wolff terms the psalmist's "desire for reconciliation."[10] Do we love God enough to tell all? Wolff argues that perhaps Israel's laments teach us today that we do not love God enough or believe enough in God's love for us.[11] Hatred is present perhaps "as long as people are mute; but as soon as they decide to express the anger that is in their heart...something is already changing and maybe even already changed."[12] Love is already at work transforming us in the honesty of our speech. Wolff's argument calls to mind the main character in Herman Melville's novel *Billy Budd*. Having just killed a man, Billy says, "I woudna hit him if I coulda spoke." Our ministering to one another has less to do with running churches and serving on committees than it does with enabling communion with God.[13]

In the same way, Nelle Morton speaks of "hearing to speech," which belongs to women's experience, that is, hearing oneself to expression, or women hearing other women to speech. This kind of hearing is "a complete reversal of the going logic," a kind of "depth hearing that takes place before the speaking—a hearing that is far more than acute listening," a hearing that evokes new speech from the one heard. Morton contends that Pentecost was about this reversal: hearing followed by speaking. This kind of hearing is theological and revolutionary and has been "long programmed out of our culture and our religious tradition"; "hearing of this sort is equivalent to empowerment." We empower by hearing to speech.[14]

This kind of hearing that empowers speaking is revolutionary theologically because it counters "those theologians who claim that God is sometimes silent, hidden, or withdrawn *(deus absconditus),* and that we must wait patiently until 'He' deigns to speak again." More empowering and realistic than this kind of silent despair would be our seeing "God as the hearing one—hearing us to our own responsible word."[15] This kind of hearing might challenge and negate the words of the theologians who have God all figured out. In this sense, God treats us as equals, hearing the speech out of us, in the lament.

Korean women are beginning to hear one another into speech in order to cut through the numbness of their self-hate and passive obedience to their fathers, husbands, and sons. Their feeling of oppression is called *han,* being "stuck" inside with no outlet for their unexpressed anger and resentment of their social powerlessness. *Han* forms a "lump" in their spirits and bodies; Korean women feel helpless and abandoned in face of overwhelming odds. Some women accept their *han* passively; Asian culture supports this acceptance, because the culture is overlaid with Buddhism, Hinduism, and Confucianism. Christian missionaries to Korea encouraged women to suffer peacefully. Some women fight *han* and engage in *han-pu-ri,* the untanglement of *han,* both in the gentle way of songs, dances, and rituals, and in militant ways involving organized political movements.[16]

Ulrike Bail suggests that Psalm 55 can help women who have been raped to name and therefore deal with the violence that has been done to them. Without naming the violence, raped women remain isolated; "no one hears my cries"[17] is the experience of many raped women. This situation suggests to me the heavy burden of silence that the raped women of Bosnia carry as victims of ethnic cleansing in the former Yugoslavia. Women in the same family who have been raped do not talk about their trauma even with one another because if the men of their family or village find out, they will be killed or cast out of town. Bail notes the "topography of violence" in Psalm 55; violence dominates the walls and central square of the city (vv. 9b, 10, 11). The city is the place and object of violence, which contradicts its true function as a place of protection. A correspondence exists between the city, a feminine noun, and a woman's body; military defeat of the city corresponds to rape of a woman's body. The "I" of verses 2–5 is also a place and object of violence, closed in with no way of escape. The psalmist images a dove (vv. 6–8) as a substitute to do what he or she can't—escape—into the desert, which serves as counterspace to her inhabited space of violence; this is a reversal of the usual associations of the wilderness with death. By the end of the psalm, the "I" is on its way to rediscovering its identity in relation to God, who is on the side of victims of violence (vv. 18–19, 22–23).

"The ability to locate oneself in language, despite absolute powerlessness, can have a liberating effect" because it ends the silence.[18]

We can learn how to hear the speech out of one another by giving permission to vent thoughts of lament and by allowing the entire process of lament to unfold. Dorothee Soelle argues that "the first step towards overcoming suffering is, then, to find language that leads out of the uncomprehended suffering that makes one mute, a language of lament, of crying, of pain, a language that at least says what the situation is." This language is missing in our liturgies today. Modern-day apathy has increased our muteness; isolation and fear have diminished our communication with one another. Communication by lament brings solidarity in which change and liberation can occur. "To become speechless, to be totally without any relationship, that is death."[19]

Black slave women in America recognized this. Christianity of the plantation bound slaves to their condition by upholding the virtues of patience, long-suffering, faith, and hope. Contemporary black womanist scholars such as M. Shawn Copeland[20] are reevaluating those virtues in light of black women's experiences in order to fashion a theology of black suffering that deals with the maldistribution, enormity, and transgenerational character of black women's suffering. Jacquelyn Grant, for example, examines the idea of "servanthood" in Christian tradition. Since black women have been the "servants of the servants"[21] in this country, their servanthood has been exploitative servitude. Grant urges Christians to reconsider the use of servant language, which can "camouflage" oppressive reality. She suggests discipleship as more empowering.

Copeland argues that a theology of black women's suffering must remember/retell, be redemptive, and be resistant. She notes the importance of language as a form of resistance for black women. Black women's slave narratives show their *sass*—their wit, courage, self-defense, speaking of truth, moral challenges—that defined themselves and dismantled the images that had been used to demean them. I see this sass as very close to the *hutzpah* of the psalm laments. Sass stands in continuity with a strand of black literature concerned with theodicy. In Alice Walker's *The Color Purple,* for example, Celie shocks her friend Shug with her view of God: "Let 'im hear me, I say. If [God] ever listened to poor colored women, the world would be a different place, I can tell you."[22] Similarly, W. E. B. DuBois puts God on trial because of black suffering: "Keep not Thou Silent, O God!…Surely you, too, art not white, O Lord, a pale bloodless, heartless thing!"[23]

The laments keep us alive and in relationship with God and one another. They teach us how to go to the depths with the sufferer. We give comfort to the one suffering by respecting the person's right to lament, instead of censuring a lament as blasphemous or unchristian. By allowing someone to express negative feelings instead of making the person feel ashamed to express them, we hear that person into speech; we empower her or him. We help to keep open the disoriented one's relationship with God through the only avenue of communication open to the person at the moment.

Some pastors have said in no uncertain terms that they do not want to open such an avenue, that the lament process is not the kind of example they want to set for their congregations. Others have shared with me their own double bind on the lament issue. Personally, many pastors yearn for the permission to express their honest feelings in front of their congregations; they are human too. Yet how difficult it is for them to embrace lament language knowing that some in their congregation would see this as weakness, as an inability to fulfill their pastoral role as example setter and moral model.

Many congregations put their ministers on a pedestal, and neither the pastor nor the congregation wants the pastor to come down. What a risk a pastor takes to be honest, to share personal feelings with those in the church. A pastor becomes very vulnerable in this way. Is there room in your view of the pastor's role for her or him to embrace the lament process? Should a pastor give permission for us to lament? Consider this question in light of the fact that Jesus listened to people's complaints and healed many without censuring them. It is cruel and dishonest to deny someone's real feelings and suppress negative thoughts. Doing so suggests that Jesus' death on the cross eliminated all human suffering and injustice, which it did not. We await the full realization of God's realm for that, and in this waiting we are not different from the psalmists. A poem by Allan Reed speaks to this tension between the crucifixion and the reality of suffering in the world on one hand and the resurrection and the promise of comfort on the other, and the need for lament to connect the two.

From Out of the Depths

I offered God my joy…
   Lying heart—whose pain and regret
   Out-shouted my song of joy.
I offered God my devotion…
   Hypocrite—to create a prayer
   Devoid of truth!
I offered God my praise…
   Foolish soul—whose wrath and hatred
   spoke louder than before.
And God seemed to hear me not.

I offered God the parts of me I feared to give:
    Demonic voices and burning curses
    from deep within my angry flesh.
And God responded:
    Look here child!
    Did you imagine
    that your pretense
    would make me believe
    that the world has changed
    Since I hung upon the cross?[24]

Think back in your own life to an experience of disorientation. How did that experience affect your relationship with God, especially as that relationship was expressed through your prayer? Did you pray angry laments? Why or why not? If not, what blocked you from appropriating the laments as a vehicle for your prayer?

When my brother died, I was very angry at God. Without the psalm laments, I doubt that I could have remained in the church and continued to teach in seminary. The laments kept me talking to God, even if all my talk was angry talk. There was comfort for me in knowing that I was not alone in my anger and my doubt, that the saints before me had prayed these psalms. Lament language can give us the words to pray when we can find none of our own. Nora Cameron offers a lament she wrote based on Psalm 42, expressing her amazement that she could produce something like this. She captures in her own way the eloquent urgency of the psalm.

As the deer longs for flowing water
So my soul longs for you, O God

PSALM 42

My soul longs for you, O God.
Unravel my knotted thoughts and feelings
That my tongue, unleashed, may speak of you in leopards' leaps
Far beyond convention's easy words
That spill like a fountain out of me.
Beyond the feather words that coo in the morning,
yet are lost by noonday prayers.
That my unfettered tongue may find the naked words behind
    convention's veil,
Words clear as the angelus bell in December's winter air,
Words like water to green the dull brown desert in our souls,
Words to speak of my beating heart relieved of fears,

Like Atlas relieved from the weight of the sky,
Steadied by your gift of peace.
Oh my soul longs to tell of you, O God.[25]

The whole process of the lament structure makes relief and healing possible. Daniel Simundson calls this the "power of negative thinking." It is sometimes necessary to work through suffering and doubt in order to maintain wholeness; otherwise, unresolved anger or questions can fester for years and eat away at our emotional and spiritual health. There have been countless times in my leading of Bible studies and retreats on the book of Psalms when participants have approached me after class and offered up their long-standing pain: "I'd like to share with you something that's been bothering me for six months." One person had been angry over the death of her sister for over a decade: "I just couldn't tell my pastor. She wouldn't understand." How many times have you felt this way—isolated, angry, and ashamed? Perhaps I was the least threatening ear because I was a stranger. What a challenge to the community of faith to become that listening ear.

The structure of the lament reminds us that God is there and that God hears, even when our inner feelings have not yet caught up with this fact and when our sense is that God does not hear. When my brother died, I prayed the laments, but when I crossed over the dotted line into "confession of trust," it was only to mouth the words that as yet had no meaning for me. They were, at most, a dim light at the end of my tunnel, a light that I could not yet embrace.

What is crucial in this lament process is that we be careful not to skip over the complaint to get to the confession of trust too quickly. Most laments may end in praise, but we "cannot short-cut the process…The agony will not go away by leaping immediately to happy thoughts. The resurrection comes only after the crucifixion."[26] This is why responsive readings in the back of hymnals that cut out the complaints of the lament are as good as useless. They are nothing more than what a person in one of my Bible studies called "pious pole-vaulting."

The pastoral question for each of us becomes "how long?" How long does it take someone to cross over from the complaint to the confession of trust in the lament in order to embrace praise after a divorce, a death, or an addiction? We are usually too ready to speak a positive word too soon. Proverbs 25:20 warns against such a practice in its pithy wisdom way: "The one who sings songs to a heavy heart is like one who takes off a garment on a cold day, and like vinegar on a wound" (modified RSV).

Most mental health professionals today speak of the stages of grieving the loss of a loved one: shock (numbness); denial ("No, this didn't happen");

anger (at people and at God: "Why me?" or "How could you do this?");
bargaining (an attempt to postpone: "I'll change if you take away my loss");
depression (reaction to past losses or preparation for impending losses);
detachment or withdrawal ("I just don't feel anything anymore"); acceptance
or reorganization (time to get on with life).[27] These stages do not unfold in
a neat, linear way; grieving is messy. How long this grief process takes is
different for each person. It took me a full two years before I could in any
way get a grip on my life again after my brother's death; for my mother it
took perhaps eight, although I could say that half of her went with my
brother to his grave.

In a 1987 University of Michigan study, up to 85 percent of the people
who had lost a spouse or child in a car accident were still grieving four to
seven years later.[28] In a 1985 report on bereavement, the National Academy
of Sciences concluded that grieving affects one's physical and mental health.
Connections between grieving and specific diseases such as heart disease
were cited, as was suppression of the immune system.[29] Unless we've been
through a grief process ourselves, we tend not to understand why grieving
takes such a long time. No less famous a person than Joe Gibbs, former
coach of the Washington Redskins, learned that when his father died. Gibbs
said that when the father of one of his reserve defensive backs had died,
Gibbs had said: "I couldn't understand why he didn't snap out of it…I even
talked to him: 'Clarence, your dad would not want you to lose your job.' So
when Clarence came on the field to say how bad he felt for me, I said: 'I
want to apologize for last year. I could not understand the way you were. I
can now.'"[30]

If we do move eventually from complaint to praise, from disorientation
to new orientation, we must remember that we do not obliterate memories
of the pain and loss; rather, we remember them in a new way. Nicholas
Wolterstorff recognizes this in a little book he wrote about dealing with the
death of his 25–year-old son, Eric, in a mountain-climbing accident.
"Everything is charged," he says, "with the potential of a reminder. There's
no forgetting."[31]

Perhaps the best thing we can do when someone suffers a loss, be it
divorce, death of a loved one, or whatever has shattered someone's
orientation, is to listen to weeping, to angry questions, to bouts of depression,
or to whatever else she or he throws at us. We need to avoid moralizing,
lecturing, and theologizing, and instead, pay attention to what Simundson
calls the "survival level" of suffering, that is, God's presence in suffering
mediated through us. We are much more comfortable with the "intellectual
level," which is concerned with giving reasons for the suffering.[32] It is easier
for us to hand a sufferer a neat intellectual explanation of why he or she is

suffering than to try to empathize with what they are feeling. That's what Job's friends did. Simundson argues that in the end, the message of Job is on the survival level, that is, "have faith," for there is no intellectual explanation for our suffering.

Wolterstorff speaks of this survival level of suffering that demands our empathy and solidarity. Joining our suffering to God's "suffering love," we can expand our sympathy "for the world's wounds"; otherwise, death wins.

> "Put your hand into my wounds," said the risen Jesus to Thomas, "and you will know who I am." The wounds of Christ are his identity. They tell us who he is. He did not lose them. They went down into the grave with him and they came up with him—visible, tangible, palpable. Rising did not remove them. He who broke the bonds of death kept his wounds…So I shall struggle to live the reality of Christ's rising and death's dying. In my living, my son's dying will not be the last word. But as I rise up, I bear the wounds of his death. My rising does not remove them. They mark me. If you want to know who I am, put your hand in.[33]

Simundson warns that we cannot simply tell people to "have faith," for that is "to tell them to do something that they cannot do. You can no more order someone to have faith in God than you can order them to stop being depressed or be six inches taller or change the color of their skin." Whether or not we ever have the kind of faith that is able to endure suffering is not something that we can will for ourselves. If it happens, as it finally did with Job or as it is structured into the lament psalms, it is a gift from God. Though we cannot make it happen, we can at least be open to the process that gives it a better chance of happening. That means that, even in suffering, we continue to address our thoughts and feelings toward God (as Job did) and that we be as honest and direct as we can.[34]

In this view, faith is not simply passive acceptance of whatever life throws at you; it is not simply the confession of trust and the vow of praise. Faith also includes what comes before the confession of trust in the lament structure: anger, questions, petitions, and motivations. As Brueggemann puts it, each part of the lament structure reflects a real moment in the relationship with God. Each part has "its own appropriate time. But one moment is not less faithful than the other."[35] This is something that people outside our churches need to hear. Douglas John Hall speaks of the "doubting faith–or faithful doubt" of "people on the edges"[36] of Christian tradition or the church. They need to understand that faith is not certitude, a "believing attitude," or mere intellectual assent. Instead, it is trust that allows freedom to doubt, which is "part of the Christian life." "God expects us to doubt;

because without doubt our belief in God becomes just as routine and artificial as happens in human relationships that have lost their vitality." It is this doubt that can help the Christian church relate to the world of doubt and disbelief. Hall insists that "if Christians were a little more open and honest about their *questions*…their *answers* might be more intriguing to those outside the churches."[37]

Well-meaning people can point to passages in the Bible that talk about rock-solid faith that never waivers, but as William Sloane Coffin said of his fellow clergy, this only proves that they know their Bibles better than the human condition.

> I know all the "right" biblical passages, including "Blessed are those who mourn," and my faith is no house of cards; these passages are true, I know. But the point is this: While the words of the Bible are true, grief renders them unreal. The reality of grief is the absence of God—"My God, my God, why hast thou forsaken me?" The reality of grief is the solitude of pain, the feeling that your heart's in pieces, your mind's a blank.[38]

How often do we use comforting words of scripture for our own protection from situations too painful to face? It takes courage to grieve honestly. The lament takes seriously our uncertainty about God when we are in the pit. It is a response to God's hiddenness that articulates that experience of hiddenness and brings it to speech. Our questions of "Why?" and "How long?" are not simply preliminary to the confession of trust or the vow of praise. The agony and uncertainty expressed in the lament structure characterize "life in the meanwhile," that is, "life lived in the period between what has happened in the past and what is hoped for in the future"[39] in our relationship with God. The lament uncovers the real doubt that emerges from the imbalance between the promises of God and the present situation.

In this sense we can say that what is expressed in the complaint, petitions, and motivations (above the dotted line in the lament structure) represents life in the meanwhile, and what is expressed in the confession and vow of praise (below the dotted line) represents the past experience of God and the future hope. Although past experience undergirds everything above the dotted line, there it is implicit only, overcome by the uncertainty of the present situation. When too much emphasis is put on the movement within the lament from complaint to praise, the lament is interpreted "less like a lament and more like another form of thanksgiving."[40] This minimizes the function of the lament as an articulation of the experience of "life in the meanwhile" and as a buffer against skepticism or atheism. The lament is directed to God with the expectation that only God can answer. Yet this problem in one's relationship with God is confronted within the religious community so that worship keeps boundaries around our experience and our despair does not exceed our tolerance and destroy us.

Both the experience of God's hiddenness and of God's presence were integral to Israel's faith. As Samuel Balentine argues, faith in God presents us with the dilemma of God's absence and presence. The prophetic or wisdom view that righteousness signals God's presence and wickedness God's absence cannot always be applied. This discrepancy between the wisdom view and reality leads to questions of "Why?" and "How long?" Ultimately, the lament structure takes into account our human condition and our need to give vent before God to what we are feeling. Rather than trying to resolve the conflict between lament and praise or trying to synthesize the two, the lament structure holds them together in tension. "Doubt and despair are not mere side-steps in an otherwise optimistic faith. They are in fact integral to the faith experience."[41] The lament structure witnesses to a determination to hold together the premises: God is good; God is all-powerful; evil exists in the world; and we are good. This is perhaps not as neat a situation as we would like, not a systematic theology, but it reflects the real experience of the life of faith.

Liturgically, we need to build in times for the honest expression of the experience of the life of faith. A chapel service created by one of my Psalms classes at Wesley Theological Seminary provides a model for just such sharing. As part of the scripture reading for the service, prior to thanksgiving and communion, the class designated a time of "Confession/Emptying," which was accompanied by two sacred dances, one for each of the scripture readings. Becky Cloud[42] introduced this part of the Lenten service with these words:

> We all experience times in our lives when we can find "no…proofs that God has spoken and that God is in control of the human situation."[43] As Christians we feel the tension of living between the inauguration of God's reign and its final realization, between the first break of dawn and the full light of day. In those shadow times of life, the faithful of Israel, like Hannah, went to the Temple seeking God and offering prayers out of their need or anxiety. We take this opportunity as the people of God gathered in this place of worship to address God in prayer
> - out of our own anger,
> - out of our own fear,
> - out of our own anxiety,
> - out of our own frustration…to ask, "My God, why?"

We make this bold act of faith out of the experience of disorder in our lives. It is the human reality to at times experience life as a pilgrimage through darkness. Though beyond our understanding why or how, it is while in the pit that God's grace most profoundly breaks through, bringing with it the experience of new life.

Our silence will be punctuated with two readings from the Psalms—51 and 22—which express both the confession of sin and the experience of the pit.

Both your confessional and questioning psalms may be offered to God by placing them in the basket as you come forward to receive communion.

After the service, the class took the purple pieces of paper that had been placed in the basket (we had passed out paper and small pencils with the worship bulletins) and burned them on the quad at Wesley while singing a hymn. It was a profoundly transformative moment for us all.

Psalm 13

Psalm 13 provides a textbook example of an individual lament. It contains all the parts of the ideal lament structure. It is a clear articulation of disorientation. Something is wrong in the psalmist's life and in her or his relationship with God. There is no confession of sin to suggest that this disorientation was deserved. The psalmist is driven to doubt and questioning.

The opening cry in verses 1 and 2 combines the address and complaint of the lament structure by asking the characteristic lament question "How long?" a question full of reproach and accusation. The question precedes the name of God, as if the pain were so great that the problem had to be expressed immediately and abruptly: "How long, Adonai? Will you forget me forever? How long will you hide your face from me? How long will I suffer pain, grief in my heart all day? How long will my enemy boast over me?"

In these two verses, Psalm 13 uses a method of repetition that is found in many of the laments, that is, rhetorical, emphatic repetition of a single word or a brief phrase. This poetic form acts "as a kind of magnifying glass, concentrating the rays of meaning to a white-hot point."[44] This intensified structure identified by Robert Alter shifts our attention away from the repeated element "How long?" to the material introduced by the repetition, the sense of God's absence, the grief, and the enemy. It is, however, the crisis in the relationship with God that is at the root of both the internal pain and the external problem with the enemy.

Alter argues that the repeated phrase never means the same thing twice. "How long?" is used four times in the opening two verses with increasing intensity and desperate urgency. Within the first line the repetition also moves the Hebrew poetry from the general to the more concrete and specific. The psalmist complains of being forgotten by God in verse 1a, and this is described more personally and concretely in verse 1b as God's hiding the divine face. This movement toward the personal can also be seen between lines; the general condition of being abandoned in verse 1 moves in verse 2 to the inward condition of the psalmist, who is burdened with cares and grief. Divine abandonment is also specified by the final "How long?" of verse 2 as it introduces the enemy.

Desperation reaches a climax at the end of verse 2. The psalmist then moves into the third part of the lament structure, the petition, with four commands addressed to God: "Look at me, answer me, Adonai, my God! Give light to my eyes lest I sleep death, lest my enemy say 'I have destroyed him; my foes gloat when I totter" (vv. 3–4). The psalmist cries to God to "notice me, pay attention to me!" It is dangerous to accuse God of forgetting and turning away, but it is more dangerous to give up on God and remain isolated from God by thinking that this doubt cannot be expressed in prayer or worship.

The psalmist's call to God to look is meant to reverse the hiding of the divine face in verse 1b. God's turning the divine face toward the psalmist would mean that the psalmist's eyes would be lightened rather than closed in the sleep of death. The psalmist reaches out to God here, uncertain whether the psalmist's life really matters to God. It is this mattering to God that gives life meaning. That the psalmist mattered to God in the past is expressed by the naming of God a second time in verse 3a: "O Adonai my God." After the expression of the raw pain and doubt, the psalmist is able to claim a past intimacy with God and remind God of what they were to each other once. This claim of past relationship that seems broken now becomes the basis or context for the petition.

The repetition of "lest" three times in verses 3 and 4 complements the repetition of "how long" in verses 1 and 2 and stresses the danger and pain of the present situation. The phrases introduced by "lest" function as motivations for God to act. Death and gloating enemies mean defeat for the psalmist and for the psalmist's God. As God's public relations agent in the world, the psalmist, by using these motivations, wants to make sure that God knows what is at stake. The general complaint back in verse 1 about God's forgetting the psalmist is intensified by the magnifying glass of reference to the sleep of death and gloating enemies.

In the midst of this painful group of motivations for God to act, the psalmist bursts forth into the confession of trust in verse 5: "But I have trusted in your *hesed;* my heart will rejoice in your salvation" (italics added).

In the midst of suffering, the psalmist holds up the past relationship of covenant loyalty with God and the future hope of exalting God once again for that loyalty. God's loyalty will be expressed by saving the psalmist from the exultation of the enemies over the psalmist's death; God will reverse the situation so that the psalmist exalts God's saving work. The psalmist crosses over from the complaint to the confession of the lament structure between verses 4 and 5, holding in tension "life in the meanwhile" with life in the past and future.

Verse 6 articulates a vow of praise, which promises in advance to tell of God's deliverance when it happens (and the psalmist asserts it will): "I will sing to Adonai, because [Adonai] has done good for me." In this final verse, God is addressed, not in anger and doubt as in verse 1, not with intimacy as a claim on the past relationship as in verse 3, but as the object of praise, of doxology. These three different uses of the divine name mark the movement within the psalm.

Yet this movement ought not be seen as a neat resolution of the psalmist's distress. Craig Broyles, for example, challenges those who would see in verses 5 and 6 a granting of what the psalmist had asked God for, so that fear has subsided and the present distress is disregarded.[45] To interpret the psalm in this way, we must assume that the psalmist drops each line for another. Poetry, however, enables us to see all the parts of the idea simultaneously rather than sequentially. Psalm poetry gives us synthetic pictures of experience. Psalmists hold on to each line until the whole poem is gathered.

This means that we ought not be too hasty to talk about mixed emotions or contradictions within a psalm. Different perspectives on the same experience are offered without any explicit resolution of apparent contradictions. This conflict may be the key to the psalm's message and to our own lives of faith as well. In our fast-paced world with its shifting values, some of us would understandably like to pin down the lament psalms; we crave resolution and a quick fix. But the psalmists saw that the life of faith is more complex than that. Psalms give the church a language that matches all our experiences; our honesty before one another and before God builds us up as the community of faith and the body of Christ. A contemporary hymn that captures the mixed emotions of the lament process is "How Long, O Lord" by Christopher Norton. "How long, O Lord…No tokens of your love I see, your face is turned away from me…I learn to praise you and to trust in your unfailing love."[46]

Psalm 41

Psalm 41 could be called the Jerusalem General Hospital chaplain's psalm. It is another individual lament. With opening words of blessing from a priest for those who care for the weak, some see it as a ritual for the healing of the sick. Verse 13 functions as the closing doxology for Book 1 of the Psalter. Instead of opening with address and complaint, Psalm 41 seems to express joyful gratitude to others in the congregation: "Happy is the one who is thoughtful of the weak; Adonai delivers that one from the day of trouble. Adonai watches over and preserves them; they are called happy in the land. You do not give them up to their enemies. Adonai sustains them on their sickbed" (vv. 1–3).

Yet in light of the confession of sin in verse 4 (which does not seem to have been accepted by God) and the lengthy complaint about enemies in verses 5–10, these opening verses are either a denial of the psalmist's true feelings or really a complaint. The irony is that this is the way it is supposed to be: God heals those who take care of the weak and protects them from enemies. But this is not the way it is now. The psalmist draws on the core testimony tradition of God as protector, wanting to believe it; but the uncertainty is too great. God is being accused here of negligence, of not delivering, watching over, and keeping from enemies, nor healing the one who helps others. This is the countertestimony.

Verse 4 expresses a confession of sin, but it is a historical account, a confession in the past: "I said, 'Adonai, grace me, heal me, for I have sinned against you.'" The implication is that the psalmist should be forgiven, given the traditional beliefs about God just expressed in verses 1–3, but that nothing has changed. The psalmist has acknowledged weakness, but Adonai has not delivered, says the psalmist. Again, the act/consequence formula is being applied by the psalmist here: You get what you deserve. If I have sinned, then I suffer at the hands of my enemies; but since my enemies still plague me, you have not accepted my confession, God. Why not? Am I as wicked as my enemies? Just look what they do (vv. 5–10).

"My enemies speak of me badly: 'When will she die and her name perish?'" (v. 5). The enemies seem just to be waiting for the psalmist to die, like vultures. They seize upon the weakness of the psalmist in suffering by whispering behind his or her back: "And if they come to see me, they utter empty words, while their heart gathers evil thoughts; they go outside and speak them. All the ones who hate me whisper together against me; they imagine the worst for me" (vv. 6–7).

No matter how well-intentioned we are when we visit sick people in the hospital, in our awkwardness we make the sufferer feel as if there is something radically and inevitably wrong with him or her. When we are the sick ones, we sometimes feel worse after a visitor than before. Visitors often speak "empty words" because they don't know any better: "You look great! You look as if you could go home tomorrow." But we suspect that as soon as they leave the room, they shake their heads and "whisper together." What they really think is: "Oh, she looks just terrible! Looks as if she could die tomorrow." These reactions are not surprising, since disease inhabits the realm of vulnerability, fear, and aloneness. Disease presents us with what David Tracy calls a "limit situation." Mark Taylor argues that "disease is the impossible embodiment of the not...disease is our chronic condition."[47] Disease is "the betrayal of the body."[48] Because it terrorizes us, we try to control it by defining and domesticating it, by distancing ourselves from it.

This distancing from disease is both spatial and psychological. It is spatial in that hospitals, clinics, asylums, and prisons treat in one place those who are ill in order to keep the disease from spreading. I was struck by how different hospital care is in China when I visited there a decade ago. In China, it is expected that the family of the sick one camp out in the hospital room, cooking for the sick one, doing laundry, tending to every need, providing comfort. Even the body language of hospital visitation in the West suggests spatial distancing. Think about those times you have visited someone in the hospital, or when you were in the hospital yourself and people came to visit you. We are a bit timid and reserved when we visit a hospital. The smells, the routine, the atmosphere are very different from what we usually experience. Things are clearly not under our control there. As visitors we tend to hang back by the doorway or plant ourselves in the corner, taking care not to get too close to the patient in the bed. This, coupled with the fact that sickness and death are disgusting to many, contributes to an awkwardness. We just can't wait to get out. We check our watches to see when visiting hours are over. Heaven forbid we should sit on the bed or hold the patient's hand or get close to the sick one in the bed.

The distancing is also psychological when we use words of self-interest: "Does it run in *your* family?" we ask, which implies it doesn't run in *mine*.[49] Or we will tell someone they look great when, in fact, they look like death warmed over. We don't want to hear how they are really feeling. To us as visitors it is as if the sick one has been taken over by something that threatens our own wholeness and health, and we want to distance ourselves from that something as much as possible. Verse 8 of Psalm 41 puts this well: "They think that a deadly thing has fastened on me, that I will not rise again from where I lie'" (NRSV). Death and sickness are personified here as a dynamic power hostile to human beings. That's why we don't sit on the bed; whatever she or he has might be catching, might overcome us too. The sick one is not whole or real, and is as good as gone, as good as dead. Even our trusted "bosom friend" sees us this way (v. 9). Our crisis in health care only exacerbates this feeling. As the length of a hospital stay decreases and more emphasis is put on home care, the inner turmoil that threatens the identity and coherence of the sick person increases, and our fear of "catching" whatever the sick have also increases. That is why new models of the health care team that include the church and parish nurses will be so important in the future.

Psalm 41 is the only one of the laments that asks for the personal power to requite enemies (all the other laments leave that to God): "But you, Adonai, grace me, and raise me up that I may repay them" (v. 10). For one who is suffering at death's door, the speaking of this wish for revenge against the insensitive ones may bring relief. The only power the psalmist has left is the power of words. Verses 11 and 12 offer the confession of trust in the sense, perhaps, of forgiveness for sin. The psalmist knows that God is "pleased with me" by the fact that the enemy is not shouting, "Look, I told you she was close to death. I knew she couldn't last!" and by a sense of being in God's presence. The wicked are those who live without God; they do not recognize their dependence on God as the psalmist does. This thought brings the psalmist comfort, for no matter what else may happen in the psalmist's life, being in God's presence is the constant comfort. God's presence will not keep the psalmist from suffering but will help him or her get through it.

Communal Laments

Communal laments are not as numerous in the Psalter nor as usable for many of us as are the individual laments. Brueggemann argues that the category of the personal has become our contemporary mode of experiencing reality. With our privatistic inclinations, we've lost our public imagination. In order to gain access to the communal laments, "we need to think through the public sense of loss and hurt and tragedy that we all have in common."[50] I suggested in the last chapter that Psalm 137 lent itself to our public use in crises such as the September 11 attacks and the Iranian hostage ordeal. Psalm 44 is another communal lament (see also Pss. 60; 74; 79; 83; 94; 129) that can articulate our public outrage over the communal dimension of suffering.

The problem with any of these communal laments is that they can feed our imperialism, a belief that we have been chosen to conquer other nations and set the world right, to our way. The communal laments also can substitute an "us versus them" mind-set for an honest critique of our internal dealings with one another in society. In this sense, communal laments are a double-edged sword. Psalm community laments can raise "the political question" about the consequences of "empire building": war, international exploitation, refugees. Does our worship allow for the voicing of these issues? J. David Pleins argues that "worship will always try to move toward praise, but in situations of communal grief, the act of worship must dare to speak to the politics of suffering."[51] Similarly, Marjorie Proctor-Smith insists that "prayer is a profoundly political act."[52] Noting both the absence of corporate prayer in feminist liturgical gatherings and the pervasiveness of violence and abuse against women, she argues that the goal of feminist liturgical prayer is resistance to patterns of domination and transformation of the church.

Paul in Romans 8:31–39 quotes one of the verses from Psalm 44. A look at why Paul does this can help us to see how Psalm 44 can help us as a nation not only to express our public hurt, but to work toward social critique and our own national transformation as well. On the surface, Romans 8 and Psalm 44 seem poles apart. The psalm complains to and accuses God, while Romans 8 affirms God's love and exults over Christ resurrected from the cross. A closer look at these two texts shows that they have more in common than just one verse of scripture. Both passages tell us something about what it means to have faith today. Psalm 44 represents our Lenten journey; Romans 8, our Easter celebration.

Psalm 44 opens with a powerful hymn to God: "We have heard with our ears O God, our parents have told us, what deeds you performed in their days, the days of old." Following this verse is a description of those divine acts in the past. The Israelite people take a long, collective look at their glorious history during the time of settlement in the promised land of Canaan. "God, you with your own hand" (v. 2) drove out the nations for our ancestors so that they could dwell in the land. Verse 4 switches from the communal "we" and "us" to the singular "I" and "my." Perhaps a representative of the people (the king?) celebrates God's sovereignty: "You are my king and my God." It is God who is responsible for Israel's salvation and victories: "For not in my bow do I trust, nor can my sword save me. But you have saved us from our foes" (vv. 6–7, NRSV).

But this review of Israel's salvation history is full of irony and bitterness in light of the complaint that bursts forth in the middle of the psalm: "Yet you have rejected us and abased us" (v. 9, NRSV). The memory of the past serves only to accentuate the agony of the present suffering of the people of Israel. Thus, the opening verse, rather than praising God, implicitly accuses God: You were once a God to be counted on, but where are you now? We in our present misery are sick of hearing about the "glorious" past.

How many Americans boast of our glorious history, not realizing that this history was one of oppression for many of our people? How many dream the American dream and find themselves shut out of it? Who can claim the ideals of a glorious past as operative right now, given the escalating homelessness of our population, the poverty of our children, the pervasive racism of our society, the drug epidemic striking at every socioeconomic bracket?

What situation of distress had provoked such despair, such anger, on the part of the Israelite people? Their present misery is described in a general way: "You have made us like sheep for the slaughter, and have scattered us among the nations" (v. 11). The community, perhaps in Babylonian exile, tries to shame God into action by asking in so many words, "What profit can you possibly get from abandoning your people like this? This is not good public relations for you." God's people bear the shame of taunts (vv. 13, 16) and of "the shaking of the head" (v. 14); they are mocked. For the United States to claim its moral superiority before the world as a God-fearing nation, we need to get our own house in order. The rapidly changing political and economic scene is causing our nation to reassess its role in the world and its treatment of its own people at home. This is the public crisis that may push us to embrace Psalm 44.

The people protest their innocence: "All this has come upon us, though we have not forgotten you or been false to your covenant—nor have our steps departed from your way, that you should have… broken us and covered us with deep darkness" (vv. 17–19). We do not deserve such treatment, Adonai. Deuteronomy 8:19 warns that the people will "perish" if they "forget Adonai your God." But the community has not forgotten (Ps. 44:17, 20); God knows that, since God "knows the secrets of the heart" (v. 21). We don't know why we are suffering: "No, for your sake we are slain all the day long and accounted as sheep for the slaughter" (v. 22). You are the culprit in our present misery, God. We suffer mysteriously because of you, because we are your people, loyal to you in a hostile world. Job makes the same protest on a personal level in Job 30—31.

The pain of Israel's undeserved suffering is poured into a harsh closing petition that very clearly accuses God of negligence: "Wake up! Why do you sleep, O Adonai? Awake!…Why do you hide your face?…Rise up! Deliver us for the sake of your *hesed*" (vv. 23–24). Elijah uses similar mocking words to dismiss the Baal god of the prophets on Mount Carmel in 1 Kings 18:27. In Psalm 44, the people refuse to believe that God will not or cannot act, so they petition God with urgency and anger. Their experience provides countertestimony to the core testimony about God's *hesed,* the word with which Psalm 44 ends: "Redeem us for the sake of your *hesed.*"

In Psalm 44, the Israelites struggle for relationship with God and won't let go. This is the point of the psalm, this not letting go of God despite, and in the midst of, our suffering, when God seems to be absent, not present to us. In Romans 8, Paul proclaims the flip side of the relationship with God: God refuses to let go of us despite God's seeming absence. We must believe that nothing can separate us from God's love in Christ: "If God is for us, who is against us?" (Rom. 8:31). Christ is God's pledge to be for us, to save, to intercede for us despite the perils we encounter in our lives of faith.

"Who shall separate us from the love of Christ?" Paul asks in Romans 8:35. This is no rhetorical question; seven forms of trial are listed. It is precisely by quoting Psalm 44 that Paul seeks to show the difficulty of the Christian life of faith: "As it is written, 'For your sake we are being killed all the day long, we are regarded as sheep to be slaughtered'" (Rom. 8:36). In light of these real dangers that Paul lists as assailing Christians, we must be careful not simply to sum up Romans 8 with the proclamation "Jesus is the answer." The problem of a Christian existence before God then and now is too complex for that. Paul saw that the pain of the life of faith is real. The psalmist also saw that the existence of the Israelites was painful when God seemed to be absent.

Both Psalm 44 and Romans 8 are saturated with experience of life in the world before God. Psalm 44's lament articulates the reality of "life in the meanwhile," the life of Lent, the period between what has happened in the past and what is hoped for in the future, that is, Easter. The faith statement undergirding Psalm 44 and proclaimed in Romans 8 is that God does not let go of us—God is for us. This is Easter. But the reality of our lives is often that God hides, and peril assails us, and we must struggle not to let go of God. This is Lent. Psalm 44, more than a hymn of praise, struggles to proclaim "God for us," even when the only words we can say to God are "for your sake we are being killed all the day long."

David Hunter has composed a communal lament entitled "Kosovo Lament" that draws on the themes articulated by Psalm 44 in a structure that corresponds to individual lament. It is a powerful communal articulation of the pain of the contemporary global situation.

Kosovo Lament

O Nameless, Holy One,
O God of our mothers and fathers,
O God of Abraham and Sarah,
Wake up!
Wake up and listen:
listen to your people, your suffering people.
We live in Kosovo; we live in Serbia, in Iraq, in the Ivory Coast,
    Indonesia, Rwanda, Lebanon, Ireland.
We are your children; we are your brothers and sisters.
The sound of bombs drowns out our cries,
and the floods of chaos overwhelm our tears.
You slaughter our sons in battle.
You rape our mothers.

You place mines in our children's path.
You take our babies and dash their heads against the rocks.
God, do you see your world?
God, do you understand?
Our sages tell us that you are suffering with us.
We are *not* comforted.
We want your action, not your compassion!
Let there be a day of the LORD!
Show the world who is in charge!
Let your justice roll down like waters.
Let your justice drown those who wage war against your people.
In your name we come to the rescue.
We watch the war on television.
The muted images allow us a peaceful dinner,
and we give thanks for our land that flows with milk and honey.
Our brothers and sisters fly the planes, dropping bombs on
targets they cannot see, on targets they need not see.
Yet, we are *here*.
We are here together this morning,
in a community, in a community of faith, love, and hope.
Would that there were in all lands today people sharing together
their meals and their lives and their suffering,
holding each other's hands until that day arrives when the sun
will shine and the rain will fall gently, and the grass will
grow again,
and the children will play on the grass, while their parents watch
with love in their hearts.
And on that day our songs of praise will echo back and forth
across the oceans,
reaching even to heaven above.
Hosannah! Hosannah![53]

Psalm 44 has also been the basis for a lament after September 11, 2001, by Karen Dize. This moving poem echoes the sections of the psalm while reflecting on the contemporary experience of terror.

An American Lament
ENDOWED BY THEIR CREATOR

We know it is true.
We have heard it in church and classroom;
We have read it in Scripture and history—
As you did for Israel

So you gave to our founding fathers this land,
From sea to sea, from coast to coast,
A land flowing with unspeakable beauty
And abundant resources.

They did not come with swords and cannons,
But with ideas and beliefs,
To worship you in freedom
To pursue life, liberty, and happiness,
To experience new life in a new land,
And you favored them above others.
You freed them from their persecution.
You smiled on all they did,
And you blessed them.

And so, you, O Lord, are my God and only King.
We, too, have seen your righteousness prevail.
There is no doubt, it was "God on our side"
That overcame the evil powers of mass annihilation.
I do not trust weapons; they cannot save me.
No, it was by your might that we turned back the dictator.
It was you who rescued the weak from tyranny.
Our victory was really your victory.

ONE NATION UNDER GOD

So how can we explain this terror?
Have you, O God, turned your back on us
And do not see this injustice?
Have you given our enemy this victory?
Did you stand by as thousands died
As innocent sheep led to slaughter,
And would not take their part?
Do their lives count for so little in your eyes?

As our borders are breached we draw closer to one another.
Yet we hear the mockery and hatred around us;
We see those celebrating our sorrow.
Our very name, America, is pronounced with contempt.
People dance and shout for joy before our screens,
In our very homes,
Denouncing us, deepening our anger, our grief,
And our confusion,
As our buildings crumble and our people die.

In God We Trust

All this has been heaped on top of us
Not unlike the rubble we witness,
And yet what have we done to deserve this?
We have not forgotten you our God.
We refute those who claim we have left your ways
And earned your wrath.
Still we feel broken and covered in deep darkness,
Marked with the ash that rains down on the great city,
Reminding us of our mortality.

God Bless America

Where are you, Lord?
You are not one to sleep,
But it is difficult to see your face in the darkness.
You are not one to forget,
But we have been brought down low,
To the dust and ashes.
We will never be quite the same—

Yet you are changeless.
Come to us once again, O Lord, our God.
Save us! Lift us from our sorrow!
Your steadfast love requires it.[54]

CHAPTER SEVEN

I'll Never Be the Same Again

Thanksgiving Psalms and Enthronement Psalms

Although each of us is different and does not move out of disorientation according to some set schedule, the hope is that we do move sometime into new orientation. This movement does not mean a return to the orientation before the pit experience. Having been in the pit, we can never be what we were before the pit; we can never be the same again. Rather, we come to a different place on the circle, or the spiral, of the life of faith. Nicholas Wolterstorff recognized this after the death of his son: "Now he's gone, and the family has to restructure itself...We have to live differently with each other. We have to live around the gap. Pull one out, and everything changes."[1]

This means that the hole in my heart caused by my brother's death can never be filled by anyone else, not even by my son Brian (who is named after my brother) or by my daughter Ariel. No matter how many times people tell me how wonderful it is that I bring healing to people through my study of the psalms, I would not hesitate for a second to trade whatever good I have done to have my brother back, alive and with me in the world.

The pit experience is never forgotten. It impinges on the present and the future. Our prayer is that we can learn to live in a new way with the memory of disorientation.

Perhaps life is more precious on the other side of the pit. New orientation, as a surprising gift from God, means that we can live with the pain of the pit experience so that it doesn't overwhelm and incapacitate us. We can once again smile and rejoice over the gift and beauty of life. We respond in awe and thanksgiving, gratitude and wonder over such a gift; and we feel compelled to tell the story of the reversal of our circumstances to anyone who will listen. Just as we need to give the details of the pit experience to help us deal with it, so, too, we need to share the details of the climb out of the pit.

Walter Brueggemann argues that the psalms of new orientation celebrate a new settlement of the theodicy issue, of the question of God's justice and the ordering of the world. The crisis is past, and the psalmist or the community looks to a new stability and order for life. Thanksgiving psalms speak of the personal experience of a new order, while enthronement psalms speak of the public experience of a new governance. Surprises and newness overcome the old way of looking at the world. This new way is inexplicable: "We do not know how such a newness happens any more than we know how a dead person is raised to new life, how a leper cleansed, or how a blind person can see"[2] (compare with Lk. 7:22; 15:24; Jn. 9:25; and Isa. 42:7, 61:1).

Thanksgiving psalms articulate this sense of newness and the surprise of the movement out of the pit of disorientation. They celebrate the gift of new orientation. Thanksgivings tell the story of the past distress and of God's saving reversal of the situation. In its form and content, the thanksgiving psalm is related both to the lament and to the hymn. Like the lament, the thanksgiving is both individual and communal. Also, we can say that the thanksgiving psalm is an expanded form of the thanksgiving already present in many laments. Laments often, but not always, include vows of praise at the end, following the confession of trust. After the psalmist's complaint, she or he declares trust in God's future help and promises to give thanks and to acknowledge before the congregation God's anticipated deliverance from the problem. Thus, the lament often moves from complaint to thanksgiving.

There is one major difference, however, between the vow of praise in the lament and in the thanksgiving psalm. The lament vow praises God for deliverance that has not yet occurred but that is hoped for and anticipated. The thanksgiving psalm, on the other hand, praises God for deliverance already experienced. The praise comes in response to what has happened, rather than in anticipation of what will happen. One is praise before the fact; the other is praise after the fact.

The psalms of thanksgiving were often sung during the offering of sacrifices in the sanctuary or the temple. The word *todah* in Hebrew means vow or freewill offering, thanksgiving (the emotion or attitude), thank offering, thanksgiving sacrifice, or song of thanksgiving. *Todah* encompasses the concrete, external action as well as the internal attitude and intention. In the Hebrew Bible, the two are never separated; a person's actions must mirror that person's inner attitude. As God declares in Psalm 50:23: "Those who bring thanksgiving as their sacrifice honor me; to those who set a way I will show the salvation of God." (NRSV, with note) To offer sacrifices or worship mechanically, without the proper inner attitude of reverence for God, means that one is not whole, not healthy. How many times do we go through the motions of worship on a Sunday morning without throwing our whole being into our worship, without having our inner attitude in sync with the sitting, singing, standing, and praying we do?

The root of the Hebrew word *todah* means "to throw or cast." Therefore, *todah* can mean to set forth, recount, recite, make known to others. When we tell the story of the pit experience and of God's delivering us from it, we witness to God's action on our behalf. We witness to God's overcoming of the chaos waters, of injustice, of the enemies. As does the praise of the hymns of orientation, only more forcefully, thanksgivings give testimony for conversion. In telling our story of wonder and awe, we are evangelists, calling people to a life of faith in this God who has saved us. We share the good news, the gospel. One cannot, indeed ought not, do that lightly. The whole person must be involved. If not, God is perceived only dimly through us by others. Hymns and thanksgivings share this evangelical aspect of giving testimony about God. Both are addressed to God and to those in the congregation and the world. Yet there is an important difference between them. The hymn praises God in general terms as one who creates the world, deals graciously with people, gives refuge in troubled times, and so forth. Hymns in this way focus on who God is. It is God's nature to be gracious, to save, and to hear prayer; and this nature is revealed to us constantly. This focus on God's general nature is reinforced by the use of active participles to talk about God, "the one who continuously does."

In the thanksgivings, however, the "I" of the psalmist is often the subject, and the verbs are finite, in the past tense. The stress is on the event from which God rescued "me"; for example, God rescued me from the pit; God did not let my enemies rejoice over me. Whereas God *acted* in the thanksgiving, God *is* in the hymn. Thanksgivings give more specific and concrete praise of God than hymns, but sometimes it is difficult to decide if hymns and thanksgivings express orientation or new orientation. In these cases, who uses them and how she or he uses them will determine which movement of faith is being expressed.

The Structure of the Thanksgiving Psalm

Like the hymn, the thanksgiving can be broken down form-critically into three parts: (1) introduction, (2) body, and (3) conclusion. In the introduction, praise and thanks are usually combined in an opening declaration or call to others to join in. The body presents the story of the individual giving thanks. A picture is drawn of the past distress and the psalmist's cry for help.

The same metaphorical language we saw in the study of laments is present in this section of the thanksgiving psalm; it makes sense that lament motifs appear in this middle section. Often English translations will use quotation marks to indicate that these are the psalmist's very words from the pit during the time of distress. Describing the pit experience helps to underscore the deliverance that God has brought about. In keeping with this emphasis on deliverance, the psalmist clearly acknowledges God as the deliverer; no one else but God could have done this for the psalmist. Often this acknowledgment is expanded into instructions for bystanders. Take heed of my experience, the psalmist says; join with me in praise for the God who has done this for me and will do the same for you.

In the conclusion, the psalmist returns to the introductory theme of praise and thanksgiving. Sometimes the opening words will be repeated. Because rescue from the pit does not mean that the psalmist will never again experience distress, the psalmist will often add a prayer for future help: If I should find myself in this situation again, God, listen to me and deliver me; don't think I don't need you anymore. This prayer for future help articulates the psalmist's real sense of dependence on God. Having been in the pit drives that point home.

Psalm 30

Communal psalms of thanksgiving include Psalms 65, 67, 107, 124, and 136; individual thanksgivings include Psalms 18, 30, 92, 103, 116, and 138. Psalm 30 presents us with a compact model of a thanksgiving psalm. Though the psalm is used at Hanukkah, the festival of the rededication of the temple in the second century B.C.E., this was probably not its original use. Israel's memory of the transformation of its pit of foreign oppression to freedom under the Maccabees is part of Israel's pattern of experience with its God of transformation, but this pattern was experienced and testified to by individuals as well.

Psalm 30 opens with the praise declaration: "I will extol you, Adonai," and moves immediately to the body, or story of the past distress in verse 1b: "For you have drawn me up and have not let my enemies rejoice over me." Verses 2 and 3 continue the story of the past distress with metaphorical language, frequent in the laments: "O Adonai my God, I cried to you for help and you healed me. O Adonai, you brought me up from Sheol, you kept me from going down into the Pit." God, the transformer of situations, reversed the psalmist's situation of distress. The verbs underscore this reversal: You drew me *up* (v. 1b) and brought me *up* (v. 3a) rather than let me go *down* to the Pit (v. 3b, italics added).

The phrases "I cried" and "you healed" in verse 2 also stress God's transformative deliverance. The cry stands at the center, between the two verbs of movement up and out of distress. The cry is the reality of the pain of the pit, which is enveloped and surrounded both theologically and structurally in these verses by God's saving actions. Each of us can concretize what it has meant in our own lives to be enveloped in this way, to be brought up from Sheol, to be healed by God, the transforming One.

The cry also speaks of intimate relationship. God is addressed three times in these first three verses. The second time, in verse 2, God is not simply addressed as Adonai, as in verses 1 and 3, but as "Adonai my God." This is an address of intimacy, claiming a past relationship and asserting at the same time the renewed relationship of the present, post-pit experience. This claim is also enveloped by the saving actions of God. The foundation of the lament is the belief that God answers prayer and hears cries of distress. This belief is confirmed and upheld by verses 1b–3.

The wonder of this deliverance as an answer to prayer pushes the psalmist to issue a sweeping call to praise in verse 4, because this good news cannot be kept secret, cannot be stored up as a personal treasure. The psalmist must testify about the God who has done this and must call others to join in the testimony: "Sing praises to Adonai, God's covenant loyal ones, and give thanks to God's holy name" (v. 4). In the same way, Psalm 40:9–10 expresses this compulsion to evangelize: "I have announced [your] righteousness in a great congregation; see, I did not close my lips; I have not hidden your saving help within my heart…I have not concealed your *hesed* and your faithfulness from a great congregation."

Verses 4 and 5 constitute a mini-hymn of their own within Psalm 30. Verse 4 would be the opening call to praise and verse 5 the reason for the praise, or the body of the hymn: "For [God's] anger is but for a moment, and when God is pleased there is life. Weeping may linger for the night, but joy comes with the morning" (v. 5). In this verse the psalmist generalizes about the life of faith and the character of God from the personal experience of God's reversal. Real pain (God's anger and the weeping it causes) is acknowledged in the life of faith, but it is seen as temporary. God's favor overcomes our pain, and joy follows. This is the good news, the gospel, that the psalmist must share. What else can we as saved creatures do but testify to the saving work of such a God?

God's grace can be seen in the divine anger that does not last. God's favor is what endures. Weeping is not the last word with the God of grace who reverses situations of distress. Here the psalmist gives instruction about God's nature to those hearing the story.

Out of the personal and specific deliverance of the psalmist, the whole community is summoned to praise this God of grace. Thus, Brueggemann argues, "As the psalm moves from reason to summons, so songs of thanksgiving move from intimate, personal experience to comprehensive, communal celebration."[3]

The psalmist addresses in verse 4 the *hasidim,* translated poorly in many English-language Bibles as "saints." This noun is related to the word *hesed,* which we have seen used so often in the psalms for God's covenant loyalty. The *hasidim* are those within the community of faith who keep covenant, who follow in the paths God has set out for them, who keep *Torah.* These are the ones who would understand and value the marvelous transformation in the life of the psalmist that has just occurred. The *hasidim* as a distinct group emerged in the time of the Maccabees, in the mid-second century B.C.E., to maintain Jewish identity in the face of death and foreign coercion. Some scholars argue that the *hasidim* were the forerunners of the Pharisees of Jesus' time. This can be a sobering corrective to the very negative and biased pictures of the Pharisees in the gospels.

The psalmist resumes the story of the past distress in verse 6, offering a more concrete picture of what happened through the actual words spoken during the time of disorientation. Actually, the psalmist begins with the time of orientation, quoting the motto we have seen in hymns of orientation (such as Ps. 46): "As for me, I said in my unconcern [my ease], 'I shall never be shaken [or totter].'" The psalmist reveals that she or he never thought that the pit was a possibility; everything was under control and secure. What the psalmist didn't realize was that this security and order were dependent on God. The realization comes in verse 7: "For you, O LORD, when you were pleased, set me up as a strong mountain. When you hid your face, I was terrified."

The movement out of orientation into disorientation is described in verses 6 and 7. The pain of life in the meanwhile gives rise to supplication and rhetorical questions in verses 8–10, which are meant to motivate God to act: "To you, Adonai, I cried and to Adonai I made appeal: 'What profit is there in my death, if I go down to the Pit? Can dust praise you? Will it tell of your faithfulness? Hear, Adonai, and grace me! Adonai, be my helper!'"

The memory of the very words said makes the pit experience real again for the psalmist and for those who hear the psalmist's story. The rhetorical questions remind God of the psalmist's public relations value in the world. At the same time, those words remind the ones listening of their duty to praise the God who gives them being.

Verses 11–12a provide a summary of the situation of transformation: "You have turned my mourning into dancing for me; you have thrown off my sackcloth and clothed me with joy, so that my whole self might sing praises to you and not be silent." The psalmist ends the body of the thanksgiving, the story of the deliverance, with a statement of reversal: mourning into dancing, sackcloth into joy clothes. The same verb, "sing praises," used in verse 12a is used in verse 4 in the call to the faithful to join the psalmist in singing praises.

Verse 1b says God did not allow the psalmist's enemies to rejoice over the psalmist; in verse 11, the same verb, "rejoice," is now used of the psalmist. The psalmist is literally clothed in rejoicing because of the deliverance God has carried out. The psalmist concludes in verse 12b with a declaration echoing the opening line, but now reinforced by the story of the reversal: "O Adonai, my God, I will give thanks to you forever." The psalmist claims an intimate relationship with God here, not as a motivation for God to act to pull the psalmist out of the pit, but as an acknowledgment that this has already happened, that God is indeed one to be counted on, now and in the future.

What is most powerful about the thanksgiving psalm is the way in which it lays out the story of a personal deliverance as the stuff of communal celebration for the faithful. How often do our personal stories become the catalyst for communal celebration in our liturgies? Sadly, we have managed to standardize and tame our personal stories of liberation or healing. We tuck away our excitement in general announcements before the call to worship or in the pastoral prayer: "So and so is recovering from her operation at home; little Johnny is recovering from his broken leg, and we are grateful." There is usually no place within the Sunday service for our personal testimonies to God's actions on our behalf. We can pray our thanks silently, but we miss the communal dimension of thanksgiving when we do. Why are we so timid about our good news? Even Mary Magdalene and the other women were afraid when they discovered the empty tomb, the greatest reversal of all; but they went out and told the disciples what they had seen. Because the psalm thanksgivings keep the memory of pit experiences and of God's rescue fresh, "each time they are sung, they invite Israel to participate in that entire history of transformation again."[4] Brueggemann insists that this participatory quality guards against the idolatry of an unchangeable God and an ideology of an unchangeable world. Thanksgivings can keep us, as they kept Israel, open to newness and transformation if we but take the risk and share them. Have we opted, instead, for control and safety in our liturgies as a protection against surprises and the newness of God's transforming power?

Psalm 47

Another psalm type that expresses new orientation is the enthronement psalm, also called the hymn to God the Sovereign. Even though form-critically this type of psalm is a hymn, not all hymns express new orientation. Enthronement psalms emerge naturally out of Israel's claim that its God is supreme as Creator of the whole earth (Ps. 104) and is especially enthroned in Zion (Pss. 46 and 48). It makes sense that Israel would argue that since its God is sovereign over all the created world, its God also claims sovereignty over other gods and peoples of the world.

Something new happens in the enthronement hymns, if we take them seriously as instruments of what Brueggemann calls "world-construction" in our liturgies.[5] Our worship not only directs our praise to heaven as a response to God but also constitutes a social act that shapes human community and the commitments we make in the world. The alternative community that emerges from the liturgical process is in tension with other kinds of community already in existence because it is shaped by the character of Adonai.

Sigmund Mowinckel argued that for Israel, the central liturgical act is the celebration of the enthronement of Adonai as sovereign during the annual New Year festival.[6] Most probably God's enthronement was celebrated liturgically, perhaps with a procession that included the ark of the covenant (2 Sam. 6:15), but whether as part of a specific festival we cannot know. The enthronement psalms construct a world over which Adonai rules, a world that challenges all other known worlds. These psalms proclaim God reigns, which J. Clinton McCann calls "the theological heart of the psalter."[7] Our use of the enthronement psalms in Christian liturgy today can challenge us, too, to create an alternative community in which Jesus Christ is truly sovereign.

Enthronement psalms include Psalms 47, 93, and 96 through 99. Psalm 47 surfaces the essential features of the type. It begins as other hymns we have seen, with an introductory call to praise in verse 1: "All you peoples, clap your hands! Shout to God with the sound of joyous shouting!" The description of a coronation in 2 Kings 11:12 notes that after the king was crowned and anointed, the people "clapped their hands" and shouted, "Long live the king." The call to praise in Psalm 47 is sweeping: "all peoples" are addressed, not just Israel, and they are to clap and shout with joy; "nations" echoes this sweep in verse 8. Artur Weiser notes how the clapping is an appropriate response to this world sovereign; it is "a thunderous echo of the divine might."[8] Everyone is called on to acknowledge God's sovereignty, which is not seen as oppressive or burdensome, but as cause for celebration.

The body of the hymn begins in verse 2 and continues through verse 4, presenting the reasons for the praise: "For Adonai Most High is awesome, a great sovereign over all the earth"; this declaration is echoed by verse 7: "For God is the sovereign of all the earth." The scope is universal; God reigns over *all* the earth. Adonai Most High in Hebrew is Adonai Elyon. Elyon is the high god of the Jebusites, a Canaanite people of pre-Davidic Jerusalem. Israel's God takes over Elyon's functions and characteristics. "Most High" echoes the verbs "gone up" in verse 5 and "highly exalted" in verse 9.[9]

In this sense we can see how the enthronement psalms are perhaps derived from songs that celebrate Israel's victory over its enemies (for example, Ex. 15 and the Song of Miriam celebrate the defeat of Pharaoh and his Egyptian army). Elyon is used frequently in the Hebrew Bible where foreign peoples, in addition to the Israelites, are present.[10] In the same way, Christian doxologies and the Gloria Patri ("Glory be to the Father") express our claims for the victory of our God over all the others.

In verses 3 and 4, reference is made to the saving history of God's actions on Israel's behalf during the settlement in Canaan: "Adonai subdues peoples under us, and nations under our feet. Adonai chooses our heritage for us, the pride of Jacob whom Adonai loves." Israel is chosen, elected by God to a special relationship with God, who carries out mighty acts for its sake. Israel's heritage is the promised land, which has been taken from the people already in it; these subjugated "peoples" are called on in the opening verse (the same noun is used) to clap and shout in joy to Adonai.

Yet, lest we think that this is simply a psalm that rubs salt into the wounds of the subjugated people and legitimates Israel's oppression of them, we must look more closely. Israel's election is a function of the grace of this awesome God who is sovereign over all the earth. It is this grace that undergirds the call to praise. The focus in verses 1–4 is on God, not Israel. There is no hint that Israel is to dominate the Gentile nations in the future. The end of the psalm makes this very clear, as we shall see.

Verses 5–7 form their own little liturgical section. They seem to indicate that some cultic drama or procession is taking place. Verse 5 declares: "God has gone up with a shout, Adonai with the sound of a trumpet." Perhaps the ark of the covenant, the invisible throne of God and symbol of God's presence in battle, is being carried in procession to the sanctuary or temple. The verb used for God's going up, *'alah,* is a technical term for the pilgrimage to Jerusalem or the holy place of worship. God has gone up to take God's rightful place as the end goal of the peoples' pilgrimages; the sovereign of all the earth is to be worshiped by all the peoples of the earth. How appropriate that early Christianity used Psalm 47 as one of the psalms for Ascension Day.

The cultic declaration in verse 5 is followed by a mini-hymn for the processional in verses 6 and 7. Verse 5 seems to be the center of the psalm. *Selah* after verse 4 sets the first section of the psalm apart from the cultic shout in verse 5. Verse 6 offers a call to praise that begins a new psalm section as it echoes verse 1. The call to praise in verse 6 commands: "Sing praises to God, sing praises! Sing praises to our sovereign, sing praises!" God is called "king" or "sovereign" also in Psalms 5:2; 10:16; 44:4; 48:2; 68:24; 84:3; 145:1; and 149:2. The body or motive for the praise is offered in 47:7a: "For sovereign of all the earth is God." Verse 7b concludes with a renewed call to praise: "Sing praises with a psalm." "Sing praises" is repeated five times in verses 6 and 7; the words "God" and "our king" are surrounded by the words "praise." Such praise of the universal sovereign is expected and deserved. The use of "sovereign [*melek*] over all the earth" in verses 2 and 7 ties the two sections of the psalm together. The peoples in verse 1 shout "with the sound of joyous shouting," while in verse 5, God goes up with a shout. The repetition of the word "earth" in verses 2, 7, and 9 also ties the psalm together and underscores the universal sovereignty of God.

Verse 8 offers the possibility for new orientation: "Elohim *malak* over the nations; God sits on [God's] holy throne." The first half of the verse is translated in many different ways: "God reigns over the nations"; "God has become sovereign over the nations"; "God has always reigned over the nations"; "God has just now become sovereign over the nations." (The other enthronement psalms use Adonai [LORD], Israel's special name for God, instead of Elohim [God].)

The emphasis in this psalm is most probably not on God's continuing reign as sovereign but rather on the action of this moment, when God just now becomes sovereign. This is what liturgy is, not just a recollection or remembering, but a making so, "an enactment of a fresh drama in this moment."[11] This is news, not merely the repeating of what has always been the case. The claim of verse 8 becomes real at this moment in the liturgy; it is genuinely new. God begins a new reign through this communal act of worship; God's reign is continually renewed in worship.

The news must be experienced, not simply affirmed. To sing "Christ the Lord Is Risen Today" on Easter Sunday morning is to make it so, to begin a new part of the liturgical year, to orient ourselves anew in the world. The church's liturgy dramatizes this new world here and now. At Christmas, which Brueggemann calls the festival of enthronement, we sing, "Joy to the world! The Lord is come…the Savior reigns"; the church enacts Jesus' coming to power in this very moment.

Brueggemann warns that "this dramatic enactment is not game playing"; rooted in memory, this "fresh announcement" changes the world.[12] It is the announcement that evokes from us new ways of being in the world. Brueggemann suggests that one can see the same dynamic at work in the experience of the death of a loved one. The death has no significance until the news is told. I remember that to be the case when my brother died. In my denial, I could not accept the news until I started telephoning the relatives to tell them what had happened. After about the fifth call, his death became more real to me, and I set about making arrangements for bringing his body home.

Because it is Adonai who has come to reign just now over all the earth, the earth is presented with the possibility just now of reflecting this divine character. In Psalms 96, 98, and 99, Adonai is great and judges the peoples with equity and righteousness. In Psalm 97, Adonai preserves and delivers the covenant loyal ones *(hasidim)*. This is good news and a source of joy. "All the earth" is called to "sing a new song" to Adonai and shout with joy in these enthronement psalms, for the world can now take on this divine character of righteousness and faithfulness.

In Psalm 47, God is awesome, the one who subdues; and "the shields of the earth belong to God" (v. 9). The "shields of the earth" (see also 2 Chron. 12:9–10) represent the earthly forces of war, symbols of political power, the subjugation of one people to another. All these belong to God and are not available to humankind. Here is a great eschatological picture of peace, much like that sketched in Psalm 46:8–9, in which God "makes wars cease to the ends of the earth, breaks the bow, and shatters the spear" and proclaims, "I am exalted!" So, too, does the psalmist end Psalm 47 with the declaration that "God is highly exalted."

This vision of peace is the possibility that the shout "God has just now become sovereign" holds out to the peoples of the earth and especially to Israel. This is the new world that can be set in motion by the liturgy of God's enthronement. Not only will peace reign in this newly constructed world, but distinctions will also be erased, as a careful reading of verse 9a reveals: "The princes of the peoples are gathered together, the people of the God of Abraham." The Hebrew text is elliptical; it lacks the word "as" or "with," which most English translations supply between the words "together" and "the people." Note that the leaders of the peoples are not called "sovereigns," because only God deserves such a title. These peoples do not become part of the people of Israel, which would imply that Israel had subjugated them: "The princes of the people are gathered together as the people of the God of Abraham." Instead, the relationship between them and Israel is left ambiguous, full of possibilities in this newly constructed world enacted in liturgy. Perhaps this ambiguity serves to check the nationalistic overtones of verse 3, recalling the universalism of God's blessing on Abraham by whom "all the families of the earth shall be blessed" (Gen. 12:1–3).

In this eschatological picture (the picture of the end time), Israel and all the world's peoples worship the God to whom they all belong. The present oppressive structures of the world are challenged by the announcement of God's universal rule. "All who share the dramatic moment of announcement and celebration are energized to live in this new world with these fresh possibilities...therefore the world can act out its true character as God's creation."[13] What would that mean for our world today if we were to acknowledge God's universal rule? How radically different our political structures would be! "Globalization" would become real, rather than the abstract term it is for many. What stands in the way of our realizing the possibilities held out by the enthronement psalms? The answers include fear of people different from us, national pride, greed, thirst for power, and ignorance.

The social liberation thrust of what Brueggemann calls the "slave memory" of the exodus stands in tension with the "grand claims of the Jerusalem liturgy" supervised by the king in the enthronement psalms. The enthronement liturgy reflects the royal establishment and serves the status quo of the temple complex, Jerusalem politics, and the Davidic dynasty. The king is in charge of this liturgy and manages it. This control can work against the transformation possible in the enthronement liturgy. Therefore, to proclaim "God reigns" or "Adonai reigns" will have a different effect depending on who announces it, hears it, and believes it. The slave will hear hope; the upper-class worshipers in Solomon's temple will hear a threat. What do we hear on Sunday mornings? What do we mean when we sing "Christ the Lord Is Risen Today" on Easter Sunday?

Although the king as "participant, sponsor, and benefactor" of the enthronement festival shapes the liturgy, thereby controlling it, the king as "creature, child, and heir" of the liturgy will be shaped by it, critiqued by it, challenged by it. The king can submit to the liturgy and embrace the world of justice and righteousness that liturgy creates rather than the world of royal power. The king has choices to make concerning his own rule in Jerusalem in light of God's universal rule. The king can choose to do on earth what God does in heaven. Isn't this the choice we can make each time we pray "Thy kingdom come, Thy will be done, On earth as it is in heaven"? Do we simply mouth words, not realizing what is at stake? "The praise of Israel is not done in a social vacuum…Praise is the beginning of political practice."[14] Do we worship on Sunday morning in a social vacuum, or do we allow the liturgy to envision for us social, political, and economic possibilities? Do we worship to escape the world or to embrace it? If we use the enthronement psalms in our liturgy, we open ourselves, our world, and the way we run our world to critique and transformation. Liturgy and worship are risky business. Are we willing to take the risk?

A Choral Reading of Enthronement Psalm 93

Psalm 93, like Psalms 97 and 99, opens with the words: "Adonai is king." Normal Hebrew word order is reversed; the subject precedes the verb to emphasize the subject, "the LORD," who "is robed in majesty" and "girded with strength." This divine king is a warrior. Only Adonai, the warrior God, can subdue the chaos waters of verses 3–4: "the floods," "the mighty waters," and "the waves of the sea"(cf. Ps. 74:12–17). God's majesty is greater than that of the chaos waters, which the Canaanites personified as gods; God wins this cosmic battle. Israel can count on this God whose "decrees are very sure [faithful]" (93:5). This God is not simply a mighty, aloof warrior, but the subject of direct, second-person address in verses 2 and 5. The affirmation of Psalm 93 counters the theological crisis expressed in Book 3 of the Psalter, and especially in Psalm 89. "The reign of God is always proclaimed amid circumstances that seem to deny it."[15]

Choral speaking of Psalm 93 can contribute to our understanding of the claims that this psalm makes upon us. The following piece by Fredericka Nolde Berger, lecturer in religion and drama at Wesley Theological Seminary, illumines the power of choral speaking for our interpretive task. Numbered parts refer to solo voices; letters refer to designated groups of people.

Psalm 93

(SCORED FOR CHORAL SPEAKING BY FREDERICKA BERGER,
BASED ON THE JERUSALEM BIBLE)

    1: The Lord is king, robed in
UNISON: majesty
    2: The Lord is robed in
UNISON: power,
    3: he wears it like a belt.
    A: You have made the world firm,

UNISON: unshakable;

    B: your throne has stood since then,

    4: you existed from the first, O Lord.

    A: The rivers raise, O Lord,

  A,B: The rivers raise their voices

A,B,C: the rivers raise their thunders;

A,B,C,D: greater than the voice of ocean,

 B,C,D: transcending the waves of the sea,

  C,D: the Lord reigns

UNISON: transcendent

    D: In the heights.

    5: Your decrees will never alter;

UNISON: holiness

    6: Will distinguish your house,

    7: O Lord,

UNISON: for ever and ever.

Berger offers the following reflection on choral speaking:

In scoring a psalm, what instrument, or sound possibilities are available? Not many, not complicated, but enough to provide interesting variety. The basic vocal instruments for choral speaking are: solo, group, unison, high voices, low voices, male, female. If you are scoring a psalm for a specific service or an already established group, consider what speakers you want to involve. How many? What balance and quality of voices? Will it be intergenerational? Your script can be custom made.

Before you commence scoring, analyze the psalm so that you can be guided in your choices by the text. What lines need to stand out, whether by being very heavy and emphatic (unison) or clear and arresting (solo)? Where are the back and forth statements (alternate between groups)? Where do the thoughts or images build or decline (adding or subtracting voices)?

If you and your group want to make the psalm truly your own in a deep way, memorize it. I can hardly overstate how memorization strengthens the presentation in worship: no distracting books or papers held by the speaker, eye contact between the speakers and the congregation, and the forceful communication that comes when you, individually and as a group, have, as God admonished Ezekiel, eaten the scroll.

When the text has been memorized, the members of your group are freed to speak it not just from the neck up, but with the entire body. You will be well advised to design some simple and subtle choreography to provide visual variety and to underline the meaning of the text. As with the scoring, there are certain basic elements: where and when the speakers stand, how they are turned (full face, one quarter, one half, back), where they look, otherwise known as focus. In these choices as well, you must be guided by the demands of the text and the scoring. Are you using groups? Do you want to have them stand separately? Do you want to have them stand at different times, or start with their backs to the congregation and turn at different times? This is a way of bringing them into the scene. Do you want to have a solo speaker separate, or in another part of the sanctuary? Do you want an antiphonal group of speakers? Where do you want the speakers to look when they are speaking? Does everyone look in the same place? When does the text suggest the need for a change in focus? You will be impressed with how effective a simple change of visual focus can be.

For Psalm 93, I separated out the attributes of the Lord and had them delivered in unison. In the dramatic part where the rivers "raise their voices" I scored a crescendo by increasing the number of voices on each line. This is followed by a decrescendo to the solo on "your decrees will never alter." In general, the solo voices give the commentary.[16]

Psalm 8

Psalm 8 is all about risk. It is about the risk God takes in sharing with human beings the care for the created order. Psalm 8 is usually classified as a hymn to God the Creator, because it expresses the theme of orientation, of a secure, well-ordered, trustworthy, no-surprise world. I would like to treat it here as a psalm of new orientation, of surprise, of new life on the other side of the pit experience. I want to focus on Psalm 8 as a tool, not of social control and the status quo, but of social critique and transformation. There is an eschatological picture in Psalm 8 that calls us back to God's intentions for us and empowers our lives as human beings. It speaks of our becoming rather than of our being. If Psalm 8 is proclaimed, heard, and believed as a psalm of divine risk, it challenges us to reconsider our way in the world and with each other.

Psalm 8 gives powerful testimony about creation (cosmology), God (theology), and human beings (anthropology). It can be broken down into the three-part hymn structure that we studied in chapter 3: introduction, body, and conclusion (or the summons to praise, the motive or reason for praise, and the renewed call to praise). The introduction in verse 1a is not a call to praise, but rather a declaration about God that would naturally evoke praise:

"O Adonai, our ruler, how majestic is your name in all the earth!" This declaration is repeated in the final verse, 9, creating a powerful envelope structure. What is inserted in the envelope of verses 1b–8 explains concretely what it means to claim that God's name is majestic.

Majesty has to do with God's all-encompassing power and presence. This is seen in the use of "all" as the main, thematic, key word of the psalm: "all the earth" in verses 1 and 9 and "all under [humankind's] feet" in verse 6. "Heavens" in verse 1b links with "earth" in verse 1a to reinforce the idea of "allness," of inclusiveness, and recalls the creation story in Genesis 1, where "heaven and earth" is the biblical idiom for "all of creation."[17] "Glory" *(hod)* in verse 1b (cf. Ps. 148:13) is often linked to the splendor of an earthly king (Ps. 21:5).

Verse 1b begins the body of the hymn, which gives the reason for the declaration and praise and which continues through verse 8. Verses 1b and 2 are difficult to translate from the Hebrew because of the words' uncertain meanings. The introduction may continue beyond verse 1a, depending on how an English translator punctuates the verses, with a period or with no period after 1b (the Hebrew text itself does not contain any periods or semicolons). The options for verses 1b and 2 include: "Thou whose glory above the heavens is chanted by the mouth of babes and infants, thou hast founded a bulwark because of thy foes, to still the enemy and the avenger" (RSV) or "You whose glory above the heavens is chanted. By the mouth of babes and infants at the breast you have founded a bulwark against your foes, to still the enemy and the avenger."

In the second translation, verse 1b is taken with the first half of verse 1 so that "heavens" and "earth" are counterpoints. Yet verse 1b can at the same time be taken with verse 2 so that God's majesty and babies are counterpoints.[18] In the second translation, the poet feels God's power working even in the praise of little children; and God's enemies, those who deny God's power and refuse to recognize the majesty of God's name, are overcome by that power. That is, God's name is majestic precisely because it is revealed in small things. Children's praise has great power. Jesus recognized this in the cries of the little children who shouted, "Hosanna to the son of David " upon his entry into Jerusalem: "'Out of the mouths of babes and sucklings thou hast brought perfect praise'" (Mt. 21:16, RSV). Compare this with Paul's remarks in 2 Corinthians 12:9. On weak infants God builds a "bulwark" (Hebrew: "strength"). Verse 2 of the psalm pulls us in from the idea of God's name, majestic throughout the whole earth, to the human being. There is dignity and challenge for the human being in this contrast.

In verses 3 and 4, the psalmist seems overwhelmed by the grandeur of creation and the Creator: "When I look at your heavens, the work of your fingers, the moon and the stars that you have set in place, what is [the human being]that you are mindful of [her], and the mortal person that you care for [him]?" Human beings seem inconsequential in comparison to the expanse of the heavens and God's creation. The difference between God the Creator and the creature is revealed by a look at the stars. I distinctly remember experiencing the awe of the psalmist in March 1997 upon emerging from a Maundy Thursday service at my local church. As the congregation filed out in silence, we stepped into the parking lot to see blazing brightly above us the Hale-Bopp comet, tail and all. We let out a collective gasp and simply stood silently for fifteen minutes watching what had not been seen for 4,200 years and would not be seen again until the year 4397. No wonder that Apollo 11 left a disc on the moon containing Psalm 8.[19]

Note that verse 3 shows a movement of specification: The psalmist looks at the heavens (3a) and then at what is contained within the heavens, the moon and the stars (3b). There is also vertical movement between verses 3 and 4; the psalmist's gaze moves down from the heavens to the earth, to human beings. The Hebrew for "man" (RSV) in verse 4a, *'enosh,* is found mostly in poetic texts and can mean humans, humankind, or a single person. It comes from a verb root that means "to be weak or sick." The Hebrew in verse 4b for "son of man" (RSV), *ben-'adam* (literally, "child of a human being") occurs frequently in Ezekiel to underscore the difference between the human, mortal, earthly being and the infinite, immortal, and powerful God (cf. Ps. 90:3; 144:3). Thus, we have a movement of intensification in the nouns of verse 4a and 4b.

This stress on the smallness and insignificance of human beings is somewhat countered by the verbs of verse 4, "remember" or "be mindful of" and "care for" or "visit," which also show a movement of intensification. This intensification juxtaposes the majesty of the creator God with the intimate care of the deliverer God. This intimate relationship between Creator and creature is underscored by the use of "work of your fingers" in verse 3a, a variation of the usual "work of your hands" found for God's creation in the psalms. "Fingers" suggests more delicate work, more care and tenderness. God is not only over all as Creator, majestically enthroned in the heavens, but is also intimately connected with creation, tending it, caring for it. This is as much a source of awe and wonder for the psalmist of Psalm 8 as it is for the psalmist of Psalm 144 (v. 3).

It is striking that the verbs "be mindful of" and "care for" in Psalm 8:4 are also found frequently in lament psalms, especially in the petitions. The psalmist pleads with God to "be mindful of me and care for me" (as in Jeremiah's lament in Jer. 15:15). The laments plead for this intimacy, which is not being experienced in the pit of disorientation. Also, Job 7:17–19 offers a bitter parody of the verbs in Psalm 8: "What is the [human being] that you make so much of him, and that you set your mind on [her], visit him every morning and test [her] every moment? How long will you not look away from me, nor let me be until I swallow my spittle?" Job would prefer it if God left him alone and didn't pay so much attention to him. For Job, God no longer seems concerned in an intimate and positive way toward God's creation. Job is not experiencing God's order and tenderness and care. God's concern has become a torment to Job, as it is for the psalmist in Psalm 39:13.

Despite the inconsequence of human beings in the vast expanse of the created order, the psalmist of Psalm 8 admits that God has given human beings an extraordinary place in creation: "Yet you have made [us] little less than God and crowned [us] with glory and splendor" (v. 5). This is royal language, the language of enthronement, but it is used for human beings, not for God or the earthly sovereign. The sense of human insignificance expressed in verse 3 is challenged by the puzzled question of verse 4 (about how God could care for such an insignificant one) and then decisively overturned by the assertion of verse 5. The "yet" of verse 5 underscores this juxtaposition of frail creature with gifted one "little less than God."

It is alarming to note how many English translators back away from the bold claim of verse 5 that God has made us "little less than God" (RSV). Some translate it "little less than gods" (cf. Ps. 82:1). This translation suggests the heavenly council or divine assembly around God's throne, perhaps like "the sons of God" in Job 1:6 or 2:1 or "the host of heaven" in 1 Kings 22:19. Other translations have "little less than a god," meaning, perhaps, the deities who don't really count in the ancient Near East. Other translations, such as Jerome's Vulgate, use "little less than angels" (the reading in the note of JPS offers "divine" instead of "angels" in the main text). This reading seems to claim a little less for humankind. All these translations are possible except "angels," for which another Hebrew word is usually used. The Hebrew in Psalm 8 is *'elohim,* one of the names for God but also the word for the gods of Canaan. The Septuagint (LXX) translates "angels" and "a little" in the temporal sense of "for a little while," which is picked up in Hebrews 2:6–8 to explain that Jesus was made lower than the angels "for a little while" until his death brought him honor and superiority over the angels.

We seem to be quite uncomfortable with the challenge of being "little less than God," yet this is what is also implied by Genesis 1, which asserts that we have been made in God's image and given dominion over creation. Perhaps in its assessment of human nature as corrupt and sinful, Christian anthropology with its "worm theology," a legacy of Augustine and the early church, leaves no room for this empowering view of humankind. J. David Pleins suggests that these verses neither humiliate nor exalt us, but rather show us living "between dust and divinity" so that we might "gain some perspective on power and poverty, history and idolatry."[20]

Verse 6 specifies the meaning of the crowning of the human creature made little less than God: "You have given [us] dominion over the works of your hands; you have put all things under [our] feet." The word for "dominion" here is not the same as the one used in Genesis 1:28. It is often used in the psalms for God's rule or mastery (see Pss. 22:28; 103:19). God delegates our authority to us. In verses 7 and 8, this dominion is detailed: "sheep, oxen, beasts of the field, birds of the air, fish of the sea." Creatures in the three spheres of the created order are named to specify what "all things under our feet" means. Again, the sense of "all," of the whole created order, is communicated. By quoting this phrase, 1 Corinthians 15:27–29 anticipates the time in which everything will come under the rule of Christ.

The discussion of the place of human beings in God's creation and of the dominion given human beings over the earth immediately calls to mind the Genesis 1 creation story. In Genesis 1:26, after God creates an orderly world out of chaos, male and female are created in God's image and given dominion over the earth. In both Genesis 1 and Psalm 8, the human being is seen as made for relationship with God, which involves human dominion over the created order. Some theologians have argued that Psalm 8 is a commentary on Genesis 1, but Brueggemann argues that the influence could be in the other direction: "The narrative derives from the doxology."[21] In one look up at the heavens, the psalmist brings into play all at once questions, awe, and sense of self. The poetry of Psalm 8 offers us a simultaneous and synthetic view of God, the world, and our place in the world, rather than a sequential or a narrative description. This view of the dignity of human beings in Psalm 8 was nothing short of revolutionary in the ancient Near East among Israel's neighbors. The gods of these other nations personified the powers of nature, such as wind, lightning, rain, the sea. All significant activity was located in the heavenly realm of the gods. The gods had dominion over the earth; humans served the gods and had to pattern their earthly life after the heavenly. Humans were servants of the gods in the ancient Near Eastern myths, doing the dirty work the gods felt themselves too good to do.

This is what makes us little less than God. The fact that God takes a risk in giving us dominion over the earth can be seen in the debate over what dominion means in Psalm 8 and Genesis 1. Phyllis Trible argues that some people insist that dominion is a license to plunder, abuse, and pollute the earth and ravage one another as we please; they blame the present ecological crisis on Genesis 1.[22] A close reading of Genesis 1, however, shows that dominion is God's good gift. We are trustees and stewards of God's creation, responsible for the ongoing health of God's world. Our separation from nature does not mean that we must be antagonistic toward it. Separation is part of the fabric of creation, night separated from day by the lights, the waters separated by the firmament, plants and animals differentiated according to their kind. Dominion is not alienation, but harmonious control. Dominion is a limited gift. It is checked and defined by the context of the affirmation of the goodness and harmony of creation. Over all is God, who establishes order and delegates responsibilities.

The very structure of Psalm 8 makes this point. The psalmist does not dwell on human significance. The envelope of praise of God's majestic name in verses 1 and 9 makes our human centeredness, our self-centeredness impossible. Lest we focus only on ourselves, the psalmist pulls us out of ourselves and back to God in verses 5–8, and in verse 9 repeats the opening declaration about God's majestic name. Human dignity points to God, who has granted that dignity. Psalm 8 focuses on God the Creator; creation and human beings are secondary, pointing back to God. Human status is framed by God's reign. This connection is underscored by the use of the Hebrew particle *mah* in both the divine envelope formed by verses 1 and 9 (translated "how") and in the human focus of verse 4 (translated "what"). This God-focus puts human beings and the created order in right relationship to God and one another. As Brueggemann puts it, "Doxology gives dominion its context and legitimacy."[23] Psalm 8 centers us on God and calls us to a dominion of responsible stewardship and trusteeship. Our modern, self-centered, technological society, which operates under the illusion that we are in control, stands challenged by the words of Psalm 8.

How can the human creature responsibly exercise dominion over all of God's magnificent creation? Walter Harrelson suggests that we can do so by being made whole, made new, opened up to the powers of divine creativity in our acts of celebration and worship.[24] In worship, the beauty and the terror of God's presence and of our mixed-up world are laid bare. Worship confronts us with the consequences of our disobedience and with the risk God has taken in giving us responsibility in our exercise of dominion. Worship does not allow us to leave the world outside at the front door of the church. In worship we examine ourselves and our lives in God's presence. Mysteriously, we are renewed for our God-given task. If liturgy constructs worlds, as Brueggemann maintains, then Psalm 8 can generate a new world, the world that God intends for us, in the very moment of its use in worship. The new world is an eschatological world of responsible stewardship and God-centeredness. It lures us. As Harrelson states: "Capacity to receive the world as God's world, capacity to exult in its good and to grieve over its wounds, capacity to take our place in its order-being-established—this is what we most profoundly want."[25] This is what awaits us in worship if we but risk it, if we want it enough. This is what makes us whole. A journey through the psalms—hymns, wisdom psalms, laments, thanksgivings, enthronement psalms—is a path to wholeness, a way of constructing this new world in our liturgies. Within this new world that God intends, we are free to become, to be all that God intends us to be; we are whole and healthy persons.

God, the Holy One, has invited us to join in this process of world building through our worship, which empowers us. The psalms used in our worship can express the full range of our humanness—our pain, our anger, our joy, our hopes, our thanks. Psalms engage us as whole persons and thus can help us to deal honestly with God, one another, and our world, making us better world builders. How we hear and use the psalms affects greatly the kind of world we build. The psalms present us with eschatological pictures, if we would but open ourselves to them, of a world even now coming into being. How full of wonder that is! Hallelujah!

APPENDIX

A Service of Silence and Lamentation for Good Friday or Holy Saturday

Jesus' first followers did not know—although they had been told—that there would be a resurrection. When he was crucified, died on the cross, and was taken down and buried, the disciples and the women who followed Jesus thought that Jesus' ministry was ended and that their relationship with him was now over. The purpose of a Good Friday or Holy Saturday service is to allow us to enter into the experience of apparent abandonment by God as Jesus expressed it in his cry from the cross and as some of his followers must surely have felt during the interim between his crucifixion and resurrection. We enter into this time of silence and lamentation as a way of affirming and entering into our own sense of abandonment and despair, which many of us experience from time to time, but which we are not always encouraged, allowed, or enabled to voice.

The sanctuary is darkened—with just enough light to see. A spotlight is on the bare cross, and its reflection is cast against the front wall of the sanctuary so that its shadow is clearly visible. The chancel has been stripped of its furnishings (candles, banners, Bible, center floral arrangements), and the few paraments left are dark and coarse…Ushers gently encourage worshipers to enter in silence.

PRELUDE *(Approximately five minutes of discordant music, begun at the designated time for worship to begin. May be preceded by more traditional but somber music as worshipers are entering. The prelude proper is designed to cause a sense of "disorientation"—thus setting the mood for what may be for many the disorientation of the worship service proper. Following the prelude, a moment of silence is kept before the presider greets the congregation.)*

GREETING
My God, my God, why have you forsaken me? *Psalm 22:1a*

LITANY OF COMPLAINT
O God, where are you?
> **We sit in darkness, longing for your presence.**

We have heard of your love. Many of us have known your love.
> **But tonight your love seems far away.**

We have heard of your Spirit. We have experienced your Spirit's warmth and energy and light.
> **But tonight we wonder if we only dreamed of your presence and your power.**

We have stood before your Word and listened to your truth for our lives. But now all is silence, and there is no word from God.

SILENCE
Allow two to three minutes of total silence.

HYMNS OF LAMENT
"Sometimes I Feel Like a Motherless Child"
"Nobody Knows the Trouble I've Seen"

CALL FOR CRIES OF ABANDONMENT
Instead of our usual call for "concerns and celebrations," tonight you are invited to lift up those people, places, and circumstances where God's absence seems more real than God's presence. The response to each offering will echo the lament of Psalm 22 with which we opened our worship service, **"My God, My God, why have you forsaken us?"**

RESPONSE TO OUR PRAYERS
"Precious Lord, Take My Hand"

DANCE OF THE ABANDONED
If your worshiping community has persons experienced in sacred dance, this would be an appropriate place in the service for music and choreography that would draw the congregation further into the experience of abandonment. Another option would be to use discordant music (similar to the opening prelude) by itself.

Scripture

Listen now to the voices of Holy Scriptures.

    Listen to the cries of abandonment and distresss.

Listen,

    and hear the sounds of your own tears, your own grief.

Lamentations 1:1–4; 2:10–13; 3:46–48; 4:4
Jeremiah 20:14–18; 31:15

Witnesses

Listen to the voices of those who followed Jesus of Nazareth.

    Listen to their cries of abandonment and distress.

Listen,

    and hear the sounds of your own grief and disillusionment.

The witnesses, dressed in dark clothing, speak from the back and sides of the sanctuary. As each one finishes speaking, he or she moves to the center chancel area under a muted spotlight and takes his or her place there in a bowed or kneeling position. When all four are in place, they form a cross. They remain standing or kneeling until the next period of silence, during which time they move silently out of view.

Sarah speaks first

My name is Sarah, and I am a witness to death.
My joy died today.

Actually, I'm more than a witness.

    I experienced death.

Not too many months ago, I became very ill;

    my body shook with fever.

    I hurt so I could hardly move.

My parents grew more and more worried

    as their prayers seemed to fall on deaf ears

    and all their loving attention seemed to no avail.

My father Jairus is an important man in our community,

    a ruler in the synagogue.

    He didn't understand why this was happening to his daughter!

He heard of a young rabbi from Nazareth.

    He went to hear him preach once at Capernaum

    Later he said that there was something unusual about Jesus' teaching,

        and he saw him actually cure a man—on the Sabbath, mind you!—

        Father wasn't sure that was right.

But as I grew weaker and father and mother were more desperate for a cure,
>   he called for the young teacher to come and lay hands on me.

I don't remember exactly what happened next.
>   Things got very confused in my mind,
>   and there there was nothing but black silence.
The next thing I knew
>   I heard the kindest voice I could ever imagine calling to me.
I opened my eyes
>   and looked into the most loving eyes I've ever seen.
I was astonished to find that I could sit up
>   and walk,
>   and eat...
>   with no pain or fever.
I danced around the room,
>   joining with joy those who had come to mourn my death.

I was brought back to life,
>   but now I'm filled with a new kind of pain and confusion,
>   and once again the sound of mourning fills the air.

My name is Sarah, and I am a witness to death.
>   I experienced death—and was called back to life and joyful living.
>   But my new life, my joy died today.

Then Benjamin speaks
My name is Benjamin, and I am a witness to death
My dreams died today.
>   I had hoped that the One crucified this day
>   would be the one who could cure my affliction.
Born with a withered hand,
>   I've suffered taunts and jeers all my life.
>   It's hard when you can't play like your friends
>   or work the way your father and uncles and cousins expect you to.
>   It's hard when the rabbis and even your parents
>   are suspicious that there must be some evil deep within you
>   because you weren't born whole and well.

I had heard stories of this Jesus of Nazareth,
>   heard that he was a miracle worker unlike any other.
I begged my parents to let me go to him for healing,
>   but they always said no.
>   I think sometimes they were afraid that to seek healing

would be a sign of unfaithfulness
or unwillingness to submit to God's punishing wrath.

I so wanted to be made well
that I finally ran away.
I caught up with some people crowding into Jerusalem for Passover,
following the healer.

I was excited,
filled with hope,
thinking that now was my chance!

But instead of having my withered hand restored to wholeness,
I spent the day watching my hopes and dreams die on a cross.
I wanted so to believe that healing and new life were possibilities.
Now I don't know what to believe—or what to do.

My name is Benjamin, and I am a witness to death.
My dreams died today.

John speaks

My name is John, and I am a witness to death.
My future died today.

I was the brightest of the disciples—Jesus' favorite—he said so himself.
And I had a big future with Jesus as he rose to prominence.
Who else, besides Peter, was asked to be present at the raising of Jairus'
daughter?
Who else was invited to climb that mountain and see Moses and Elijah?
Who else, besides Peter, of course, did he take with him
when he went to the garden to pray—
Was that only yesterday? a few hours ago?

If Peter was going to be the muscle, the driving force behind Jesus' kingdom,
someone was going to have to supply the brains,
and that was clearly going to be me.
You can ask any of the other disciples.
I had gifts they didn't have.

But none of that matters.
It's all over now,
three years of hard work and sacrifice—for nothing.

But it was worth it just to know him.
It was worth it just to have heard him teach
and to have seen all the things we were privileged to see.

He really was a prophet and healer like no other.
　　But his kingdom—our kingdom—that we hoped for,
　　that's gone.
　　It will never come to pass now.

Yes, I will care for his mother.
　　I'll love her as my own mother.
　　Together we will cherish his memory.
　　　　We'll never, ever forget.

We might as well live in the past.

My name is John, and I am a witness to death.
My future died today.

Johanna speaks last
My name is Johanna, and I am a witness to death.
My past died forever today.

I have lived as a woman of some means.
　　My husband manages Herod's personal estate.
　　We were used to comfort and respect.
But, if you must know, demons tormented me.
　　I would be fine one moment
　　　　and filled with a terrifying spirit the next.
And despite our comfortable home and active social life,
　　my days seemed more and more empty and meaningless.

Then I went with some of my friends,
　　almost on a lark,
to hear a Jewish teacher who claimed he had the key to abundant life.
I was captured by the truth of his teaching
　　and went to hear him again and again whenever I could.
　　I began to serve the poor
　　　　and found more joy in that than in any of the parties I used
　　　　to attend.

One day I was able to get really close to him.
　　He spoke to me, and it was as though he knew all about me.
　　He rebuked the evil spirit that had tormented me,
　　　　and somehow, following him gave my life meaning and purpose.

I became committed to following him and serving his God
　　and joined a company of women who had similar stories to tell
　　　　of the way he had transformed their lives.

Now he is dead,
> and I'm not sure what will happen to the newfound purpose
> and meaning
>> I've experienced as one of his followers.

I do know that I will continue to keep vigil.
I will mourn and watch with Mary his mother, and Mary of Migdal, and the others.

My name is Johanna, and I am a witness to death.
My past died forever today,
> and all I could do is mourn and wail and keep watch.

RESPONSIVE READING
Psalm 22:1–18 *(Consider using a sung response.)*

AN INVITATION TO SILENT REFLECTION
If we cannot be honest here, where can we be honest?
If we cannot be honest before God,
> is it worth being honest anywhere?

If we cannot bring our pain to this holy place,
> where can we take our pain?

SILENCE
Allow two to three minutes of silence.

DISMISSAL
My God, my God, why have you forsaken me?
That is how we began our time of worship together this evening.
Old Testament scholar Walter Brueggemann has said that this haunting,
> plaintive, terrible cry is in its essence "an act of hope, knowing
> that full communion is the measure of being a finished self in
> the presence of God."[1]

If we can only be finished selves in the presence of God,
> perhaps living for a little while
>> with the sense of how very unfinished,
>> how very needy,
>>> we are,
> we will draw ever closer to the mysterious absence
>> we have invoked tonight.

My God, my God, why have you forsaken me?

We have lingered over this cry this evening.
> We have heard its echo in the pages of scripture.

We have heard its echo in our own lives and in our own world.
We have tried to enter into the despair and loneliness
    of those who heard the One
        they thought was their Master and Savior
        cry out with those words
            as he took his final breath.

As you leave in the dark and silence this evening,
    may that cry echo in your heart
    and may you hear in that cry
        the voice of hope.

Go in peace to pray and meditate on this fearful and holy night.

The congregation is dismissed into a darkened narthex. There is no postlude.

Notes

CHAPTER 1
Praying the Psalms, Praying into Wholeness

[1]Roland Murphy, "The Faith of the Psalmist," *Interpretation* 34 (1980): 237.

[2]My thanks to my former student, Rev. John Wesley Moore, a Lakota who has enriched many of my classes with Native American insights, for calling my attention to this saying.

[3]Kathleen D. Billman and Daniel L. Migliore, *Rachel's Cry: Prayer of Lament and Rebirth of Hope* (Cleveland: United Church Press, 1999), 1–3.

[4]Ibid., 4. Similarly, J. Clinton McCann, "The Book of Psalms: Introduction, Commentary, and Reflections," *The New Interpreter's Bible*, vol. 4 (Nashville: Abingdon Press, 1996), 674, notes that "the inseparability of cross and resurrection is analogous to the way in which lament and praise are finally inseparable in the psalms."

[5]Patrick Miller, *Interpreting the Psalms* (Philadelphia: Fortress Press, 1986), 67.

[6]Torah is Hebrew for "instruction," or "guidance." The Greek translation is "law," but this is too narrow. In Judaism, Torah refers especially to the first five books of Moses, or the Pentateuch, which contain law, poetry, narrative, myths, geneologies, saga, and so forth.

[7]Walter Brueggemann, "Bounded by Obedience and Praise: The Psalms as Canon," in *The Psalms and the Life of Faith,* ed. Patrick D. Miller (Minneapolis: Fortress Press, 1995), 211.

[8]Ibid., 213.

[9]Renita Weems, *Listening for God: A Minister's Journey through Silence and Doubt* (New York: Simon & Schuster, 1999), 25. "No one is ever prepared to endure the long silence that follows intimacy."

[10]Samuel E. Balentine, *The Hidden God: The Hiding of the Face of God in the Old Testament* (Oxford: Oxford University Press, 1983), 166.

[11]Billman and Migliore, *Rachel's Cry,* 30.

[12]A typical example of this emphasis is offered by L. J. Baggott, *The Seven Penitential Psalms: A Book of Lenten Studies* (London: A.R. Mowbray & Co., 1963). Baggott writes that "the purpose of this little book is to help the sincere Christian in deepened devotional endeavour towards true penitence and renewal" (p. 8); these seven laments have great "purifying power."

[13]Billman and Migliore, *Rachel's Cry,* 28.

[14]Murphy, "The Faith of the Psalmist," 236.

[15]Martin E. Marty, *A Cry of Absence: Reflections for the Winter of the Heart* (San Francisco: HarperSanFrancisco, 1993), xi.

[16]Darrell J. Fasching, "Faith and Ethics after the Holocaust: What Christians Can Learn from the Jewish Narrative Tradition of *Hutzpah*," *Journal of Ecumenical Studies* 27, no. 3 (Summer 1990): 454. Fasching argues that the more complex model of faith in Judaism supported the moral resistance of the Jews in the Holocaust, while its absence in Christianity led to accommodation and compromise with the Nazis. A reconstruction of Christian faith and ethics in light of the *Shoah* (destruction, rather than Holocaust, which means burnt offering) must take into account the dialectical complexity of Jewish faith.

[17]See also Arthur Waskow, *God-Wrestling* (New York: Schocken Books, 1978).

[18]See Billman and Migliore, *Rachel's Cry*, 33–40 for a discussion of lament in the New Testament, though lament is conceived primarily as passionate petition, not *hutzpah.*

[19]For what follows, see Belden E. Lane, "*Hutzpa K'Lapei Shamaya:* A Christian Response to the Jewish Tradition of Arguing with God," *Journal of Ecumenical Studies* 23, no. 4 (Fall 1986): 583–84.

[20]Elaine Pagels, *Adam, Eve, and the Serpent* (New York: Random House, 1988) supports Lane's analysis indirectly. She argues that the Christian movement became more powerful under the emperor Constantine, so that by the mid-fourth century, Christian teaching shifted from a celebration of human freedom to an emphasis on the universal bondage of original sin. Sinners do not pray with *hutzpah.*

[21]Compare the comment from Terence Fretheim: "Prayer gives God more room in which to work, makes God more welcome, creates more relational space (less distance) for God." See Terence Fretheim, "Prayer in the Old Testament: Creating Space in the World for God," in *A Primer on Prayer,* ed. Paul R. Sponheim (Philadelphia: Fortress, 1988), 52.

[22]The Reverend Dr. Victoria Bailey is a Doctor of Ministry graduate of Wesley Theological Seminary. This service was prepared as a liturgical response to an immersion experience in Poland and the Holocaust sites in which she participated with me as part of the Spirituality and the Suffering of God D.Min. program at Wesley Theological Seminary. Used by permission of the author.

[23]Billman and Migliore, *Rachel's Cry,* 14.

[24]Walter Brueggemann, "From Hurt to Joy, from Death to Life," *Interpretation* 28 (1974): 4.

[25]Robert Wuthnow, *After Heaven: Spirituality in America since the 1950s* (Berkeley: The University of California Press, 1998).

[26]Even the liturgical Psalter (for which I served as a reader/reviewer before its final editing) in the *United Methodist Hymnal* (Nashville: The United Methodist Publishing House, 1989) is guilty of this practice. Despite the fact that laments such as Psalms 13 and 137 stand, thankfully, in their entirety, others such as 44 and 77 do not. In the case of Psalm 44, only verses 1 to 8 are included, which declare God's saving acts in the past; this testimony serves to heighten the anguish of the following excluded verses, which describe God's very different present conduct. The contrast functions as the basis for the psalmist's appeal.

[27]Lester Meyer, "A Lack of Laments in the Church's Use of the Psalter," *Lutheran Quarterly* (Spring 1993): 67–78.

[28]This is a modification of an exercise found in the excellent manual by Donald Griggs, *Praying and Teaching the Psalms* (Nashville: Abingdon Press, 1984).

[29]See "Religious Images in Culture: Designing a Seminary Course in Theology and the Arts," an interview with Linnea Wren by Kimberly Vrudny in *Arts: The Arts in Religious and Theological Studies* 12, no. 2 (2000): 12–15.

[30]Patrick Ellis, Ph.D. candidate in liturgical studies at Drew University, shared this insight in a class on the psalms he took with me for his M.T.S. degree at Wesley Seminary.

[31]This reminder came as part of a presentation to the Wesley Seminary faculty by the Reverend Dr. Peggy Johnson, Distinguished Faculty, Deaf Ministry, during the fall 2000 semester.

[32]William L. Holladay, "How the Twenty-third Psalm Became an American Secular Icon" in *The Psalms through Three Thousand Years: Prayerbook of a Cloud of Witnesses* (Minneapolis: Fortress Press, 1993), 359–71. As Wayne Roosa argues in his discussion of the Bible's influence on cultural formation, "the immense significance and reach of the Bible's content has so deeply permeated the Western psyche that much of our mental furniture in terms of image, language and form is descended from it," Wayne Roosa, "At the Intersection of Contemporary Art and Biblical Themes," *Arts: The Arts in Religious and Theological Studies* 12, no. 2 (2000): 5. The poet Maya Angelou, in her inaugural poem for President Clinton in 1992, declared, "I am that Tree planted by the River," alluding to "the tree planted by streams of water" in Psalm 1:3. See Maya Angelou, *On the Pulse of the Morning* (New York: Random House, 1993).

[33]Weems, *Listening for God,* 18–19.

[34]Ibid., 20.

[35]For what follows, see Samuel E. Balentine, *Prayer in the Hebrew Bible: The Drama of Divine-Human Dialogue* (Minneapolis: Fortress Press, 1993), 251–52. See also Billman and

Migliore, *Rachel's Cry,* 60–66, which argues that Barth's piety was shaped by his understanding of the victory of God's grace in Jesus Christ over sin, suffering, and death, which puts all our sorrow already behind us. Only God has the right to complain; Jesus' misery encompasses and transcends all of ours. See chapter 3, "The Prayer of Lament in the Christian Theological Tradition," in which the piety of Augustine, Luther, Calvin, and Moltmann, in addition to Barth, is discussed in relation to their uses of lament.

[36]Weems, *Listening for God,* 16, 20.

[37]Dr. William B. McClain is Mary Elizabeth McGehee Joyce Professor of Preaching at Wesley Theological Seminary. He was an associate of Dr. Martin Luther King, Jr., during the civil rights movement. See also Marjorie Proctor-Smith, *Praying with Our Eyes Open: Engendering Feminist Liturgical Prayer* (Nashville: Abingdon Press, 1995).

[38]Balentine, *Prayer in the Hebrew Bible,* 9.

[39]Patrick D. Miller, *They Cried to the Lord: The Form and Theology of Biblical Prayer* (Minneapolis: Fortress Press, 1994), 1.

[40]A notable exception is *The Book of Psalms for Singing* (Pittsburgh: The Board of Education and Publication, Reformed Presbyterian Church of North America, 1973), which offers all 150 psalms in rhymed meter in the tradition of the Genevan and Scottish Psalters of the early 1600s.

[41]Elaine Ramshaw, *Ritual and Pastoral Care* (Philadelphia: Fortress Press, 1987): 31–32. Douglas J. Hall offered a similar critique in 1976 when he noted that Christianity was the "official religion of the officially optimistic society." See Douglas J. Hall, *Lighten Our Darkness: Toward an Indigenous Theology of the Cross* (Philadelphia: Westminster, 1976), 112. See also Robert J. Lifton and Greg Mitchell, *Hiroshima in America: Fifty Years of Denial* (New York: Putnam's Sons, 1995). Kathleen Norris notes how the laments do not make "comfortable reading" and go "against the American grain" of optimism and denial. This creates special problems for American women, who are culturally conditioned to deny their pain and smooth things over. See "The Paradox of the Psalms," in *Out of the Garden: Women Writers on the Bible,* ed. Christina Buchmann and Celina Spiegal (New York: Fawcett Columbine, 1994), 224.

[42]The Reverend Robin K. White is pastor of Faith Presbyterian Church in Baltimore, Maryland, and an M.Div. graduate of Lancaster Theological Seminary with a degree in music from Ithaca College. The Reverend Dana Schlegel of Lititz, Penn., choreographed and performed a liturgical dance for both Psalms 13 and 113 using the music of Robin White. His liturgical dance pieces appear on the Kaleidoscope Videocassette, which accompanied the first edition of this book (New York: United Church Press, 1991).

[43]Hailstork's cantata was performed by The Heritage Chorale of New Haven, Conn., with Jonathan Q. Berryman, conductor, and Gregory Hopkins, tenor, at Woolsey Hall, Yale University, on January 20, 2001, for the "Up with a Shout!" conference at Yale. This concert also featured the premiere of Stephen Paulus' "Psalm 1" as well as performances of Leonard Bernstein's "Chichester Psalms" and Richard Smallwood's "Total Praise," wonderfully powerful psalms music.

[44]See Robert Wuthnow, *The Crisis in the Churches: Spiritual Malaise, Fiscal Woe* (New York: Oxford University Press, 1997). Fear of unemployment and work that does not satisfy have fueled a spiritual crisis in America.

[45]Lauren Winner, "A Return to Tradition? Gen X Revisited," *Christian Century* (November 8, 2000): 1146.

[46]Ibid., 1148.

[47]Harold Kushner, *Who Needs God?* (New York: Summit Books, 1989), 9. Kushner argues that it is the psalms that provide the kind of nourishment that our souls crave.

[48]Laura Sessions Stepp, "Doing the Kindly Thing: John Q. Citizen as a Good Samaritan," *The Washington Post,* Style Plus, 15 March, 1994: E5. On the best-seller list of paperback nonfiction that same year were Stephen Covey's *The Seven Habits of Highly Effective People,* a management manual, and William Bennett's *The Book of Virtues,* an anthology of moral tales.

[49]David Willis, "Contemporary Theology and Prayer," *Interpretation* 34 (1980): 250–64. Willis argues for the strong correlation between a theologian's doctrine of prayer and his or her doctrine of God.

[50]Norris, "The Paradox of the Psalms," 222.

[51]Ibid.

[52]Don Saliers, "Prayer and the Doctrine of God in Contemporary Theology," *Interpretation* 34 (1980): 278.

[53]Harold Kushner, *When Bad Things Happen to Good People* (New York: Schocken Books, 1981).

[54]Ibid., 108–9.

[55]Balentine, *Prayer in the Hebrew Bible,* 5.

[56]Ann Weems, *Psalms of Lament* (Louisville: Westminster John Knox Press, 1995), xvi.

[57]Ibid., xv.

[58]Miller, *They Cried to the Lord,* 1.

[59]See for example, Donald Gowan, *Reclaiming the Old Testament for the Christian Pulpit* (Atlanta: John Knox Press, 1976). Gowan treats the Psalms in the epilogue, arguing that "we ought to pray them and sing them rather than preach them" (146) according to their original function and that a sermon would sound "very pedestrian and dull" in comparison with the psalm text from which it is drawn!

[60]See *And the Angels Wept: From the Pulpits of Oklahoma City,* ed. Marsha B. Bishop and David P. Polk (St. Louis: Chalice Press, 1995). My colleague at Wesley Theological Seminary Dr. William B. McClain shared in a recent faculty meeting that he surveyed what texts were preached on Sunday, December 15, 1993, when the church in Atlanta was bombed, killing children. Almost all the black preachers chose Hebrew Bible texts, with the eighth-century prophets particularly prominent, while almost all the white preachers chose New Testament texts, especially the pastoral epistles. Clearly, homiletic use of the Bible is contextual. See Henry Mitchell, *The Recovery of Preaching* (San Francisco: Harper and Row, 1977).

[61]Erhard Gerstenberger, "Enemies and Evildoers in the Psalms: A Challenge to Christian Preaching," *Horizons in Biblical Theology* 4–5 (1982–83): 77. Even Claus Westermann, who argues that we must take psalms as they are, maintains that some psalms contain features that "we cannot directly adopt as our own prayer, in particular the petitions against enemies" in individual laments. See Westermann, *The Living Psalms* (Grand Rapids, Mich.: Eerdmans, 1989), 2.

[62]Susan Stevens, an artist who works in stained glass and other media, was Artist-in-Residence at Wesley Theological Seminary during the 1989–90 academic year. She created these paraments for a worship service conducted by my psalms seminar in Oxnam Chapel at Wesley Seminary.

[63]Brian Wren, *What Language Shall I Borrow?: God-Talk in Worship: A Male Response to Feminist Theology* (New York: Crossroads, 1991), 115.

[64]Ibid., 3.

[65]Rebecca Chopp, "Writing Women's Lives," *Memphis Theological Seminary Journal* 29, no. 1 (Spring 1991): 3–13.

[66]What many feminist and liberationist theologies have in common is their starting point with the body and feelings rather than with the mind and knowledge. See Beverly W. Harrison, "The Power of Anger in the Work of Love," *Union Seminary Quarterly Review* 36 (Supplement 1981): 48. She argues that feminists "recognize that all our knowledge, including our moral knowledge, is body-mediated knowledge…When we cannot feel, we literally lose our connection to the world." Similarly, Jose Comblin, *Retrieving the Human: A Christian Anthropology,* trans. Robert R. Barr (Maryknoll, N.Y.: Orbis Books, 1990), argues in his liberation anthropology that "the privileged forget their bodies…For the poor, the liberation of humanity is the liberation of suffering, crushed, humiliated bodies." Even John Wesley maintained that "our bodies help to constitute who we are." Thus, a restoration of the created order through God's grace included the restoration of health to the physical body. Members of Wesley's societies visited the sick every other day, and Wesley established medical

dispensaries in English cities to diagnose and treat the sick. See E. Brooks Holifield, *Health and Medicine in the Methodist Tradition: Journey toward Wholeness* (New York: Crossroad, 1986).

[67]Billman and Migliore, *Rachel's Cry,* 72.

[68]Arlo Duba, "Psalms, the Scripture and the Church," *Liturgy* 3, no. 3 (1983): 35.

[69]Norris, "The Paradox of the Psalms," 228.

[70]Ibid., 229.

[71]Renita Weems, *Listening for God,* 22.

[72]Barbara Brown Taylor, *When God Is Silent: The 1997 Lyman Beecher Lectures on Preaching* (Boston: Cowley Publications, 1998), 39.

[73]Ibid., 101.

[74]Patrick Miller, *Interpeting the Psalms,* 21.

CHAPTER 2
The Synagogue, the Church, and the Psalms

[1]For a thorough analysis of the use of the Psalter through history, see William L. Holladay, *The Psalms Through Three Thousand Years: Prayerbook of a Cloud of Witnesses* (Minneapolis: Fortress Press, 1993).

[2]I use the term Hebrew Bible for what Christians call the Old Testament as a way of reminding us that the first part of our Bible, written originally in Hebrew, is also canon, that is, normative, for more than one community of faith, that is, the Jews. The adjective *old* in Old Testament can carry negative unconscious baggage for Christians. For example, old can mean worn out, inferior, superceded. The use of *Old* Testament can make it easy for Christians to forget that Jews address different questions to scripture and allow the witness of the first part of the Christian Bible to inform their lives in different ways than Christians do. See Denise D. Hopkins, "God's Continuing Covenant with the Jews and the Christian Reading of the Bible," *Prism* 3, no. 2 (1988): 60–75.

[3]Roy Harrisville, "Paul and the Psalms: A Formal Study," *Word and World* 5, no. 2 (1985): 168.

[4]J. Clinton McCann, "The Book of Psalms: Introduction, Commentary, and Reflections," *The New Interpreter's Bible*, vol. 4 (Nashville: Abingdon Press, 1996), 672.

[5]The Hebrew word *hesed* is usually translated as "steadfast love" or "mercy," but is better translated as "covenant love" or "loyalty." I use the terms B.C.E., Before the Common Era, and C.E., the Common Era, in place of the confessional terms B.C., Before Christ, and A.D., Anno Domino, Year of our Lord, in order to encourage dialogue between Christians and people of other faiths, especially Jews, who do not confess Jesus as Lord.

[6]Holladay, *The Psalms Through Three Thousand Years*, 139–40. Jews today always recite the superscription as part of the psalm; indeed, it is the first verse of the psalm in numbering in Jewish Bibles. Christians do not consider the superscription to be part of the psalm text.

[7]Michael D. Goulder, *The Psalms of the Sons of Korah* (Sheffield, England: Journal for the Study of the Old Testament Press, 1982), 103–5.

[8]Shaye Cohen, *From the Maccabees to the Mishnah* (Philadelphia: Westminster Press, 1987).

[9]Raphael Posner, Uri Kaploun, and Shalom Cohen, eds., *Jewish Liturgy, Prayer and Synagogue Service Through the Ages* (Jerusalem: Keter Publishing House, 1975), 18–19. Fixed, or statutory, prayer is recited to fulfill an obligation to pray rather than to mark a special occasion or event. *Midrash* (searching) is a term for rabbinic biblical interpretation. *Talmud* (study) is rabbinic commentary on the *Mishnah* (a collection of legal statements from the rabbis edited in the second century C.E.), produced in both Palestine and Babylonia between the third and sixth centuries C.E.

[10]Geoffrey Wainwright, *Doxology: The Praise of God in Worship, Doctrine, and Life* (New York: Oxford University Press, 1980), 210.

[11]Quoted in Massey H. Shepherd, *The Psalms in Christian Worship, A Practical Guide* (Minneapolis: Augsburg, 1976), 37. James W. McKinnon notes the critique of the assumption that Christians used the Psalter as their hymnbook from the beginning in direct continuity with synagogue practice in "The Book of Psalms, Monasticism, and the Western Liturgy," in *The Place of the Psalms in the Intellectual Culture of the Middle Ages* (Albany: State University of New York, 1999), 43–58. McKinnon argues that a "new consensus" has emerged about psalm singing in church and synagogue. Formalized synagogue services were not created until after the destruction of the temple in 70 C.E., with the psalms being treated as readings rather than hymns until that time, and being sung in the home at meals, as in early Christianity. Further, the church of the first two centuries sang newly composed hymns rather than the biblical psalms; singing psalms during the Daily Offices did not develop until Constantine. Given the fragmentary and ambiguous nature of evidence from the first and second centuries, McKinnon believes that this critique is overstated and that there is no reason to exclude the singing of psalms.

[12]Adela Yarbro Collins, for example (paper delivered at the conference "Up with a Shout! The Psalms in Jewish and Christian Religious, Artistic and Intellectual Traditions" at Yale University, January 20–23, 2001) argues that "psalms" were not necessarily canonical psalms, but rather, religious songs used in communal worship reflecting the pluralistic social situation of the congregation. Thus, the hymn in Philippians 2 was modeled on the prose hymn *(encomium)* composed for deities by the office of the *theologos*. For the sake of the gospel, Paul as *christologos* adapted this Greek form to honor Jesus instead of the emperor.

[13]See Peter Jeffrey, "Philo's Impact on Christian Psalmody" (paper delivered at the "Up with a Shout!" conference).

[14]Brian Daley, "'To Sing with Understanding': The Aims and Strategies of Early Christian Interpretation of the Psalms" (paper presented January 22, 2001, at the "Up with a Shout!" conference).

[15]Shepherd, *The Psalms in Christian Worship*, 39.

[16]Cohen, *From the Maccabees to the Mishnah*, 68–69. A third prayer, which did not parallel the sacrificial offerings, was recommended but not required. It is uncertain to what extent the rabbinic injunctions reflected the actual situation in the Second Temple period. The *Tamid* was God's "daily food," an honoring of God's presence in the temple.

[17]Shepherd, *The Psalms in Christian Worship*, 54–55. In a manual of church order (c. 200 C.E.), Hippolytus of Rome outlined the six prayer times: (1) dawn—pray upon rising; (2) third hour (9 a.m.)—recall that Christ was nailed to the cross; (3) sixth hour (noon)—darkness covered the earth; (4) ninth hour (3 p.m.)—the Lord was pierced and died; (5) evening—pray before sleep; (6) midnight—arise and pray, for at this hour the Bridegroom comes. Shepherd notes that we do not know how many Christians followed this discipline or what exactly they prayed when they did; possibly the psalms were recited, along with the Lord's Prayer and Bible passages.

[18]Robert Taft, "Christian Liturgical Psalmody: Origins, Development, Decomposition, Collapse" (paper presented January 21, 2001, at the "Up with a Shout!" conference).

[19]Holladay, *The Psalms Through Three Thousand Years*, 178–79.

[20]Ibid., 184.

[21]See Robert E. Webber, *The Prymer: The Prayer Book of the Medieval Era Adapted for Contemporary Use* (Boston: Paraclete Press, 2000).

[22]Donad Hustad, "The Psalms as Worship Expression: Personal and Congregational," *Review and Expositor* 81, no. 3 (1984): 414. Holladay, *The Psalms Through Three Thousand Years*, 196, notes that in the preface to his commentary on psalms, Calvin called the Psalter "An Anatomy of all the Parts of the Soul…for there is not an emotion of which any one can be conscious that is not here represented as in a mirror."

[23]"All People That on Earth do Dwell," words by William Kethe, music by Louis Bourgeois, *Chalice Hymnal* (St. Louis: Chalice Press, 1995), no. 18.

[24]Serene Jones, "Calvin's Commentary on the Psalms: Songs to Live and Die By" (paper presented January 22, 2001, at the "Up with a Shout!" conference).

[25]This psalm sing was led by Mark Brombaugh and organist William Porter at the United Church on the Green in New Haven, Connecticut, as part of the "Up with a Shout!" conference.

[26]Gilbert Bond, "Psalms in a Contemporary African-American Church" (paper presented at the "Up with a Shout!" conference).

[27]In the same way, the new *United Methodist Hymnal* brings together Methodist and Evangelical United Brethren hymns and traditions, which had been circulating independently.

[28]Confusion surrounds the numbering of verses within a psalm. Some English translations, notably JPS (Jewish Publication Society), follow the Hebrew numbering by including the superscription as the first line of the psalm, but most begin verse numbering after the superscription. The Septuagint (LXX) also divides the psalms differently from the Hebrew text. In the Hebrew, Psalms 9 and 10 are two separate psalms, but in the LXX they are combined, as are Psalms 114 and 115. On the other hand , the LXX splits in two Psalms 116 and 117, whereas they are one in the Hebrew. Consequently, the LXX numbering of Psalms 9—116 does not follow that of the Hebrew text.

[29]McCann, "The Book of Psalms," 658.

[30]Patrick Miller, *Interpreting the Psalms* (Philadelphia: Fortress Press, 1986), 45.

[31]Gerald Wilson, *The Editing of the Hebrew Psalter*, Society of Biblical Literature Dissertation Series 76 (Chico, Calif.: Scholars Press, 1985), 142–43, 170–72.

[32]Ibid., and also Gerald Wilson, "The Use of Royal Psalms at the 'Seams' of the Hebrew Psalter," *Journal for the Study of the Old Testament* 35 (1986): 85–94.

[33]Wilson, "The Use of Royal Psalms," 92.

[34]Wilson, *The Editing of the Hebrew Psalter,* 207.

[35]McCann, "The Book of Psalms," 664.

[36]Ibid. This is a form of canonical criticism pioneered by Brevard Childs, "Psalm Titles and Midrashic Exegesis," *Journal of Semitic Studies* 16 (1971): 137–50. Childs argues that the final literary form of the biblical texts is normative for our interpretation of them. Canonical criticism freeze frames a text at one particular point in its history and robs the text of its polyvalence or multiplicity of voices.

[37]Walter Brueggemann, "Response to J. Mays, 'The Question of Context,'" in *The Shape and Shaping of the Psalter*, ed. J. Clinton McCann (Sheffield: Journal for the Study of the Old Testament Supplement Series 159, 1993), 32.

[38]J. David Pleins, *The Psalms: Songs of Tragedy, Hope, and Justice* (Maryknoll, N.Y.: Orbis Books, 1993), 5.

[39]Now available as Hermann Gunkel, *Introduction to Psalms: The Genres of the Religious Lyric of Israel,* Mercer Library of Biblical Studies, trans. James D. Nogalski (Macon, Ga.: Mercer University Press, 1998).

[40]Claus Westermann, *Praise and Lament in the Psalms* (Atlanta: John Knox Press, 1981), 122.

[41]Walter Brueggemann, *The Message of the Psalms* (Minneapolis: Augsburg, 1984), 19.

[42]The Reverend Chris Suerdieck is an M.Div. graduate of Wesley Seminary and pastor of Sleepy Hollow United Methodist Church in Falls Church, Virginia.

[43]James H. Cone, "Sanctification, Liberation, and Black Worship," *Theology Today* 35 (1978–79): 141.

[44]The Reverend Glenda Gay Beach Condon is a graduate of Wesley Theological Seminary and pastor of West Liberty United Methodist Church in Whitehall, Maryland.

[45]Robert Hughes, *The Culture of Complaint: The Fraying of America* (New York: Oxford University Press, 1993), 9.

CHAPTER 3
Your Hallelujahs Don't Have to Be Hollow Anymore

[1]Ronald Clements, *In Spirit and In Truth* (Atlanta: John Knox Press, 1985), 13–14.

[2]Donald Saliers, in an address to the Virginia State Pastors' Convocation of the United Methodist Church, January 9, 2001, in Blackstone, Virginia.

[3]Patrick Miller, *Interpreting the Psalms* (Philadelphia: Fortress Press, 1986), 64.

[4]Bruce C. Birch, *Singing the Lord's Song: A Study of Isaiah 40—55* (Nashville: Abingdon Press, 1989), 83.

[5]Walter Brueggemann, *The Message of the Psalms* (Minneapolis: Augsburg, 1984), 55. This motivation assumes a kind of parity in the relationship between God and the psalmist.

[6]Birch, *Singing the Lord's Song,* 83–85.

[7]James H. Cone, "Sanctification, Liberation, and Black Worship," *Theology Today* 35 (1978–79): 141, 146.

[8]Claus Westermann, *Praise and Lament in the Psalms* (Atlanta: John Knox Press, 1981), 116–42.

[9]Miller, *Interpreting the Psalms,* 66.

[10]C. S. Lewis, *Reflections on the Psalms* (New York: Harcourt Brace & Co., 1958), 94, 97.

[11]Walter Brueggemann, "From Hurt to Joy, from Death to Life," *Interpretation* 28 (1974): 13–18.

[12]Miller, *Interpreting the Psalms,* 68.

[13]This is another modification of a praying exercise from Donald Griggs' manual, *Praying and Teaching the Psalms* (Nashville: Abingdon Press, 1984).

[14]Brueggemann, *The Message of the Psalms,* 68.

[15]Ibid., 27.

[16]Geoffrey Wainwright, *Doxology: The Praise of God in Worship, Doctrine, and Life* (New York: Oxford University Press, 1980), 425.

[17]Ibid., 118–21.

[18]Brueggemann, *The Message of the Psalms,* 28.

[19]Cone, "Sanctification," 140.

[20]Walter Brueggemann, *Israel's Praise: Doxology Against Idolatry and Ideology* (Philadelphia: Fortress Press, 1988).

[21]J. David Pleins, *The Psalms: Songs of Tragedy, Hope, and Justice* (Maryknoll, N.Y.: Orbis Books, 1993), 75.

[22]Saliers, address to the Virginia State Pastors' Convocation. Karen Baker-Fletcher, another speaker at this conference, expands the understanding of liturgy to mean service or work on behalf of the public good.

[23]Wainwright, *Doxology,* 8.

[24]Brueggemann, *The Message of the Psalms,* 19.

[25]Miller, *Interpreting the Psalms,* 70.

[26]Brueggemann, *The Message of the Psalms,* 30.

[27]Miller, *Interpreting the Psalms,* 71.

[28]J. Clinton McCann, "The Book of Psalms: Introduction, Commentary, and Reflections," *The New Interpreter's Bible,* vol. 4 (Nashville: Abingdon Press, 1996), 1150.

[29]Katherine Sakenfeld, *Faithfulness in Action: Loyalty in Biblical Perspective* (Philadelphia: Fortress Press, 1985).

[30]Frederick Gaiser, "The Emergence of the Self in the Old Testament: A Study in Biblical Wellness," *Horizons in Biblical Theology* 14, no. 1 (June 1992): 1–29, argues that the word *nephesh,* translated "self" here ("soul" in most English translations), is the only Hebrew anthropological term seen as a distinct entity so that it becomes addressable and engages in dialogue. "My soul/self" occurs 102 times in the psalms. The self becomes

recognizable in the isolation of pride or loss, but the goal of the self is return to community with a knowledge of self.

[31]Miller, *Interpreting the Psalms,* 73.

[32]Pleins, *The Psalms,* 83.

[33]Ibid., 78.

[34]Brueggemann, *The Message of the Psalms,* 36.

[35]Bernhard Anderson, *Out of the Depths: The Psalms Speak for Us Today,* rev. and enl. (Philadelphia: Westminster Press, 1962), 53.

[36]Ibid., 148.

[37]Robert Davidson, *The Vitality of Worship: A Commentary on the Book of Psalms* (Grand Rapids, Mich.: William B. Eerdmans, 1998), 438.

[38]McCann, "The Book of Psalms," 1226. McCann quotes James L. Mays, *Psalms,* Interpretation (Louisville: John Knox, 1994), 421.

[39]Pleins, *The Psalms,* 149.

[40]The Reverend David Nesselrodt, pastor of Friendship United Methodist Church in Falls Church, Virginia, posted this declaration on the signboard in front of his church.

[41]Artur Weiser, *The Psalms* (Philadelphia: Westminster Press, 1962), 481.

[42]James Pritchard, *Ancient Near Eastern Texts Relating to the Old Testament,* 3d ed. (Princeton, N.J.: Princeton University Press, 1969), 369–73.

[43]McCann, "The Book of Psalms," 1096.

[44]Harvey Guthrie, Jr., *Israel's Sacred Songs* (New York: Seabury Press, 1978), 61ff. Guthrie's book has been reprinted by University Press of America.

[45]Leslie A. Allen, *Psalms 101—150,* Word Biblical Commentary, vol. 21 (Waco, Tex.: Word Books, 1983), 34.

[46]Jon Levenson, *Creation and the Persistence of Evil: The Jewish Drama of Divine Omnipotence* (San Francisco: Harper & Row, 1988). Levenson argues that Genesis 1 describes creation without opposition rather than *creatio ex nihilo* (creation out of nothing). The point of creaton is the emergence of a stable community in a benevolent and life-sustaining order out of the precariousness of life.

[47]"Bless the Lord, My Soul and Being," words by Fred R. Anderson, music by C. Hubert H. Parry, *The Presbyterian Hymnal: Hymns, Psalms, and Spiritual Songs* (Louisville: Westminster/John Knox Press, 1990), no. 224.

[48]Patrick Miller, "The Psalms as a Book of Theology" (paper presented Jan. 21, 2001, to the conference "Up with a Shout! The Psalms in Jewish and Christian Religious, Artistic and Intellectual Traditions" at Yale University, January 20–23, 2001).

[49]"All Things Bright and Beautiful," words by Cecil F. Alexander, *Chalice Hymnal* (St. Louis: Chalice Press, 1995), no. 61.

[50]"O Worship the King," words by Robert Grant, *Chalice Hymnal* (St. Louis: Chalice Press, 1995), no. 17.

[51]Brueggemann, *The Message of the Psalms,* 33.

[52]Catherine Kapikian is Director of the Henry Luce III Center for Arts and Religion at Wesley Theolgoical Seminary. Her work on Psalm 104 is in fine wool, trapunto technique, framed in wood and plexiglass, 7 1/4 x 3 3/4'. It hangs in the sanctuary of Bethesda Presbyterian Church in Bethesda, Maryland.

[53]"A Mighty Fortress Is Our God," words by Martin Luther, *Chalice Hymnal* (St. Louis: Chalice Press, 1995), no. 65.

[54]Guthrie, *Israel's Sacred Songs,* 66–69.

[55]Joseph Campbell with Bill Moyers, *The Power of Myth,* ed. Betty Sue Flowers (New York: Doubleday, 1988), 40. Unfortunately, Campbell argues (p. 31) that the myth of the West does not function today, because it is based on the Bible and its view of the universe that belongs to the first millenium B.C.E.: "It does not accord with our concept either of the universe, however, or of the dignity of man [sic]." I

would argue, rather, that our Western myth is in trouble precisely because it is not based on the Bible, but on an Enlightenment view of inevitable progress and human control. The mechanical, Newtonian universe, however, has given way to chaos theory that postulates that chaos is built into the order of creation that is still unfolding. The Bible appropriately interpreted can help us to recover what Campbell sees as the "mystical function" of myth, "realizing what a wonder the universe is, and what a wonder you are, and experiencing awe before this mystery" (p. 31). The psalms lift up the dignity of the human being and our awe before the Creator. See my treatment of Psalm 8 in chapter 7.

[56]Cain Hope Felder, *Troubling Biblical Waters: Race, Class, and Family* (Maryknoll, N.Y.: Orbis Books, 1989), 37–48.

[57]McCann, "The Book of Psalms," 864–65.

[58]Ibid., 865.

[59]Davidson, *The Vitality of Worship*, 153.

[60]Pleins, *The Psalms*, 119.

[61]Robert Alter, *The Art of Biblical Poetry* (New York: Basic Books, 1985), 121.

[62]McCann, "The Book of Psalms," 866.

[63]Peter Craigie, *Psalms 1—50,* Word Biblical Commentary, vol. 19 (Waco, Tex.: Word Books, 1983), 343.

[64]Walter Harrelson, *From Fertility Cult to Worship* (Garden City, N.Y., Doubleday, 1969; reprint, Missoula, Mont.: Scholars Press, 1980), 137–47.

[65]Ibid., 138.

[66]Ibid., 150.

[67]My thanks to Dee Ann Dixon, a 1991 M. Div. graduate of Wesley Theological Seminary and pastor of New Street UMC in Shepherdstown, W. Va., for this insight.

CHAPTER 4
You Get What You Deserve, Don't You?

[1]James L. Crenshaw, *The Psalms: An Introduction* (Grand Rapids, Mich.: William B. Eerdmans, 2001), 94.

[2]Walter Brueggemann, *The Message of the Psalms* (Minneapolis: Augsburg, 1984), 38.

[3]J. Clinton McCann, "The Book of Psalms: Introduction, Commentary, and Reflections," *The New Interpreter's Bible*, vol. 4 (Nashville: Abingdon Press, 1996), 752.

[4]For what follows, see John Collins, *Proverbs/Ecclesiastes*, Knox Preaching Guides (Atlanta: John Knox Press, 1980), 1–14.

[5]Norman Vincent Peale, *Thought Conditioners* (Pawling, N.Y.: Peale Center for Christian Living, 1951, 1988), 16, 24.

[6]McCann, "The Book of Psalms," 684.

[7]Brueggemann, *The Message of the Psalms*, 38–39; 183n. 32.

[8]McCann, "The Book of Psalms," 683.

[9]Fred Craddock, "Hearing God's Blessing," *The Christian Century* (January 24, 1992): 74.

[10]Peter Craigie, *Psalms 1–50,* Word Biblical Commentary, vol. 19 (Waco, Tex.: Word Books, 1983), 61.

[11]Robert Alter, *The Art of Biblical Poetry* (New York: Basic Books, 1985), 115–17.

[12]Eli Ezry, *Praying for Recovery: Psalms and Meditations* (Deerfield Beach, Fla.: Simcha Press, 2000), 18–19.

[13]Robert Davidson, *The Vitality of Worship: A Commentary on the Book of Psalms* (Grand Rapids, Mich.: William B. Eerdmans, 1998), 12.

[14]Brueggemann, *The Message of the Psalms*, 42.

[15]Crenshaw, *The Psalms,* 111.

[16]Ibid., 117.

[17]Robert Cole, *The Shape and Message of Book III (Psalms 73–89),* Journal for the Study of the Old Testament Supplement Series 307 (Sheffield: Sheffield Academic Press, 2000), 17.

[18]Ibid., 10–15.

[19]Walter Brueggemann and Patrick Miller, "Psalm 73 as a Canonical Marker," *Journal for the Study of the Old Testament* 72 (1996): 45–56.

[20]Walter Brueggemann, "Bounded by Obedience and Praise: The Psalms as Canon," *Journal for the Study of the Old Testament* 50 (1991): 81.

[21]Crenshaw, *The Psalms,* 116.

[22]McCann, "The Book of Psalms," 968.

[23]J. David Pleins, *The Psalms: Songs of Tragedy, Hope, and Justice* (Maryknoll, N.Y.: Orbis Books, 1993), 164–67.

[24]Karen Cassedy, in an unpublished exegesis of Psalm 73. She is a 1995 M.Div. graduate of Wesley Theological Seminary.

[25]Martin Buber, "The Heart Determines: Psalm 73," in *Theodicy in the Old Testament,* Issues in Religion and Theology, vol. 4, ed. James L. Crenshaw (Minneapolis: Fortress Press, 1983), 111.

[26]McCann, "The Book of Psalms," 969.

[27]Crenshaw, *The Psalms,* 124.

[28]Davidson, *The Vitality of Worship,* 235.

CHAPTER 5
Complaining in Faith to God

[1]Roland Murphy, "The Faith of the Psalmist," *Interpretation* 34 (1980): 236.

[2]The Reverend David G. Bowen is a D.Min. candidate at Wesley Theological Seminary. He is pastor of First United Methodist Church in Austell, Georgia.

[3]Walter Brueggemann, *The Message of the Psalms* (Minneapolis: Augsburg, 1984), 22.

[4]Craig Broyles, *The Conflict of Faith and Experience in the Psalms,* JSOT Supplement Series 52 (Sheffield, England: Sheffield Academic Press, 1989), 14.

[5]Harold Kushner, *When Bad Things Happen to Good People* (New York: Schocken Books, 1981), 88.

[6]Broyles, *Faith and Experience,* 113.

[7]Michael Podesta, Graphic Design, Inc., 8847 Eclipse Drive, Suffolk, VA 23433. Used by permission.

[8]Robert Davidson, *The Vitality of Worship: A Commentary on the Book of Psalms* (Grand Rapids, Mich.: William B. Eerdmans, 1998), 291.

[9]Wayne Oates, *The Presence of God in Pastoral Counseling* (Waco, Tex.: Word Books, 1986), 105–6.

[10]Eli Ezry, *Praying for Recovery: Psalms and Meditations* (Deerfield Beach, Fla.: Simcha Press, 2000), 5.

[11]Brueggemann, *The Message of the Psalms,* 78.

[12]Ibid., 80–81.

[13]Walter Brueggemann, *The Theology of the Old Testament: Testimony, Dispute, Advocacy* (Minneapolis: Fortress Press,1997).

[14]Murphy, "The Faith of the Psalmist," 238.

[15]Erhard Gerstenberger, "Enemies and Evildoers in the Psalms: A Challenge to Christian Preaching," *Horizons in Biblical Theology* 4–5 (1982–83): 61–77.

[16]Erich Zenger, *A God of Vengeance? Understanding the Psalms of Divine Wrath* (Louisville: Westminster/John Knox, 1996), 37.

[17]Gerald T. Sheppard, "'Enemies' and the Politics of Prayer in the Book of Psalms," *The Bible and the Politics of Exegesis,* ed. David Jobling, Peggy Day, and Gerald Sheppard (Cleveland: Pilgrim Press, 1991), 73.

[18]Ibid., 75.

[19]David Biggs, Associated Press, "Debate over Abortion Rights Revives Hell as Topic of Religious Discussion," *The Washington Post,* 24 February 1990.

[20]Lee Porter, *By the Waters of Babylon,* 1992, 58 x 52", collection of the artist.

[21]Dorothee Soelle, *Suffering,* trans. E. Kalin (Philadelphia: Fortress Press, 1975), 4.

[22]Brueggemann, *The Message of the Psalms,* 168–69.

[23]Ibid., 171.

[24]Ibid., 175.

[25]Ibid., 77.

[26]Dietrich Bonhoeffer, *The Cost of Discipleship,* trans. R. H. Fuller (New York: Macmillan, 1963), 45, 54.

[27]Brueggemann, *The Message of the Psalms,* 176.

[28]Broyles, *Faith and Experience,* 70–73.

[29]Ibid., 66.

[30]Pierre Wolff, *May I Hate God?* (New York: Paulist Press, 1979), 25.

[31]Daniel Simundson, *Faith Under Fire: Biblical Interpretations of Suffering* (Minneapolis: Augsberg, 1980), 48.

[32]Robert McAfee Brown, *Creation Dislocation: The Movement of Grace* (Nashville: Abingdon Press, 1980), 89.

[33]Elie Wiesel, *Night* (New York: Bantam Books, 1982), 61.

[34]Kushner, *When Bad Things Happen,* 108.

[35]Ibid., 37.

[36]William Sloane Coffin, Jr., "My Son Beat Me to the Grave," *AD Magazine* (June 1983): 25–26.

[37]Richard F. Vieth, *Holy Power, Human Pain* (Bloomington, Ind.: Meyer-Stone Books, 1988), 17–25.

[38]Jürgen Moltmann, *The Crucified God: The Cross of Christ as the Foundation and Criticism of Christian Theology* (London: SCM Press, 1974).

[39]Anson Laytner, *Arguing with God: A Jewish Tradition* (Northvale, N.J.: Jason Aronson, 1990).

[40]David R. Blumenthal, *Facing the Abusing God: A Theology of Protest* (Louisville: Westminster/John Knox, 1993), 259.

[41]Broyles, *Faith and Experience,* 113.

[42]Ibid., 131.

[43]Lee Porter, *Cleanse Me with Hyssop,* 2000, Psalm 51:7, 26 x 26", collection of Susan and Peter Kilborn. Porter created this quilt against the backdrop of Christian use at the time of Lent.

[44]Brueggemann, *The Message of the Psalms,* 104.

[45]Dr. James D. Siddons is pastor of Forest Road United Methodist Church in Lynchburg, Virginia. He has a Ph.D. in musicology and is an internationally recognized expert in European and Asian Medieval and Modern Music. Most recently he was awarded a Fulbright Grant for research in Japanese music. The music for Psalm 130 draws on fifteenth-century Flemish polyphony and modern jazz for its style. It premiered on March 12, 1989, at Quaker Memorial Presbyterian Church in Lynchburg, Virginia, conducted by Hadley Hunt. Since 1989, Dr. Siddons has been setting all 150 psalms to original or arranged music based on his own translations of the Hebrew.

[46]Claus Westermann, "The Role of the Lament in the Theology of the Old Testament," *Interpretation* 28, no. 1 (1974): 33.

[47]Simundson, *Faith Under Fire,* 50.

⁴⁸Brueggemann, *The Message of the Psalms,* 55.

⁴⁹Ibid.

⁵⁰Ibid.

CHAPTER 6
Life in the Meanwhile

¹Walter Brueggemann, *The Message of the Psalms* (Minneapolis: Augsburg, 1984), 56.

²William L. Holladay, *The Psalms through Three Thousand Years: Prayerbook of a Cloud of Witnesses* (Minneapolis: Fortress Press, 1993), 359.

³*Psalm Twenty-Three,* illus. Tim Ladwig (Grand Rapids, Mich.: Eerdmans Books for Young Readers, 1997).

⁴Brueggemann, *The Message of the Psalms,* 154–55.

⁵Dr. Jan Fuller Carruthers is a D.Min. graduate of Wesley Theological Seminary. She is currently chaplain at Hollins College in Virginia.

⁶Walter Brueggemann, "From Hurt to Joy, from Death to Life," *Interpretation* 28 (1974): 10, 13.

⁷Ibid., 18.

⁸Claus Westermann, "The Role of the Lament in the Theology of the Old Testament," *Interpretation* 28, no. 1 (1974): 27.

⁹Elaine Emeth is a 1998 M.Div. graduate of Wesley Theological Seminary. She is pastor of Westminster United Methodist Church in Westminster, Maryland.

¹⁰Pierre Wolff, *May I Hate God?* (New York: Paulist Press, 1979), 57.

¹¹Ibid., 34.

¹²Ibid., 57.

¹³My thanks to the Reverend Dr. Marcia Cox for this insight from Melville in a Doctor of Ministry class I taught at Wesley Seminary.

¹⁴Nelle Morton, *The Journey Is Home* (Boston: Beacon Press, 1985), 127–28.

¹⁵Ibid., 129.

¹⁶Chung Hyun Kyung, *Struggle to Be the Sun Again* (Maryknoll,N.Y.: Orbis Books, 1990), 36–52.

¹⁷Ulrike Bail, "'O God Hear My Prayer': Psalm 55 and Violence against Women," in *Wisdom and Psalms: A Feminist Companion to the Bible* (2d series), ed. Athalya Brenner and Carole Fontaine (Sheffield, England: Sheffield Academic Press, 1998), 244.

¹⁸Ibid., 257.

¹⁹Dorothee Soelle, *Suffering* (Philadelphia: Fortress Press, 1975), 70, 76.

²⁰M. Shawn Copeland, "Wading through Many Sorrows: Toward a Theology of Suffering in Womanist Perspective," in *A Troubling in My Soul: Womanist Perspectives on Evil and Suffering,* ed. Emilie M. Townes (Maryknoll, N.Y.: Orbis Books, 1993), 109–29.

²¹Jacquelyn Grant, "The Sin of Servanthood and the Deliverance of Discipleship," in *A Troubling in My Soul: Womanist Perspectives on Evil and Suffering,* ed. Emilie M. Townes (Maryknoll, N.Y.: Orbis Books, 1993), 200.

²²Alice Walker, *The Color Purple* (New York: Harcourt Brace Jovanovich, 1992), 187.

²³W. E. B. DuBois, "Litany at Atlanta," in *The Seventh Son: The Thought and Writings of W. E. B. DuBois,* vol. 1, ed. Julius Lester (New York: Random House, 1971), 425. See also William Jones, *Is God a White Racist?: A Preamble to Black Theology* (New York: Anchor/Doubleday, 1973).

²⁴Allan Reed, "From Out of the Depths," *The Journal of Pastoral Care* 4, no. 4 (Winter 1991): 364.

²⁵Nora Leake Cameron is an Episcopalian M.T.S. graduate of Wesley Theological Seminary.

²⁶Daniel Simundson, *Faith Under Fire: Biblical Interpretations of Suffering* (Minneapolis: Augsburg, 1980), 61.

[27]Elizabeth Kübler-Ross, *On Death and Dying* (New York: Macmillan, 1969). A physician describes five stages of coping for those who are terminally ill: denial and isolation, anger, bargaining, depression, and acceptance. Those grieving the loss of a loved one "undergo different stages of adjustment similar to the ones described for our patients" (149).

[28]Cited in Rhoda Donkin, "Facing Life Alone Again," *Washington Post Health*, 10 January 1989, 16.

[29]Ibid.

[30]Ken Denlinger, "Gibbs: 'Emotional Marathon'," *The Washington Post*, 12 November 1989, B1.

[31]Nicholas Wolterstorff, *Lament for a Son* (Grand Rapids, Mich.: William B. Eerdmans,1987), 98.

[32]Simundson, *Faith Under Fire*, 97.

[33]Wolterstorff, *Lament for a Son*, 92–93.

[34]Simundson, *Faith Under Fire*, 98.

[35]Brueggemann, *The Message of the Psalms*, 56.

[36]Douglas John Hall, *Why Christian?: For Those on the Edge of Faith* (Minneapolis: Fortress Press, 1998), vii, ix.

[37]Ibid., 92, 93.

[38]William Sloane Coffin, Jr., "My Son Beat Me to the Grave," *AD Magazine* (June 1983): 26.

[39]Samuel E. Balentine, *The Hidden God: The Hiding of the Face of God in the Old Testament* (Oxford: Oxford University Press, 1983), 166.

[40]Ibid.

[41]Ibid., 173.

[42]Becky Cloud is an M.Div. graduate of Wesley Theological Seminary. She is an elder in the Virginia Annual Conference of the United Methodist Church and pastor of Redwood UMC in the Danville District.

[43]Bernhard Anderson, *Out of the Depths: The Psalms Speak for Us Today*, rev. and enl. (Philadelphia: Westminster Press, 1962), 69.

[44]Robert Alter, *The Art of Biblical Poetry* (New York: Basic Books, 1985), 63.

[45]Craig Broyles, *The Conflict of Faith and Experience in the Psalms*, JSOT Supplement Series 52 (Sheffield, England: Sheffield Academic Press, 1989), 31–34.

[46]"How Long, O Lord," by Christopher Norton, 1989, in *Renew! Songs and Hymns for Blended Worship* (Carol Stream, Ill.: Hope, 1995), 87. The one deviation from Psalm 13 in this piece presents itself in stanza 3, line 1: "How long, O Lord, but you forgive." Psalm 13 is not a penitential lament; the element of confession, and by implication, forgiveness, is absent.

[47]Mark C. Taylor, *Nots* (Chicago: University of Chicago Press, 1993), 6.

[48]Ibid., 215.

[49]Ibid., 216.

[50]Brueggemann, *The Message of the Psalms*, 68.

[51]J. David Pleins, *The Psalms: Songs of Tragedy, Hope, and Justice* (Maryknoll, N.Y.: Orbis Books, 1993), 42, 44.

[52]Marjorie Proctor-Smith, *Praying with Our Eyes Open: Engendering Feminist Liturgical Prayer* (Nashville: Abingdon Press, 1995), 9.

[53]David Hobart Hunter is an M.Div. graduate of Wesley Theological Seminary, a member of the Unitarian Universalist Church of Delaware County in Media, Pennsylvania, and a former attorney, Voting Section, Civil Rights Division, of the U.S. Department of Justice. This poem was given at the Unitarian Fellowship of the Chester River on Sunday, March 28, 1999.

[54]Karen Dize is an M.Div. student at Wesley Theological Seminary. She wrote this lament in December, 2001.

CHAPTER 7
I'll Never Be the Same Again

[1]Nicholas Wolterstorff, *Lament for a Son* (Grand Rapids, Mich.: William B. Eerdmans,1987), 99.

[2]Walter Brueggemann, *The Message of the Psalms* (Minneapolis: Augsburg, 1984), 175.

[3]Walter Brueggemann, *Israel's Praise: Doxology Against Idolatry and Ideology* (Philadelphia: Fortress Press, 1988), 148.

[4]Ibid., 148.

[5]Ibid., 29.

[6]Sigmund Mowinckel, *The Psalms in Israel's Worship* (New York: Abingdon Press, 1962; Sheffield, England: JSOT Press, 1992).

[7]J. Clinton McCann, "The Book of Psalms: Introduction, Commentary, and Reflections," *The New Interpreter's Bible,* vol. 4 (Nashville: Abingdon Press, 1996), 868.

[8]Artur Weiser, *The Psalms,* Old Testament Library (Philadelphia: Westminster Press, 1962), 376.

[9]Robert Davidson, *The Vitality of Worship: A Commentary on the Book of Psalms* (Grand Rapids, Mich.: William B. Eerdmans, 1998), 155.

[10]Peter Craigie, *Psalms 1—50,* Word Biblical Commentary, vol. 19 (Waco, Tex.: Word Books, 1983), 349.

[11]Brueggemann, *Israel's Praise,* 34.

[12]Ibid., 36.

[13]Ibid., 38.

[14]Ibid., 55.

[15]McCann, "The Book of Psalms," 1055.

[16]Fredericka Nolde Berger, "Inhabiting the Psalms through Choral Speaking: Lord, you have been our dwelling place in all generations." Unpublished paper, © 2000 by Fredericka Berger.

[17]Robert Alter, *The Art of Biblical Poetry* (New York: Basic Books, 1985), 119.

[18]Davidson, *The Vitality of Worship,* 37. Davidson argues that verse 1b can be taken with either verse 1a or verse 2; I argue that it can do both at the same time.

[19]McCann, "The Psalms," 711.

[20]J. David Pleins, *The Psalms: Songs of Tragedy, Hope, and Justice* (Maryknoll, N.Y.: Orbis Books, 1993), 76.

[21]Brueggemann, *The Message of the Psalms,* 183n. 29.

[22]Phyllis Trible, "Ancient Priests and Modern Polluters," *Andover-Newton Quarterly* 12 (1971).

[23]Brueggemann, *The Message of the Psalms,* 38.

[24]Walter Harrelson, *From Fertility Cult to Worship* (Garden City, N.Y.: Doubleday, 1969), 96–97.

[25]Ibid., 99.

APPENDIX
A Service of Silence and Lamentation
for Good Friday or Holy Saturday

[1]Walter Brueggemann, *Texts Under Negotiation: The Bible and Postmodern Imagination* (Minneapolis: Fortress Press, 1993), 43.